T0214345

Communications in Computer and Information Science 929

Commenced Publication in 2007
Founding and Former Series Editors:
Phoebe Chen, Alfredo Cuzzocrea, Xiaoyong Du, Orhun Kara, Ting Liu,
Dominik Ślęzak, and Xiaokang Yang

More information about this series at http://www.springer.com/series/7899

El Hassan Abdelwahed · Ladjel Bellatreche
Djamal Benslimane · Matteo Golfarelli
Stéphane Jean · Dominique Mery
Kazumi Nakamatsu · Carlos Ordonez (Eds.)

New Trends in Model and Data Engineering

MEDI 2018 International Workshops
DETECT, MEDI4SG, IWCFS, REMEDY
Marrakesh, Morocco, October 24–26, 2018
Proceedings

 Springer

Editors
El Hassan Abdelwahed
Cadi Ayyad University
Marrakesh, Morocco

Ladjel Bellatreche
ISAE-ENSMA
Chasseneuil-du-Poitou, France

Djamal Benslimane 🆔
LIRIS Lab
University Lyon 1, IUT
Villeurbanne Cedex, France

Matteo Golfarelli
Computer Science and Information
Technology
University of Bologna
Cesena, Italy

Stéphane Jean
ISAE-ENSMA
Chasseneuil-du-Poitou, France

Dominique Mery
LORIA
Nancy, France

Kazumi Nakamatsu
University of Hyogo
Himeji, Japan

Carlos Ordonez
University of Houston
Houston, TX, USA

ISSN 1865-0929   ISSN 1865-0937 (electronic)
Communications in Computer and Information Science
ISBN 978-3-030-02851-0   ISBN 978-3-030-02852-7 (eBook)
https://doi.org/10.1007/978-3-030-02852-7

Library of Congress Control Number: 2018958519

This Springer imprint is published by the registered company Springer Nature Switzerland AG
The registered company address is: Gewerbestrasse 11, 6330 Cham, Switzerland

Preface

This volume presents the proceedings of the scientific workshops that were held in conjunction with the 8th International Conference on Model and Data Engineering (MEDI 2018), which took place in Marrakech, Morocco, October 24–26, 2018.

Four workshops were selected on a wide range of topics that fall into the main area of the MEDI 2018 conference:

- The Model and Data Engineering for Social Good Workshop (MEDI4SG 2018)
- The International Workshop on Modeling, Verification, and Testing of Dependable Critical Systems (DETECT 2018)
- The Second International Workshop on Cybersecurity and Functional Safety in Cyber-Physical Systems (IWCFS 2018)
- The International Workshop: Formal Model for Multifaceted Systems (REMEDY)

Workshop proposals were submitted and the selection of appropriate workshops was carried out by Djamal Benslimane, Jean Stéphane, and Kazumi Nakamatsu. Each selected workshop was managed by its chairs and had its own Program Committee. An introduction to the selected workshops is presented in the next pages.

We would like to thank the workshop chairs for their nice work and the Program Committee members of the different selected workshops for their contribution to evaluating submitted papers.

For readers of this volume, we hope you will find it both interesting and informative. We also hope it will inspire and embolden you to greater achievements and to look further into the challenges that still lie ahead in our digital society.

October 2018

El Hassan Abdelwahed
Ladjel Bellatreche
Djamal Benslimane
Matteo Golfarelli
Stéphane Jean
Dominique Mery
Kazumi Nakamatsu
Carlos Ordonez

Contents

IWCFS 2018 Workshop

REMEDY 2018 Workshop

Short Paper

DETECT 2018 Workshop

Introduction to the International Workshop on Modeling, Verification and Testing of Dependable Critical Systems (DETECT 2018)

The International Workshop DETECT 2018 (Modeling, Verification and Testing of Dependable Critical systems) took place in Marrakesh, Morocco, on October 24, 2018, in conjunction with the International Conference on Model and Data Engineering (MEDI 2018).

Owing to their heterogeneity and variability, critical systems require the expertise of modeling, verification, and testing to ensure their dependability and safety. DETECT Workshops aim to provide a friendly and inclusive area with a great sense of community that presents excellent opportunities for collaboration. DETECT 2018 was mainly based on the model-based system engineering paradigm and presented novel research where human safety is dependent on the precise operation of the system.

This volume contains the papers selected for presentation at the workshop. The acceptation rate was 31%. Indeed, DETECT 2018 received 19 submissions. Each submission was reviewed by at least three Program Committee members. The committee decided to accept six papers. We note that the accepted papers address not only the theoretical results, but also methodological results that can play an important industrial transfer role.

DETECT 2018 would not have succeeded without the support and the cooperation of the Program Committee members and also the external reviewers, who carefully reviewed and selectted the best contributions. We would like to thank all the authors who submitted the papers, the reviewers and the Organizing Committee members for their investment and involvement in the success of DETECT 2018. The EasyChair was used for the management of DETECT 2018 and it provided a very helpful framework for the submission, review, and volume preparation process.

October 2018

Yassine Ouhammou
Abderrahim Ait Wakrime

DETECT 2018 Workshop Chairs

Yassine Ouhammou   LIAS/ISAE-ENSMA, France
Abderrahim Ait Wakrime   IRT Railenium, France

DETECT 2018 Program Committee

Abderrahim Ait Wakrime	IRT Railenium, France
Mohamed Bakhouya	International University of Rabat, Morocco
Youness Bazhar	ASML, The Netherlands
Jamal Bentahar	Concordia University, Canada
Alessandro Biondi	Scuola Superiore Sant'Anna, Italy
Rachida Dssouli	Concordia University, Canada
Mamoun Filali-Amine	IRIT, France
Mohamed Ghazel	IFSTTAR, France
Abdelouahed Gherbi	ETS Montreal, Canada
Paul Gibson	Telecom sudParis, France
Emmanuel Grolleau	LIAS/ISAE-ENSMA, France
Geoff Hamilton	Dublin City University, Ireland
Jameleddine Hassine	KFUPM, KSA
Rafik Henia	Thales, France
Slim Kallel	University of Sfax, Tunisia
Yassine Ouhammou	LIAS/ISAE-ENSMA, France
Mehrdad Saadatmand	RISE SICS Västerås, Sweden
Laurent Voisin	Systerel, France

Steady-State Performability Analysis of Call Admission Control in Cellular Mobile Networks

Sana Younes$^{(\boxtimes)}$ and Maroua Idi

Tunis El Manar University, Campus Universitaire El-Manar, 2092 Tunis, Tunisia
sana.younes@fst.utm.tn, maroua.idi@etudiant-fst.utm.tn

Abstract. In this paper we propose a performability model of multi-class Call Admission Control (CAC) in cellular mobile networks. A performability model is a combination between availability model and performance model. A pure performance model, by ignoring failure and recovery, overestimates the performance measures of the considered system. On the other hand, a pure availability model is too conservative since performance considerations are not taken into account. We extend a previous work by proposing a composite model which considers performance changes associated with failure and recovery of radio channels in a CAC schema. We use the probabilistic model checking to perform the analysis of the performability model that we propose in this work. We first construct a composite multidimensional Continuous Time Markov Chain (CTMC) of the considered CAC schema containing both performance and failure-recovery events. Then we specify Quality of Service (QoS) requirements through the CTMC using the Continuous Stochastic Logic (CSL). Finally, we quantify the steady-state performability measures by checking CSL formulas using the PRISM model checker.

Keywords: CAC · CTMC · Failure · Performability · CSL · PRISM

1 Introduction

This paper deals with formal verification of performability model of CAC in cellular mobile network. CAC is a mechanism regulating cellular network access to ensure QoS provisioning. It determines whether a call should be accepted or rejected at the base station (BS). A BS covers a geographic area (cell) and each cell is equipped with a limited number of channels to serve user's requests. Due to the lack of radio resources, a call can be rejected. There are two major types of calls that can arrive to a cell: new calls (NC) from within and handoff calls (HC) coming from neighboring cells. The majority of CAC schemes gives priority to HCs over NCs because from the user's point of view it is more annoying to drop a HC in progress than blocking a NC. In addition, nowadays and future cellular network are required to serve different classes of traffic and each class has different QoS requirements. These classes are defined by several standards

© Springer Nature Switzerland AG 2018
E. H. Abdelwahed et al. (Eds.): MEDI 2018 Workshops, CCIS 929, pp. 5–16, 2018.
https://doi.org/10.1007/978-3-030-02852-7_1

[1, 16]. Recently, many works propose multiservices CAC schemes and classify traffic mainly into two classes [2, 7, 18]: real time (RT) class which can contain voice, streaming and interactive applications such as voice over IP, and non-real time (NRT) class which can contain non interactive applications such as web services and file transfers. All these works prioritize RT class over NRT class because RT class has stringent QoS requirements compared to NRT class.

In this context we have proposed in [17] a performance analysis of multi-services CAC schemes. However, we neglect the possibility of failure of radio channels. Likewise, the majority of works that propose CAC schemes ignores the eventuality of failure of channels, which does not comply with the reality. Indeed, there are various factors causing channel failure. These failures can be permanent or transient. The permanent channel failures are caused by equipment degradation. Whereas, the transient channel failures are caused by many propagation factors, such as channel interference, multipath fading and shadowing [14]. All these causes can cause the rejection of ongoing calls and increase the call dropping probability.

We propose to extend our work in [17] by taking into account the possibility of failure of radio channels. In this former work we have proposed a pure performance model of some investigated CAC schemes, and we have compared their performances. These pure performance models are optimistic and not realistic because they evaluate the system under ideal conditions without taking into account the failure and recovery events in the system. On the other hand, the pure availability models focus on the availability and/or reliability and do not take into account performance considerations. The performability model is a combination of the pure performance model and the pure availability model, considers performance changes associated with failure and recovery behaviors. We recall that the performability is a concept defined by Meyer in [12]. It was introduced to describe the capability of systems to operate in a degraded mode. In order to obtain more realistic performance measures, we should consider changes in performances associated with failure and recovery events. In this paper we develop a performability model of a CAC schema proposed in [17] taking into account performance changes due to failure related events. In order to ensure the continuity of the ongoing call, we add to the performability model a recovery strategy which consists in replacing an occupied failed channel by an idle channel, if one is available. We note that this recovery strategy was proposed and investigated in [10, 11, 15] but only in the context of a single class of service. Therefore, we propose to adapt this strategy considering RT and NRT classes.

Probabilistic model checking (PMC) is a probabilistic extension of the model checking formal verification technique. It is used to analyze stochastic systems and has been used in different domains [9] such as wireless communication protocols and distributed algorithms. PMC requires two inputs: a description of the system (model) and a specification of the system under investigation (requirement) expressed in temporal logics. Unlike discrete event simulation techniques which compute approximate results by generating large numbers of samples,

PMC computes exact results by checking formulas under a probabilistic model which is constructed by generating exhaustively all reachable states.

The aim of this work is to use the probabilistic model checking to analyze performability of a CAC schema proposed in a previous work. We develop a composite CTMC model of this schema by considering both performance and failure-recovery related events. We express performability measures with CSL (Continuous Stochastic Logic) formulas. CSL [3] is a branching-time logic that provides an ample means to specify state as well as path-based performance and availability measures for CTMCs in a unambiguous way. This logic is a probabilistic extension of CTL (Computational Tree Logic) [4]. We note that in this paper we will focus on steady-state formulas of CSL since we are interested on the evaluation of steady-state performability measures.

The main contributions of this paper are:

1. We extend a previous work by taking into account the possibility of failure of the channel in use. In order to ensure the continuity of the ongoing call, we adapt an existing recovery strategy, proposed in the context of one single class of traffic, to support the two classes RT and NRT. Likewise the studied CAC schema, we give priority to RT class in this adapted recovery strategy.
2. We develop a performability model containing both performance and failure-recovery events and we specify QoS requirements using CSL logic.
3. We use the PRISM model checker to perform modelling, specification and quantification of the performability measures by checking CSL formulas.

The paper is organized as follows. Section 2 is devoted to the related works. In Sect. 3, we give a brief introduction to CTMC model and CSL logic. In Sect. 4, a performability model of the considered CAC schema is presented. In Sect. 5, we give numerical results. Finally, we make our conclusions in Sect. 6.

2   Related Works

Several works [2, 7, 18] propose CAC schemes and evaluate their performances in the context of no failure of channels. In this section we focus on the main works that evaluate performance of schemes which consider performance and failure-recovery events. In [6, 10, 11, 15], authors propose analytic performability models of their proposed schemes in the context of one cell. All these schemes prioritize HCs over NCs by using guard channels and treat the failed calls with the same priority as a HC, in the sense that both of them can access any idle channel.

In [10], authors consider a permanent single channel failures and propose a two channel recovery schemes: in the first one they suppose that only a channel in use can fail and that an idle channel never fails. The last assumption is released in the second recovery strategy. Indeed, a failed channel is switched to an idle channel, if one is available and the call continues. Otherwise, the call with a failed channel is queued until an idle channel is available. For comparison purposes, a pure performance model is also presented under the assumption that the channels in a wireless network never fail. A method for multiple channel recovery for time division multiple access (TDMA) in wireless system with base repeaters is discussed in [11] where permanent and transient failure recoveries are considered. It should be noted that the authors use the same principle of recovery in [10]. The novelty of [15] compared to the previous works is the use of control channel. The failure of the control channel will cause the failure of the whole system. In this case, the system selects a channel from the rest of the non-failed channels to substitute the failed control channel. If all non-failed channels are busy, then one of them is forcefully terminated and is used as the control channel. In [6], a quantitative assessment of survivability of cellular networks, considering channel and infrastructure failures, is conducted. Indeed, the traffic is classified into RT and NRT classes and the authors use guard channels to give priority to RT calls. In [13], a performance model for CAC and the availability model for a heterogeneous wireless network environment is developed. The model handles the conversation traffic, the interactive traffic and the background traffic.

3 Preliminaries

In this section we briefly recall the basic concepts of CTMCs. Then, we present the CSL logic. For more details we refer to [8] for CTMC and to [3] for CSL.

3.1 Labelled Continuous Time Markov Chains

A CTMC can be viewed as a finite state machine where transitions are labelled with rates of exponential distributions. Let AP be a finite set of atomic propositions. A labelled CTMC $\mathcal{M}$ is a tuple $(S, \mathbf{R}, L)$ where S is a finite set of *states*, $\mathbf{R} : S \times S \rightarrow \mathcal{R}^+$ is the *rate matrix* and $L : S \rightarrow 2^{AP}$ is the *labelling* function which assigns to each state $s \in S$, the set $L(s)$ of atomic propositions that are valid in s. The infinitesimal generator $\mathbf{Q}$ can be easily deduced as $\mathbf{Q}(s, s') = \mathbf{R}(s, s')$ if $s \neq s'$ and $\mathbf{Q}(s, s) = -\sum_{s' \in S} \mathbf{R}(s, s')$. A path through a CTMC is an alternating sequence $\sigma = s_0 t_0 s_1 t_1 \cdots$ with $\mathbf{R}(s_i, s_{i+1}) > 0$ and $t_i \in \mathcal{R}^+$ for all $i \geq 0$. t_i represents the amount of time spent in state s_i. Let us denote by $path_s$ the set of paths through $\mathcal{M}$ starting from the state s. For a CTMC, there are two types of state probabilities: transient probabilities where the system is considered at time t and steady-state probabilities when the system reaches an equilibrium if it exists. Let $\mathbf{\Pi}_s^{\mathcal{M}}(s')$ be the steady-state probability to be in state s' starting from the initial state s. If $\mathcal{M}$ is ergodic, $\mathbf{\Pi}_s^{\mathcal{M}}(s')$ exists and it is independent of the initial distribution that we will denote by $\mathbf{\Pi}^{\mathcal{M}}(s')$. Let $\mathbf{\Pi}^{\mathcal{M}}$ be the steady-state probability vector. For $S' \subseteq S$, we denote by $\mathbf{\Pi}^{\mathcal{M}}(S')$ the steady-state probability to be in states of S', $\mathbf{\Pi}^{\mathcal{M}}(S') = \sum_{s' \in S'} \mathbf{\Pi}^{\mathcal{M}}(s')$.

3.2 Temporal Logic CSL

Specifications for CTMC models can be written in CSL [3] which is an extension of CTL [4] with two probabilistic operators. Let $p \in [0, 1]$, $\lhd \in \{\leq, \geq, <, >\}$ and

I be an interval of real numbers. In the sequel, we denote by S_ϕ the set of states that satisfy ϕ property and by $\models$ the satisfaction relation.

The syntax of CSL is defined by:

$$\phi ::= true \mid a \mid \phi \wedge \phi \mid \neg \phi \mid \mathcal{P}_{\triangleleft p}(\phi \, \mathcal{U}^I \phi) \mid \mathcal{S}_{\triangleleft p}(\phi)$$

$\mathcal{P}_{\triangleleft p}(\phi_1 \, \mathcal{U}^I \phi_2)$ asserts that the probability measure of paths satisfying $\phi_1 \, \mathcal{U}^I \phi_2$ meets the bound given by $\triangleleft p$. Whereas, the path formula $\phi_1 \, \mathcal{U}^I \phi_2$ asserts that ϕ_2 will be satisfied at some time $t \in I$ and that at all preceding time ϕ_1 holds. $\mathcal{S}_{\triangleleft p}(\phi)$ asserts that the steady-state probability of S_ϕ meets the bound $\triangleleft p$.

The semantic of CSL for boolean operators is identical to CTL. We give the semantics of the probabilistic formulae. Let $Prob^{\mathcal{M}}(s, \phi_1 \mathcal{U}^I \phi_2)$ denote the probability measure of all paths σ starting from s ($\sigma \in paths_s$) satisfying $\phi_1 \, \mathcal{U}^I \phi_2$.

$$s \models \mathcal{P}_{\triangleleft p}(\phi_1 \, \mathcal{U}^I \phi_2) \quad \text{iff} \quad Prob^{\mathcal{M}}(s, \phi_1 \mathcal{U}^I \phi_2) \triangleleft p$$

$$s \models \mathcal{S}_{\triangleleft p}(\phi) \quad \text{iff} \quad \mathbf{\Pi}^{\mathcal{M}}(S_\phi) = \sum_{s' \in S_\phi} \mathbf{\Pi}^{\mathcal{M}}(s') \triangleleft p \tag{1}$$

In this paper, we will use $\mathcal{S}_{\triangleleft p}(\phi)$ to define and quantify steady-state measures of the studied system. We will use also the steady-state reward formula $\mathcal{E}_J(\phi)$ that belongs to CSRL logic. Continuous Stochastic Reward Logic (CSRL) [5] is an extension of CSL by adding constraints over rewards. $\mathcal{E}_J(\phi)$ asserts that the long run reward rate in S_ϕ lies in J (J is an interval of real numbers). $\rho : S \to \mathcal{R}^+$ is a *reward structure* that assigns to each state $s \in S$ a reward $\rho(s)$.

$$s \models \mathcal{E}_J(\phi) \text{ iff} \sum_{s' \in S_\phi} \mathbf{\Pi}^{\mathcal{M}}(s') \cdot \rho(s') \in J \tag{2}$$

4   Performability Model

Now we present the performability model of the studied CAC schema to obtain more realistic performance measures by considering failure and recovery events.

4.1   System Description

We consider a single cell and two classes of services: RT and NRT. The RT class is prioritized over the NRT class. For each class, we distinguish NCs and HCs. The radio resources are divided into: NRT channels and RT channels. According to the studied schema, RT channels serve only RT calls whereas NRT channels can serve both NRT and RT calls. Indeed, this schema was proposed in [17] and was called RTP-CAC (Real Time Priority-CAC). A pure performance model of this schema was developed and was analyzed by computing performance measures in terms of NC blocking/HC dropping probabilities and the bandwidth occupation rate for each class. It was observed that this schema provides good performances comparing to the other investigated scheme. Therefore, we choose this schema to be extended in order to quantify more realistic performance measures.

Let us recall the basic concept of this considered schema: RT calls can use NRT channels if there is no RT available channels. Whereas, NRT calls are served only by NRT channels. HCs are prioritized over NCs for each class by reserving guard channels used only by HCs and RT calls have the higher priority. Let C_1 (resp. C_2) be the total number of NRT (resp. RT) channels. Let g_1 (resp. g_2) be the number of guard channels reserved exclusively for HCs NRT (resp. RT). A NRT NC is blocked if the number of available channels in NRT channel part is less or equal to $C_1 - g_1$. Whereas, A NRT HC is dropped if the number of occupied channels in NRT channel part is equal to C_1. Concerning RT class, if $C_2 - g_2$ channels are occupied and a RT NC arrives to BS, it is not blocked and can take a NRT channel. In case of occupation of $C_1 - g_1$ channels (authorized for NRT NC) then the RT NC will be blocked. A RT HC can take NRT channel if all C_2 channels are occupied. But if the number of busy NRT channels is equal to C_1 then it will be dropped.

In this paper we call this schema which ignores the failures of channels WoF-CAC (Without Failure-CAC). And we call it extension with the possibility of failures, FR-CAC (Failure Recovery-CAC). This latter schema is developed considering the failure and recovery strategy that we present in the sequel.

4.2 Failure and Recovery Strategy

Recall that the aim of the paper is to develop a formal model FR-CAC extended from WoF-CAC by considering the possibility of the failure of a channel during a service period. We assume that an idle channel can never fail. In order to let the ongoing call continue, we consider a recovery strategy. This involves a reduction of the dropping/blocking probabilities for NRT and RT classes. We adapt an existing recovery strategy [10,11,15], proposed in the context of one single class of traffic, to support the two classes RT and NRT. Similarly to WoF-CAC which gives priority to RT calls over NRT calls, we prioritize the RT class in the adapted recovery strategy. Indeed, when an occupied RT channel fails, the ongoing call (can be only an RT call), is switched to an idle RT channel. If all RT channels are occupied, then the call is switched to an idle NRT channel. If all NRT channels are occupied, the call is dropped. Let us remark that this RT call is treated as well as a RT HC. On the other hand, if an occupied NRT channel fails, the ongoing call (can be RT or NRT call) is switched to a NRT available channel if one is available otherwise this call is dropped. Similarly, we can note that this ongoing call is treated with the same priority of an NRT HC.

4.3 Composite CTMC

We present the composite CTMC of FR-CAC. We assume that the arrival processes for different traffic are independent and follow Poisson distribution with rates: λ_{Nh} for NRT HCs, λ_{Nn} for NRT NCs, λ_{Rh} for RT HCs, λ_{Rn} for RT NCs. We denote by $\lambda_N = \lambda_{Nh} + \lambda_{Nn}$ (resp. $\lambda_R = \lambda_{Rh} + \lambda_{Rn}$) arrival rate of NRT (resp. RT). We suppose that: the holding time of channels is exponentially distributed with mean $1/\mu$, the failure rate of the channel is a Poisson distribution with rate λ_F and the channel repair is exponential time distribution with the mean $1/\mu_r$.

Based on these Markov assumptions, FR-CAC can be modeled by a multi dimensional homogeneous CTMC where the state space is given by:

$$S_{FR-CAC} = \{(c_1, p_1, c_2, p_2) \mid 0 \le p_1 \le c_1 \le C_1; 0 \le p_2 \le c_2 \le C_2\}$$

In state (c_1, p_1, c_2, p_2), c_1 (resp. c_2) represents the number of busy NRT (resp. RT) channels. p_1 (resp. p_2) represents the number of failed NRT (resp. RT) channels. Transition rates $\mathbf{R}(s; (\bar{c}_1, \bar{p}_1, \bar{c}_2, \bar{p}_2))$ from the state $s = (c_1, p_1, c_2, p_2)$ to the state $(\bar{c}_1, \bar{p}_1, \bar{c}_2, \bar{p}_2)$ are defined as:

- A call arrives to occupy a NRT channel, for all $0 \le p_1 \le c_1; 0 \le p_2 \le c_2$

$$\mathbf{R}(s; (c_1 + 1, p_1, c_2, p_2)) = \begin{cases} \lambda_N & \text{if}(0 \le c_1 < C_1 - g_1; 0 \le c_2 < C_2 - g_2) \\ \lambda_N + \lambda_{Rn} & \text{if}(0 \le c_1 < C_1 - g_1; C_2 - g_2 \le c_2 < C_2) \\ \lambda_N + \lambda_R & \text{if}(0 \le c_1 < C_1 - g_1; c_2 = C_2) \\ \lambda_{Nh} & \text{if}(C_1 - g_1 \le c_1 < C_1; 0 \le c_2 < C_2) \\ \lambda_{Nh} + \lambda_{Rh} & \text{if}(C_1 - g_1 \le c_1 < C_1; c_2 = C_2) \end{cases}$$

- A failure happens in an active NRT channel and the ongoing call is switched to an NRT channel.

$$\mathbf{R}(s; (c_1 + 1, p_1 + 1, c_2, p_2)) = (c_1 - p_1)\lambda_F \text{ if } (0 \le p_1 < c_1 < C_1; 0 \le p_2 \le c_2 \le C_2)$$

- A failure happens in an active NRT channel and the ongoing call is rejected because all NRT channels are busy.

$$\mathbf{R}(s; (c_1, p_1 + 1, c_2, p_2)) = (c_1 - p_1)\lambda_F \text{ if } (0 \le p_1 < c_1 = C_1; 0 \le p_2 \le c_2 \le C_2)$$

- An active non-failing NRT channel is released.

$$\mathbf{R}(s; (c_1 - 1, p_1, c_2, p_2)) = (c_1 - p_1)\mu \text{ if } (0 \le p_1 < c_1 \le C_1; 0 \le p_2 \le c_2 \le C_2)$$

- A failed NRT channel is repaired.

$$\mathbf{R}(s; (c_1 - 1, p_1 - 1, c_2, p_2)) = p_1\mu_r \text{ if } (0 < p_1 \le c_1 \le C_1; 0 \le p_2 \le c_2 \le C_2)$$

- A call arrives to occupy a RT channel, for all $0 \le p_1 \le c_1; 0 \le p_2 \le c_2$.

$$\mathbf{R}(s; (c_1, p_1, c_2 + 1, p_2)) = \begin{cases} \lambda_R & \text{if}(0 \le c_1 \le C_1; 0 \le c_2 < C_2 - g_2) \\ \lambda_{RH} & \text{if}(0 \le c_1 \le C_1; C_2 - g_2 \le c_2 < C_2) \end{cases}$$

- A failure happens in an active RT channel and the ongoing call is switched to a RT channel.

$$\mathbf{R}(s; (c_1, p_1, c_2 + 1, p_2 + 1)) = (c_2 - p_2)\lambda_F \text{ if } (0 \le p_1 \le c_1 \le C_1; 0 \le p_2 < c_2 < C_2)$$

- A failure arrives in an active RT channel and the ongoing call is switched to occupy a NRT channel.

$$\mathbf{R}(s; (c_1 + 1, p_1, c_2, p_2 + 1)) = (c_2 - p_2)\lambda_F \text{ if } (0 \le p_1 \le c_1 < C_1; 0 \le p_2 < c_2 = C_2)$$

- A failure arrives in an active RT channel and the ongoing call is rejected because all channels (RT and NRT) are occupied.

$$\mathbf{R}(s; (c_1, p_1, c_2, p_2 + 1)) = (c_2 - p_2)\lambda_F \text{ if } (0 \le p_1 \le c_1 = C_1; 0 \le p_2 < c_2 = C_2)$$

- A non-failing active RT channel is released.

$$\mathbf{R}(s; (c_1, p_1, c_2 - 1, p_2)) = (c_2 - p_2)\mu \text{ if } (0 \le p_1 \le c_1 \le C_1; 0 \le p_2 < c_2 \le C_2)$$

- A failed RT channel is repaired.

$$\mathbf{R}(s; (c_1, p_1, c_2 - 1, p_2 - 1)) = p_2\mu_r \text{ if } (0 \le p_1 \le c_1 \le C_1; 0 < p_2 \le c_2 \le C_2)$$

4.4   Formal Specification of Steady-State QoS Requirements

In order to check CSL formulas that specify QoS requirements in terms of NC blocking probability and HC dropping probability for NRT and RT classes, we need to label CTMC states with atomic propositions that characterize the state. Let $AP = \{\text{NRT\_Block}, \text{RT\_Block}, \text{NRT\_Drop}, \text{RT\_Drop}\}$. NRT_Block (resp. RT_Block) is assigned to states in which NRT (resp. RT) NC is blocked. NRT_Drop (resp. RT_Drop) is assigned to states in which NRT (resp. RT) HC is dropped. Satisfaction sets of these atomic propositions are formally defined in FR-CAC by:

$$
\begin{aligned}
S_{\text{NRT\_Block}} &= \{(c_1, p_1, c_2, p_2) \mid C_1 - g_1 \le c_1 \le C_1 \& 0 \le p_1 \le c_1 \& 0 \le p_2 \le c_2 \le C_2\} \\
S_{\text{RT\_Block}} &= \{(c_1, p_1, c_2, p_2) \mid C_1 - g_1 \le c_1 \le C_1 \ \& \ 0 \le p_1 \le c_1 \ \& \\
& \qquad C_2 - g_2 \le c_2 \le C_2 \& 0 \le p_2 \le c_2\} \\
S_{\text{NRT\_Drop}} &= \{(c_1, p_1, c_2, p_2) \mid c_1 = C_1 \ \& \ 0 \le p_1 \le c_1 \ \& \ 0 \le p_2 \le c_2 \le C_2\} \\
S_{\text{RT\_Drop}} &= \{(c_1, p_1, c_2, p_2) \mid c_1 = C_1 \& 0 \le p_1 \le c_1 \& c_2 = C_2 \& 0 \le p_2 \le c_2\}
\end{aligned}
$$

Let note that these sets are defined similarly for WoF-CAC in [17] without considering p_1 and p_2 because in WoF-CAC a state is defined by (c_1, c_2).

Since in this work we focus on the computation of steady-state performability measures, we check first $\mathcal{S}_{=?}(\phi)$ to determine the dropping/blocking probabilities. Then we check $\mathcal{E}_{=?}(true)$, which belongs to CSRL, to determine the mean occupation rate of channels.

$\mathcal{S}_{=?}(\phi)$ The verification of this formula is given by the Eq. 1. In order to compute steady-state dropping and blocking probabilities for each class of traffic we check the following formulas: $\mathcal{S}_{=?}$(RT_Block) (resp. $\mathcal{S}_{=?}$(NRT_Block)) spec-ifies the expected steady-state blocking probability for NRT (resp. RT) NC. $\mathcal{S}_{=?}$(RT_Drop) (resp. $\mathcal{S}_{=?}$(NRT_Drop)) specifies the expected steady-state drop-ping probability for NRT (resp. RT) HC.

$\mathcal{E}_{=?}(true)$ To determine the mean occupation rate of NRT channels (resp. RT channels) we enrich models with the reward function $\rho_{NRT}(s)$ (resp. ρ_{RT}). In FR-CAC, we assign to each state $s = (c_1, p_1, c_2, p_2)$ the reward values $\rho_{NRT}(s) = 100(c_1 - p_1)/C_1$ and $\rho_{RT}(s) = 100(c_2 - p_2)/C_2$. In the model WoF-CAC, we assign to each state $s = (c_1, c_2)$ the reward values $\rho_{NRT}(s) = 100c_1/C_1$ and $\rho_{RT}(s) = 100c_2/C_2$. We check $\mathcal{E}_{=?}(true)$ to quantify the occupation rate of NRT (resp. RT) channels by considering ρ_{NRT} (resp. ρ_{RT}) and using Eq. 2. Let note that for FR-CAC model we consider only the active channels that are occupied by ongoing calls and we do not count failed channels.

5   Numerical Results

We compute the steady-state performability measures of the composite model FR-CAC in order to give more realistic measures in terms of the NC blocking probabilities, HC dropping probabilities and the channels occupation rate of RT and NRT classes. We compare theses measures with performance measures com-puted over the pure performance model WoF-CAC. This comparison shows the efficiency of the recovery schema that we propose. We use the probabilistic model checker PRISM [9] to construct and solve CTMCs of FR-CAC and WoF-CAC schemes. This tool is a high-level modeling language and formulas are checked automatically. Numerical results are obtained with the following parameters: the number of RT channels (resp. NRT channels) is 50 (resp. 30), $g_2 = 5$, $g_1 = 3$, the traffic intensity of NRT class is: $\lambda_{Nh} = \lambda_{Nn} = 10$ and the arrival rate of RT HC is 20. The time unit is 1 min, the channel holding time $\mu = 1$, the arrival rate of channel failure $\lambda_F = 0.1$ and the reparation rate is $\mu_r = 0.5$.

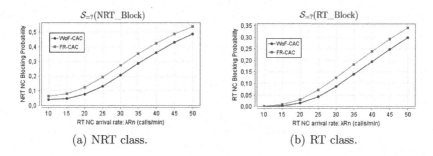

(a) NRT class.   (b) RT class.

Fig. 1. Steady-state NC blocking probabilities.

We vary the arrival rate of RT NC from 10 to 50 and we plot in Fig. 1(a) (resp. 1(b)) the steady-state NC blocking probability for NRT (resp. RT) class

and in Fig. 2(a) (resp. 2(b)) the steady-state HC dropping probability for NRT
(resp. RT) class. Clearly, these probabilities for both FR-CAC and WoF-CAC
models increase when the traffic load increases. Results show also that the call
blocking probability values for both classes are higher than call dropping probability values because the scheme give priority to HCs over NCs. Moreover, it is
observable that these probabilities are higher for FR-CAC than for WoF-CAC
and this is expectable because in FR-CAC which is a composite of availability and performance models, a call is dropped or blocked due to two reasons:
channels are occupied (performance reason) or channels are failed (availability
reason). The former type of loss is captured by WoF-CAC. Moreover we can
observe that relatives curves to FR-CAC and WoF-CAC are near especially for
blocking probabilities Fig. 1(a) and (b). We can deduce that the recovery strategy can reduce the dropped/blocked probabilities caused by failures.

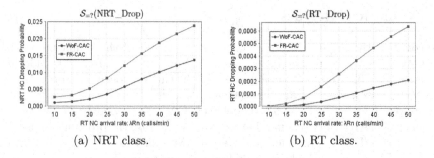

(a) NRT class.   (b) RT class.

Fig. 2. Steady-state HC dropping probabilities.

In Fig. 3(a) (resp. Fig. 3(b)), we present the mean channels occupation rate of
NRT (resp. RT) channels against increasing the RT NC arrival rate. Recall that
in FR-CAC we count only the active channels containing ongoing calls without
counting the failed ones. Obviously, when the traffic load increase the mean
channels occupation rate increases for FR-CAC and WoF-CAC. This is trivial

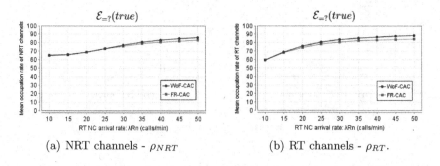

(a) NRT channels - ρ_{NRT} (b) RT channels - ρ_{RT}.

Fig. 3. Steady-state channels occupation rate.

because when the number of calls increases the number of occupied channels increases too. In addition, it can be observed that the mean occupation rate of active channels of the performability model FR-CAC and the pure performance model WoF-CAC is nearly the same due the use of recovery strategy. Indeed, in FR-CAC when an active channel fails it is replaced by an idle one which let the number of active channels almost the same in the FR-CAC and WoF-CAC.

6   Conclusion

In this paper we have presented a formal analysis of a composite performance and availability model of a multi-service CAC schema. The aim is to compute more realistic measures by considering the possibility of failures of active channels. In order to reduce the dropping and blocking probabilities of respectively HCs and NCs for both NRT and RT classes we have proposed a recovery strategy.

The Probabilistic model checking is used to construct CTMC models. We have used CSL logic to express performance requirements in terms of the blocking probabilities, the dropping probabilities and the mean bandwidth occupation rate. We have compared the performability measures obtained through the performability model with performance measures obtained through the pure performance model. Results show that the recovery strategy in the performability model can reduce the dropping and the blocking probabilities and can maintain the same level of the bandwidth utilization obtained by the performance model.

In the future we will extend this work by performing additional performance measures related to the transient behavior of the system as reliability. These measures are non traditional in the evaluation of CAC schemes and can be performed by the use of the time bounded path formula of CSL.

References

1. Alasti, M., Neekzad, B., Hui, J., Vannithamby, R.: Quality of service in WiMAX and LTE networks. IEEE Commun. Mag. **48**(5), 104–111 (2010)
2. AlQahtani, S.A.: Delay aware and users categorizing-based call admission control for multi-services LTE-A networks. AJSE **41**(9), 3631–3644 (2016)
3. Aziz, A., Sanwal, K., Singhal, V., Brayton, R.: Model checking continuous time Markov chains. ACM Trans. Comp. Logic **1**(1), 162–170 (2000)
4. Clarke, E.M., Emerson, A., Sistla, A.P.: Automatic verification of finite-state concurrent systems using temporal logic specifications. ACM Trans. Program. Languag. Syst. **8**(2), 244–263 (1986)
5. Haverkort, B., Cloth, L., Hermanns, H., Katoen, J.P., Baier, E.C.: Model checking performability properties. In: Proceedings of the DSN, pp. 103–112. IEEE CS Press (2002)
6. Jindal, V., Dharmaraja, S., Trivedi, K.S.: Markov modeling approach for survivability analysis of cellular networks. IJPE **7**(5), 429 (2011)
7. Khdhir, R., Mnif, K., Belghith, A., Kamoun, L.: An efficient call admission control scheme for LTE and LTE-A networks. In: ISNCC, pp. 1–6. IEEE (2016)

8. Kulkarni, V.G.: Modeling and Analysis of Stochastic Systems. Chapman & Hall, London (1995)
9. Kwiatkowska, M., Norman, G., Parker, D.: Probabilistic model checking in practice: case studies with PRISM. ACM SIGMETRICS Perform. Eval. Rev. **32**(4), 16–21 (2005)
10. Ma, Y., Han, J.J., Trivedi, K.S.: Channel allocation with recovery strategy in wireless networks. Trans. ETT **11**(4), 395–406 (2000)
11. Ma, Y., Han, J.J., Trivedi, K.S.: A method for multiple channel recovery in TDMA wireless communications systems. Comput. Commun. **24**(12), 1147–1157 (2001)
12. Meyer, J.F.: On evaluating the performability of degradable computing systems. IEEE Trans. Comput. **29**(8), 720–731 (1980)
13. Siddamallaiah, R.B.H., Subramanian, G., Satyanarayana, P.S.: Unified performance and availability model for call admission control in heterogeneous wireless networks. IJCNS **3**(04), 406 (2010)
14. Tarkaa, N.S., Mom, J.M., Ani, C.I.: Drop call probability factors in cellular networks. IJSER **2**(10), 1–5 (2011)
15. Trivedi, K.S., Ma, X., Dharmaraja, S.: Performability modelling of wireless communication systems. IJCS **16**(6), 561–577 (2003)
16. WiMAX Forum: WiMAX QoS Whitepaper, September 2006
17. Younes, S., Benmbarek, M.: Performance analysis of multi-services call admission control in cellular network using probabilistic model checking. In: Barkaoui, K., Boucheneb, H., Mili, A., Tahar, S. (eds.) VECoS 2017. LNCS, vol. 10466, pp. 17–32. Springer, Cham (2017). https://doi.org/10.1007/978-3-319-66176-6_2
18. Zarai, F., Ali, K.B., Obaidat, M.S., Kamoun, L.: Adaptive call admission control in 3GPP LTE networks. IJCS **27**(10), 1522–1534 (2014)

An MDA Approach for the Specification of Relay-Based Diagrams

Dalay Israel de Almeida Pereira[1]($\boxtimes$), Ouahmed Malki[1], Philippe Bon[1], Matthieu Perin[2], and Simon Collart-Dutilleul[1]

[1] Univ Lille Nord de France, IFSTTAR, COSYS, ESTAS,
59650 Villeneuve d'Ascq, France
{dalay.pereira,ouahmed.malki,philippe.bon,
simon.collart-dutilleul}@ifsttar.fr
[2] Institut de Recherche Technologique Railenium, 59300 Famars, France
matthieu.perin@railenium
http://www.ifsttar.fr/en/welcome/, http://railenium.eu/en

Abstract. A railway interlocking system is one example of a critical system, and therefore it must have a high level of reliability in order to avoid problems that may result on the loss of people's lives. However, many railway systems are still specified using historical relay-based diagrams, whose analysis are made by human inspection, which is error prone. This paper constitutes a first step towards using Model Driven Architecture (MDA) in order to specify railway interlocking systems. This work proposes a restructuring methodology starting from relay-based diagrams to produce formalized machine-readable XML models. This is performed by formalizing industrial formalisms and knowledge into a complete Domain Specific Language UML meta-model that is latter used to automatically generate an XSD using Model-to-Text transformation. The conforming XML models may then be understood by different stakeholders and used as input for automated analysis tools.

Keywords: Model-driven architecture · Restructuring
Reverse engineering · Domain specific languages · UML · XML
Railway systems

1 Introduction

The use of increasingly complex applications is demanding a greater investment of resources in system specification. Furthermore, high field reliability is an highly desirable attribute of any product, system or plant [7]. Railway Interlocking systems (RIS) is an example of critical systems, where reliability may be the differentiating factor determining its success or the occurrence of significant

Results are part of FUI 21 LCHIP project, founded by French National Research Agency (ANR).

E. H. Abdelwahed et al. (Eds.): MEDI 2018 Workshops, CCIS 929, pp. 17–29, 2018.
https://doi.org/10.1007/978-3-030-02852-7_2

negative consequences (like the loss of people's lives, for instance). These systems must have strict requirements for security and safety, in order to protect the user [17]. In this case, the use of advanced modelling techniques in order to model these RIS may be a crucial factor in order to improve safety and reliability.

In the Model Driven Development (MDD), the models are the primary artefact of the system development process. The most known example of MDD is the Model Driven Architecture (MDA) [21], which separates the specification of system functionality from the specification of its implementation. Created by the Object Management Group (OMG), one of the primary activities to be performed in MDA is the definition of a domain specific meta-model, which *"may make it possible to describe properties of a particular platform"* [19]. In this context a model is defined as an instance of a meta-model.

Despite the demand for new methodologies of specification, many railway systems are still specified by historical relay-based diagrams, which is a Domain Specific Language (DSL) describing how the physical elements of these systems are connected (relays, electrical wires, dipoles, etc). These languages are usually described without any explicit formalisation, thus lacking a meta-model and semantics description. Furthermore, in order to analyse the safety of these systems, one must inspect the relay-based specification and draw conclusions, which is not satisfactory for critical systems, since it is error prone [16].

This work proposes a restructuring [9] methodology starting from relay-based diagrams to produce formalized machine-readable XML models using a UML meta-model.

First section presents the previous works in the matter at hand, and the used formalisms. The first step of the method, presented in Sect. 3, is to reverse engineering [9], the industrial relay-based DSL, reviewed and then formalized into the UML [3] DSL meta-model. The second step, explained in Sect. 4, consists in the automated concretization of the meta-model into XSD/XML in order to obtain a specification that can be understood by many stakeholders and which will also be processed by computer software. Finally, a discussion on the proposed approach and a conclusion are developed in Sects. 5 and 6.

2   Related Works and Formalism Used

2.1   MDA

The Model Driven Architecture is a framework for system development where models are the primary artefact. It is the most know example of MDD [21] and it uses UML (Unified Modelling Language) in order to specify and visualize the code. MDA separates the operation specification of a system from the details of the way that system uses the capabilities of its platform. As a result, by using MDA, one is able to make specifications of platform independent models (PIM), whose implementation may be proceeded into one of many different platforms by model transformation.

In the MDA context, a model *"consists of sets of elements that describe some physical, abstract, or hypothetical reality"* [18]. A modelling language consists of its abstract syntax (the vocabulary of concepts and how they can be connected), concrete syntax (model as a diagram or a structured textual form) and semantics (additional information to explain the meaning of the abstract syntax) [8]. In the execution of a MDA process, it is necessary to accomplish two main activities. Firstly, one may formalize the knowledge by gathering relevant requirements of the domain, abstract it into some set of concepts and then express it into a model. The second activity is the transformations of this model into other models or its implementation.

Model transformations (MTs) are a way how models can be manipulated. The general idea of a model transformation is the translation from a source model (conforming with the source meta-model) into a target model (conforming with the target metamodel). *"The transformation specification is defined at the level of metamodels whereas its execution operates on the model level"* [6]. According to [11], there are many reasons for using MDA in the system development, some of them are: improvement of productivity, lower maintenance costs and reduced quality assurance costs, for instance.

Besides Model-to-Model (M2M) transformation, a model can also be used as input for Model-to-Text (M2T, e.g. [2]) transformation to produce text-based formats. This latter process allows the specification of an abstract model in a concrete language as a way to process it within computerized tooling suite.

2.2 Meta-modelling Formalism

There are many meta-modelling formalisms present in the literature nowadays: UML [3], Ecore [23], XMF [10], Kermeta [12], MOF [20], etc. Comparing these formalisms is not an easy task, since they have generally been designed for different needs, capacities and specificities that are not comparable [13]. In order to chose a formalism for meta-modelling the relay-based diagrams, some criteria were relevant:

- The language must be understandable for the majority of the project partners,
- The language must make it possible to model the abstract semantics of the relay schemas,
- The language must be best equipped for the generation of concrete textual semantics.

Considering these criteria, UML is the best candidate, since it is known by the partners and its semantics reduced to basic principles is sufficiently precise and rich to meet the needs of modelling. Besides, there are many tools that facilitate the (partial) generation of concrete semantics. In this work, the meta-model was developed in the Papyrus[1] open-source tool of the Eclipse platform.

---

[1] https://www.eclipse.org/papyrus/.

2.3   Model-To-Text Transformation

The transition from an abstract syntax into a concrete syntax requires strong modelling decisions in order to organize data and allow the specification of a model which conforms with the meta-model, decreasing the possibility of inconsistencies. Several possibilities are available to produce the concrete syntaxes, like those presented in [13] and [24]. A previous work proposed in [4] focuses on the behavioural translation of Relay-based specification into a formal language to perform complete system analysis. The aim of this work is thus different as we aim at providing an human readable exchangeable file across the project members.

In order to define and describe the structure of XML documents, one may define a XSD schema (XML Schema Definition), whose components constrain and document the meaning, usage and relationships of the XML constituent parts [14]. So, it is possible to define a XSD schema from our meta-model in order to support the specification of relay-based diagrams in XML.

In order to generate the XSD schema, we chose to use the Acceleo Query Language (AQL) [15], which is a language used to navigate and query a model. Acceleo[2] is the open-source Model-to-Text (M2T) implementation of the OMG MOF2Text norm [2] in the Eclipse platform. The transformation allows us to define characteristics of the XML specifications in the XSD schema. These characteristics are, for instance, the type of the objects, the patterns and restrictions to be followed (for the names of the objects, for instance) or the relations between the objects.

2.4   Relay-Based Specification

In the railway field, in an environment where the trains are not computer-controlled, the transmission, reception and use of information inside the system are made by electromechanical switching elements. The most widely used element is the Electromechanical Relay [22], which is composed by a electromagnet and one or more mobile mechanical parts (contacts). A contact may connect different wires by changing its position when affected by the electromagnet inside a relay. The different combinations of different power sources, contacts and relays allows the creation of several different systems.

In order to describe relay-based systems, one may use relay-based diagrams, which are drawings presenting all the elements of a system and their interconnections (similar to the diagram depicted on Fig. 1, for instance). In fact, the relay-based diagrams are undirected graphs. Two elements (nodes) are connected when there is a cable (arc) whose each extremity makes contact with each of these two elements. The cables have a explicit and unequivocal syntax: it physically connects the elements of the system in order to allow the passage of electric current.

However, the elements tend to be more complex as a consequence of its different nature and representations. The Table 1 presents some of the elements

---

[2] http://www.eclipse.org/acceleo/.

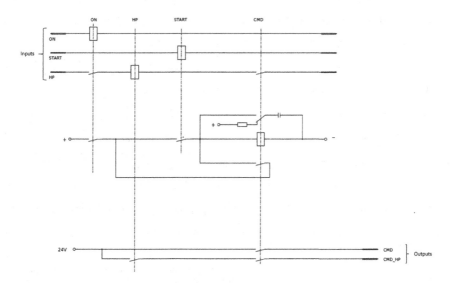

Fig. 1. Relay-based diagram example pointing the inputs and outputs

that may be used in a relay-diagram. The complexity of its representation arises by the fact that an element may be described by many graphical representations (contacts), or a graphical representation may describe a whole family of elements (blocks), for instance.

In the relay diagram graph, the elements can be connected by cables, which can be represented by a full or a dotted line. The former represents the passage of continuous current and the later describes the passage of alternating current. Furthermore, there is another relation between the nodes, more specifically, between contacts and relays denoted by a vertical mixed fine line. This last notation represents the functional and mechanical link between a relay and its associated contacts.

In the railway industry, a project of a train system specified by relay diagrams contains several sheets of specification. Each sheet describes a small part of the system and contains a diagram similar to the one presented on Fig. 1. Two diagrams in two different sheets are connected by their inputs and/or outputs and the union of all sheets describes the whole system of a project.

3   Meta-modelling

The meta-model of the relay-based diagram presents the elements that may be used in a specification and their possible interconnections. The meta-model is depicted on Fig. 2 and comes from the deep analysis of a representative set of Relay diagrams (concrete syntax) associated with domain-related knowledge provided by field experts from the SNCF, the French National Railway

Table 1. Elements that may be used in a relay-based diagram.

	Electrical Terminal or inputs (Sources, in french) with negative or positive poles of 24Vdc.
Circuits issus du poste ③	Supply from another station or inputs (Circuit issus du poste, in french). A priori not stable (can be set to - or to + for communication).
	Two position relays (Relais, in french) with one or two coils (bistable).
	Junction points between arcs (Liasons, in french).
R 08	Dipole-resistance couple (couple de dipôle rèsistance, in french).
BKF2	Functional blocks, used as substitutes for other commonly used diagram sheets.
	Some of the possible representations of Contacts

Company (Société Nationale des Chemins de fer Français). The *Project* ("Projet"[3]) object is the root of the model, so, there must exist only one project in the specification of a system. A project comprises several sheets ("Folios"). All

---

[3] In this section French translation have been added in quotes to help readability of the shown diagrams.

the sheets together form a complete and autonomous unit of meaning: a railway automation control-command. In each Folio one can find elements, which are represented by nodes ("noeuds"). A node can be specialised to relay, contact, block, dipole, terminal or an other element, as presented in the meta-model.

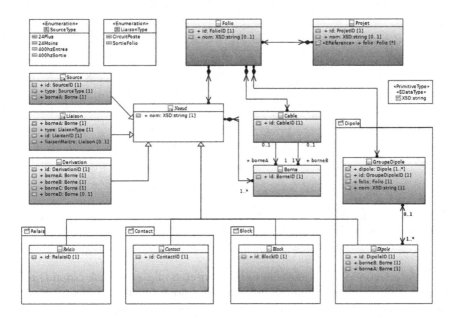

Fig. 2. Meta-model of the relay-based specification

Each node has one or more pins ("bornes") which are connected to cables. The connection between two pins of two different nodes represents the arc between two elements. This decision allows us to anonymise the end of the cables and make their use independent of the context (when it is possible). Pins are part of the nodes and their use are refined into specific properties (for example, BorneA or BorneB) in order to differentiate all the pins of a node.

Relays ("relais"), contacts and dipoles use inheritance to define the different subtypes of these objects, as it is presented in Fig. 3, this is the case when the number of bornes and/or the internal variables vary from one subtype to another. A relay can be monostable ("neutre") or bistable ("basculeur"), which are related to a fixed contact ("contact neutre") or a movable contact ("contact translateur"), respectively. A dipole can be a button, a resistance or a capacitor, for instance. When the differences are only semantic (their meanings to the human reader) then an enumeration typing explaining the types has been preferred to limit the number of objects, which is how the terminals ("sources") are defined.

In order to connect more than two elements at the same time by cables, a junction ("liaison") must be used. This element can be connected to three or

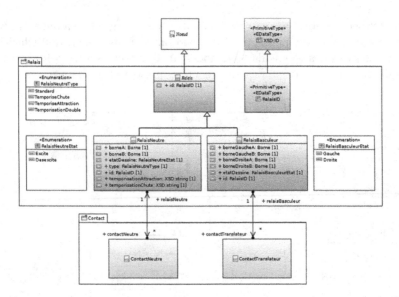

Fig. 3. Relay inheritance in order to represent relays monostable ("Neutre") or bistable ("Basculeur")

four different nodes, allowing them to be connected all together. A *GroupDipoles* element represents another set of arcs linking dipoles together, which represents that these elements must operate always together.

An example of an instance of a system which was specified conforming to this metamodel is presented in Fig. 4. This instance represents The control line "HP" of the diagram presented in Fig. 1.

4   XML Generation Using Model to Text (M2T) Principles

The XSD file allows the direct specifications of XML conforming with the metamodel we defined. Using the Eclipse platform it is possible to validate the XML files as the designer is specifying the system, showing errors when there is something inconsistent with what is defined in the XSD. By using these tools, a system designer can make corrections on the specification as soon as errors appear, which allows the creation of a XML specification conforming with our meta-model.

The generation of the XSD schema is conforming to the following principles:

– **Types** are translated into *xsd:simpleType* based on an analysis of their names. In the model, to ease the transformation, all specific xsd-related types have been prefixed with "XSD:" String. For example, names of Nodes are described in the model using specific type "XSD:String" that is translated into the standard *xsd:String* type of xsd norm in the resulting XSD file.

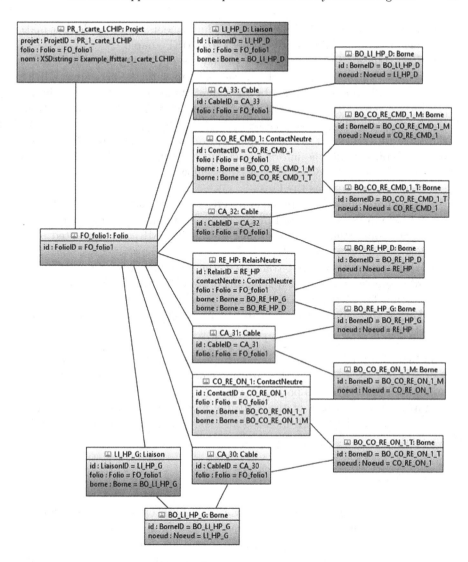

Fig. 4. Part of the instantiation of the diagram presented on Fig. 1

- **Enumerations** are translated into *xsd:simpleType* that extends *xsd:NCName* with a restriction over values based on the enumeration values. Enumerated values not starting with a letter (eg: "24Plus" for 24 volt plus power supply entry) are prefixed with an underscore to ensure *NCName* compatibility.
- **ID** are translated using a specific set of rules, as identifiers and links between objects are really concrete syntax specific:
  - An unique couple of *xsd:ID* and *xsd:IDREF* is created for each ID type that inherits from the "XSD:ID" type in the model,

- Both the ID and IDERF in the couple implement a shared rule that make them distinguishable from another ID/IDREF couple,
- Each time an instance reference to another one (non composite relation in the UML meta-model) the target is swap with the according IDREF of the "id" property owned by the target typing Class. For example, the reference to a "Borne" in a "Cable" is translated in the XSD by an IDREF associated to the Borne Class.

- **Classes** are translated into a couple *xsd:complexType* and *xsd:element*, the first one contains all the informations and it is also typing the latter. The type associated to the Class is created as follows:
  - Name is the same as the Class;
  - Set of non composition-related properties are translated into *xsd:attribute*, following rules for Types, Enumeration and ID/IDREF presented before;
  - Set of components (composition relations in UML) are translated using a *xsd:sequence* of elements;
  - Abstract classes are not translated, the generalizations are flattened as all properties (both owned and gained from generalization) are taken into account for each Class translation.
- **Packages** are explored to transform containing objects but they are not directly translated.

Another set of formatting and organising rules (using folding mock elements to help experts to read the XML) are implemented in the transformation but they are not detailed in this paper.

Figure 5 presents a part of the XML file modelling the running example of this paper (Fig. 1). This XML model is also the concrete textual representation of the model presented in Fig. 4.

5 Discussion

The meta-model we presented in this work has been created by the efforts of a group of researchers together with SNCF. The final goal of this project is the translation of relay-based specification into B [5], a formal language, which allows the verification and validation of systems according to defined properties. For evaluation purposes, some relay diagrams provided by SNCF (real industrial cases) has been successfully expressed in the meta-model and specified in XML. The relay meta-model and the XML specifications have been validated by SNCF. The names of the objects and the relation between them has been defined according to the relay-based diagrams used in industry and the experience on the field shared with us by SNCF.

The specification of relay-based diagrams in XML can cause many positive impacts in the industry:

- It can be understood by computers, as consequence it can be translated into formal models by the use of transformation languages (like QVT [1], for instance);

```
<?xml version="1.0" encoding="UTF-8"?>
  <lchip:Projet nom="Example_Ifsttar_1_carte_LCHIP"
  id="PR_1_carte_LCHIP" xmlns:lchip="http://lchip.xsd"
  xmlns:xsi="http://www.w3.org/2001/XMLSchema-instance">
...
    <Folio id="FO_folio1">
...
      <Cable borneB="BO_LI_HP_G" borneA="BO_CO_RE_ON_1_T" id="CA_30"/>
      <Cable borneB="BO_CO_RE_ON_1_M" borneA="BO_RE_HP_G" id="CA_31"/>
      <Cable borneB="BO_RE_HP_D" borneA="BO_CO_RE_CMD_1_T" id="CA_32"/>
      <Cable borneB="BO_CO_RE_CMD_1_M" borneA="BO_LI_HP_D" id="CA_33"/>
...
      <ContactNeutre relaisNeutre="RE_ON" id="CO_RE_ON_1" nom="Contact
      ON 1" etatDessine="Repos">
      <borneMobile id="BO_CO_RE_ON_1_M"/>
      <borneRepos id="BO_CO_RE_ON_1_R"/>
      <borneTravail id="BO_CO_RE_ON_1_T"/>
      </ContactNeutre>
...
      <ContactNeutre relaisNeutre="RE_CMD" id="CO_RE_CMD_1" nom="Contact
      CMD 1" etatDessine="Repos">
        <borneMobile id="BO_CO_RE_CMD_1_M"/>
        <borneRepos id="BO_CO_RE_CMD_1_R"/>
        <borneTravail id="BO_CO_RE_CMD_1_T"/>
      </ContactNeutre>
...
      <Liaison nom="Liaison ON_G" id="LI_HP_G" type="CircuitPoste">
        <borneA id="BO_LI_HP_G" />
      </Liaison>
      <Liaison nom="Liaison ON_G" id="LI_HP_D" type="CircuitPoste">
        <borneA id="BO_LI_HP_D" />
      </Liaison>
...
      <RelaisNeutre id="RE_HP" nom="Relais HP" type="Standard"
      etatDessine="Desexcite" temporisationChute=""
      temporisationAttraction="">
        <borneA id="BO_RE_HP_G"/>
        <borneB id="BO_RE_HP_D"/>
      </RelaisNeutre>
...
    </Folio>
...
</lchip:Projet>
```

Fig. 5. Part of the XML specification of the diagram described on Fig. 1

- There is the possibility of generating programming code directly from the XML specification, which can be used for animation or validation purposes, or the implementation of a computer controlled system;
- It can be understood by many stakeholders.

6   Conclusion

In this paper we propose the creation of a meta-model for relay-based diagrams and the use of XML as a concrete language for their specification. There are many benefits of using XML for the specification of railway relay-based systems, some of them are: the possibility of implementing and animating these systems, the fact that this is a technology widely known in industry and the possibility of using XML specifications as input for computer programs. This latter benefit may allows us to implement a tool for the automatic translation from relay-based diagrams into a formal language in order to prove their correctness.

As a reverse engineering process, we defined the meta-model based on the diagrams and the knowledge offered by the industry (SNCF). The final result of this process is a meta-model which can be used in order to guide the specification of Relay-based systems. In order to use XML as a concrete specification language, we used Acceleo to derived a XSD schema from the meta-model, which allows the direct specification of XML conform with the relay-based meta-model.

Two different examples used in industry has been specified using our approach with success. The meta-model and the XML specifications has been validated by SNCF. In order to improve the safety and the reliability of the railway systems, we plan to expand our approach in some future works.

In order to prove the correctness of a relay-based specification of a railway system, one must specify it in a formal language. Due to their mathematical background and support tools, the use of formal languages allows the specification and proof of systems. The translation of relay-based diagrams into a formal language (B-method), is in our near future agenda. Then, we intend to build a tool that allows the automatic transformation of relay-based specification and, furthermore, its automatic verification. After this last step, we aim to give a feedback about the correctness of the specification to the designer of the relay-based specifications.

References

1. Meta object facility (mof) 2.0 query/view/transformation specification. OMG Standard ptc/07-07-07, Object Management Group (OMG) (2007)
2. MOF Model to Text Transformation Language, v1.0. OMG Specification formal/2008-01-16, Object Managment Group (OMG), January 2008
3. Unified Modeling Language v2.5. OMG Specification, Object Management Group (OMG), March 2015
4. Aanæs, M., Thai, H.P.: Modelling and verification of relay interlocking systems. Master Thesis, Technical University of Denmark, DTU Informatics, Asmussens Alle, Building 305, DK-2800 Kgs. Lyngby, Denmark (2012)

5. Abrial, J.R.: The B-book: Assigning Programs to Meanings. Cambridge University Press, New York (1996)
6. Amrani, M., et al.: Formal verification techniques for model transformations: a tridimensional classification. J. Object Technol. **14**(3) (2015)
7. Barnard, R.: 3.2. 2 what is wrong with reliability engineering? In: INCOSE International Symposium, vol. 18, pp. 357–365. Wiley Online Library (2008)
8. Cetinkaya, D., Verbraeck, A.: Metamodeling and model transformations in modeling and simulation. In: Proceedings of the Winter Simulation Conference, pp. 3048–3058. Winter Simulation Conference (2011)
9. Chikofsky, E.J., Cross, J.H.: Reverse engineering and design recovery: a taxonomy. IEEE softw. **7**(1), 13–17 (1990)
10. Clark, T., Willans, J.: Software language engineering with XMF and XModeler. In: Computational Linguistics: Concepts, Methodologies, Tools, and Applications, pp. 866–896. IGI Global (2014)
11. Duby, C.K., Solutions, P.: Accelerating embedded software development with a model driven architecture®. Technical report, Pathfinder Solutions (2003)
12. Fleurey, F., Drey, Z., Vojtisek, D., Faucher, C., Mahé, V.: Kermeta language - reference manual (2010)
13. Fondement, F.: Concrete syntax definition for modeling languages. Ph.D. thesis, École polytechnique fédérale de Lausanne (EPFL), Lausanne, SW (2007)
14. Gao, S., Sperberg-McQueen, C.M., Thompson, H.S., Mendelsohn, N., Beech, D., Maloney, M.: W3C XML schema definition language (XSD) 1.1 part 1: structures. W3C Candidate Recommendation **30**(72), 16 (2009)
15. Goubet, L., Delaigue, L.: Acceleo user guide (2008)
16. Haxthausen, A.E.: Towards a framework for modelling and verification of relay interlocking systems. In: Calinescu, R., Jackson, E. (eds.) Monterey Workshop 2010. LNCS, vol. 6662, pp. 176–192. Springer, Heidelberg (2011). https://doi.org/10.1007/978-3-642-21292-5_10
17. Hinchey, M., Coyle, L.: Evolving critical systems: a research agenda for computer-based systems. In: 2010 17th IEEE International Conference and Workshops on Engineering of Computer Based Systems (ECBS), pp. 430–435. IEEE (2010)
18. Mellor, S.J.: MDA Distilled: Principles of Model-driven Architecture. Addison-Wesley Professional, Boston (2004)
19. Mellor, S.J., Scott, K., Uhl, A., Weise, D.: Model-driven architecture. In: Bruel, J.-M., Bellahsene, Z. (eds.) OOIS 2002. LNCS, vol. 2426, pp. 290–297. Springer, Heidelberg (2002). https://doi.org/10.1007/3-540-46105-1_33
20. Overbeek, J.: Meta Object Facility (MOF): investigation of the state of the art. Master's thesis, University of Twente (2006)
21. Parviainen, P., Takalo, J., Teppola, S., Tihinen, M.: Model-driven development processes and practices. Technical report, VTT Technical Research Centre of Finland (2009)
22. Rétiveau, R.: La signalisation ferroviaire. Presse de l'école nationale des Ponts et Chaussées (1987)
23. Steinberg, D., Budinsky, F., Merks, E., Paternostro, M.: EMF: Eclipse Modeling Framework. Pearson Education, London (2008)
24. Vu, L.H., Haxthausen, A.E., Peleska, J.: A Domain-specific language for railway interlocking systems, pp. 200–209. Technische Universität Braunschweig, Braunschweig, Germany (2014)

A Problem-Oriented Approach to Critical System Design and Diagnosis Support

Vincent Leildé[2(✉)], Vincent Ribaud[1], Ciprian Teodorov[2],
and Philippe Dhaussy[2]

[1] Lab-STICC, team MOCS, Université de Bretagne Occidentale,
Avenue le Gorgeu, Brest, France
Vincent.Ribaud@univ-brest.fr
[2] Lab-STICC, team MOCS, ENSTA-Bretagne, rue François Verny, Brest, France
{vincent.leilde,ciprian.teodorov,philippe.dhaussy}@ensta-bretagne.fr

Abstract. For critical software applications, dependability and safety are required features that should respect security principles. To cope with these constraints, the design activity should use methods that foster knowledge sharing and reuse, in particular security problems and their solutions. In this paper, we present a new problem-oriented method that follows a step-wise building of the solution. Problems are reused using various mechanisms, and a solution is conceived, verified and diagnosed. We wish to illustrate the approach, building a secure SCADA architecture.

Keywords: Problem oriented method · Diagnosis · Security patterns

1 Introduction

Critical software systems are pervading our daily lives and sustain many different domains (transportation, avionics, health-care or information management). To improve their dependability and safety, regardless their complexity, critical software design should be carried out with respect to security principles.

Over time, knowledge about security issues has been captured into patterns, a packaged solution to a recurrent problem in a specific context [6]. A security pattern is a reusable solution for a recurring security problem. It is used to analyze, construct and evaluate secure systems [14]. It provides detailed guidelines about the application of an architectural solution for a particular problem of security. Several research works address security issues using security patterns, and we exploit as a case study the approach set by Obeid [12]. The author secures SCADA systems through the composition of the SCADA architecture with security patterns. Safety and security requirements of the composition are then validated through model-checking.

Our research work is focused on methods and tools intended to ease verification activities, especially diagnosis activities. Briefly stated, our approach aims

© Springer Nature Switzerland AG 2018
E. H. Abdelwahed et al. (Eds.): MEDI 2018 Workshops, CCIS 929, pp. 30–39, 2018.
https://doi.org/10.1007/978-3-030-02852-7_3

to address diagnosis issues with a general diagnosis ontology [10], a management system to perform and enable verification and diagnosis activities [9], and a domain-oriented method [11].

Fernandez's seminal work [5] proposes to design a SCADA system using security patterns. Built on this proposal, Obeid's work proposes to formalize security requirements using safety properties. Then, a model-checker is used to verify the combination between security patterns and architecture. Both authors do not address practical implementation issues. The research work presented in this paper shows how Obeid's case study can benefit from our combination and diagnosis proposals and how he could build a secure SCADA architecture through successive iterations, reusing security *problem cases* (package of solutions addressing a problem) from a pattern-based knowledge base. This work relies on the method we proposed in [11] that addresses the issues of building and reusing verified components and configurations (set of components). Configurations assemble components thanks to three combination mechanisms (property-based, pattern-based and component-based). The present work uses only the pattern-based mechanism.

A software organization that manages quality should have a corporate infrastructure that links together and transcends single projects by capitalizing on successes and learning from failures [2]. These tasks require to manage past diagnosis experiences (gathering a set of heterogeneous artifacts) and to correlate discovered abnormalities with experiences. This can be achieved with a knowledge management system together with a well-defined method. To some extent, the method we use in this paper borrows the Twin Peaks idea of performing round trips between problem and solution spaces [8], with the goal to improve the verification process. It should help the engineer to bring closer high-level information and abnormalities observations. It focuses on a progressive constitution of a *problem cases* knowledge base, containing both problems and solutions, that can be reused. Solutions package formal designs and verification runs, and *problem cases* are formalized with a set of properties together with various structured solutions. Section 2 overviews the method and discusses how *problem cases* is a support to design. In Sect. 3, we show an application of the method to secure a SCADA system with security patterns. Section 4 concludes the study.

2 A Problem-Oriented Approach

2.1 Overview of the Method

The method proposes a progressive understanding and solving of the problem. First, this should help the designer to find efficiently a solution to his problem, by decomposing the problem in smaller subproblems, and reusing existing solutions. Second, it should help the verifier to understand the root causes of abnormalities for a selected solution, by providing diagnosis with relevant information. This section describes the process used to formalize problems and the different steps of the process flow. The step-wise method is presented by the activity diagram in Fig. 1. The method is reiterated until a satisfactory solution is achieved. The method conforms to a metamodel (an excerpt is given in Fig. 2) and method elements are briefly defined in Sect. 2.2.

Let us consider an example. Suppose a board game with one board and two players. The board asks an infinite number of questions to each player, in a non deterministic manner. If the player has a right answer, it increases its score by one point, otherwise no point is awarded. The match ends when a player reaches 3 points. The game is not fair because in some cases, the board can ask more questions to one player rather the other. The method steps are illustrated below.

Figure 1 and steps explanation are extracted from [11].

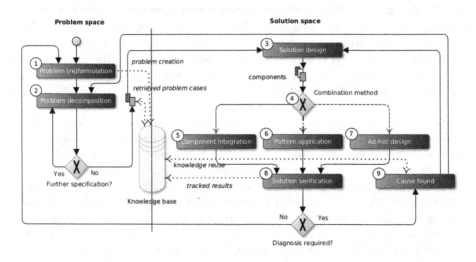

Fig. 1. Method steps

(1) The problem is formulated as a set of properties and constraints (architectural or technical choices). For instance, "at the end of the game, each player has played the same number of times". (2) The problem is decomposed into subproblems, either known problems - called *problem cases* - selected from a knowledge base, or unknown situations. For instance, we may decide that fairness can be achieved by reusing a turn mechanism, available as a *problem case*. (3) When the need for a concrete view occurs, we move towards the solution space. The solution elements are organized. For instance, we introduce the turn *problem case* into the solution in progress. (4) We consider how to combine the selected *problem case* with the solution[1]. The *problem case* may be either (5) composed with other parts of the solution, (6) applied as a pattern, or acts only as specifications and (7) an ad-hoc design is left to the engineer. (8) At this point, we built a part of the expected solution; hence we are able to start a verification cycle. When abnormalities are observed, it triggers a diagnosis process.

---

[1] Each kind of combination is represented with a particular arrow shape.

Verification results are stored in the knowledge base. (9) When the diagnosis process is performed, knowledge about *problem cases* can be used to ease the process. The design is corrected, and the verification endeavor repeated. In some cases, the selected *problem case* does not suit, hence we have to backtrack and rework the *problem cases* combination, and it might be useful to keep track of the failed attempt.

The step-wise method is repeated several times while useful components can be combined. The engineer is left with a reduced problem for which no known solutions exist and where a classical design and verification activities have to be performed.

The method space is divided in two parts, the problem space, related to the problem elaboration, and the solution space, related to the design and verification of the solution. Whereas the problem elaboration produces specifications to the solution design, the resulting solution produces expanded specifications (stemming from design choices) to the problem space. The mutual enrichment is inspired from the Twin Peak model [8], a software iterative development process that focuses on the combination of problem structures and solution structures.

2.2   Problem Cases for System Design

Decomposing a complex problem into smaller problems that are more manageable and easier to solve, is a natural way to reduce the design complexity. When past experiences are available, the method can be improved by analogical reasoning, i.e. reusing past known problems. But it raises the issue about the capture of problems and how they have been solved.

A problem is reified as a *problem case*, that aims to understand and capture both problems and solutions during the design of a software system. Engineers thus constitute a reusable base of expertise related to their engineering domain. A *problem case* is a combination of subproblem cases, which are made of various *problem elements*, essentially related to system objects, for instance, *states*, *transitions, verification runs* or *properties*. A *problem case* can be of different kinds, a *component-based*, a *pattern-based*, or a *property-based*. An excerpt of the *problem case* conceptual model is given by Fig. 2, but readers should refer to [11] for more information about *problem cases*.

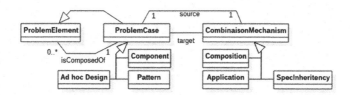

Fig. 2. Excerpt of problem case conceptual model

During reuse, *problem cases* are combined together. Combination can be of different kinds, for instance *component integration, pattern application* and *ad hoc design. Component integration* is the most easy way for reusing a problem case, as it requires few adaptations. When the component is too generic, the counterpart is a lack of efficiency. Besides, the *pattern application* generally requires manual implementations. A pattern is a well-defined guidance for a recurring problem, but the solution must be adapted to the context. With *ad hoc design*, only specifications are reused, and the solution design is left to the user. Thus, the kind of *problem case* has an impact on the reuse efficiency.

3   Application

We reuse a case study extracted from the work of [12]. The approach aims at securing architectures by applying security patterns together with a security policy. The approach has been demonstrated on several kinds of architectures.

3.1   Domain Description

We suppose that a knowledge base has been built from the domain together with previous experiences. The base contains a set of *problem cases* structured as security patterns. The author [12] defines a security pattern as a list of formal properties, a name, a list of functionalities, a description of the problem it is intended to solve, a static and a dynamic structure of the solution and some examples of use.

The authorization *problem case* (*AUTH*) implements operation controls for a resource (read, write, execution). *AUTH* ensures that a resource access by an entity *Ent*, for an operation *OpRes*, is granted. When an access is authorized, the access is realized, otherwise counter-measures are triggered.

The structure of the *problem case* is depicted in Fig. 3. Function *hasRight (e: Ent, opRes: OpRes):Boolean* returns true if the entity *e* can perform the *opRes.oper* operation on the *opRes.res* resource (either the resource is not protected for this operation or the entity has an explicit permission for this operation).

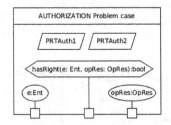

Fig. 3. Authorization problem case structure

AUTH includes also the problem specification described with two LTL properties. *PRTAuth1*: when an access request respects the access rights, the resource access is finally realized. *PRTAuth2*: a resource access must respect access rights.

$$PRT\,Auth1 : \forall c \in Auth, \forall e \in Ent, \forall opRes \in OpRes,$$
$$[evtVerify(c, AccReq(e, opRes)) \wedge right(c, e, opRes) \Rightarrow \Diamond evtAccess(c, e, opRes)]$$

$$PRT\,Auth2 : \forall c \in Auth, \forall e \in Ent, \forall opRes \in OpRes,$$
$$[evtAccess(c, e, opRes) \Rightarrow right(c, e, opRes)].$$

3.2   Problem Formalization

The Fig. 4, issued from [12], represents a unsecured SCADA architecture composed of four entities, a global controller (GC), two local controllers ($LC1$ and $LC2$), and a communication network ($NETWORK$) that links together GC, $LC1$ and $LC2$. The local controller $LC1$ owns the resource $RES1$, while the local controller $LC2$ owns the resource $RES2$. Some $READ$ and $WRITE$ operations on a resource are granted to an entity according to its role. Different roles are $ADMIN$ ($READ$ and $WRITE$ access to $RES1$ and $RES2$), $GCOWNER$ ($READ$ access to $RES1$ and $RES2$), $LC1OWNER$ ($READ$ and $WRITE$ access to $LC1$) and $LC2OWNER$ ($READ$ and $WRITE$ access to $LC2$).

The architecture can be seen at a higher abstraction level, as a set of NET and $ACCESS$ components. A NET component is an abstraction of a $NETWORK$ entity that forwards messages to other components. An $ACCESS$ component is an abstraction of $LC1$, $LC2$ and GC entities that manage access to resources. An $ACCESS$ component behaves as depicted in Fig. 4.

In the figure, the transitions between states conforms to the Event-Condition-Action scheme represented as $Si \xrightarrow{\{Event\}[Condition]Action} Sj$. Si and Sj are *states*, arrows stand for *transitions*, labeled with *events* that cause *transitions* to be triggered. A *condition* is a boolean expression, and an *action* represents a statement such as a variable assignment or event sending. When an *event* occurs, the guard *condition* is evaluated and the *transition* is fired only if the *condition* is true, and the *action* is performed.

Each $ACCESS$ component starts with an *Idle* state, where it waits for a request (req). If a request is received and if the request is properly addressed to the component ($req.target==id$), the resource is accessed ($Access$) and the component replies ($sending$). When the request is not intended to the component ($req.target!=id$), the component forwards the request to other connected components through the network. In our case, when the environment ENV wants to access to an element of the architecture, it sends a message to GC together with an indication about the target (either $RES1$ or $RES2$), and the corresponding operation ($READ$ or $WRITE$). When GC receives requests from the environment(ENV), GC forwards the request to $LC1$ or $LC2$ through the $NETWORK$. $LC1$ or $LC2$ receives and processes requests from the $NETWORK$, and replies to or acknowledges the request.

To guarantee integrity and confidentiality constraints about $LC1$ and $LC2$, security mechanisms are applied. The security mechanisms must guarantee two properties: -$PRT1$, when a component sends a request that respects the access rights for accessing a resource, the access must be realized. -$PRT2$, any resource access must respect the access rights.

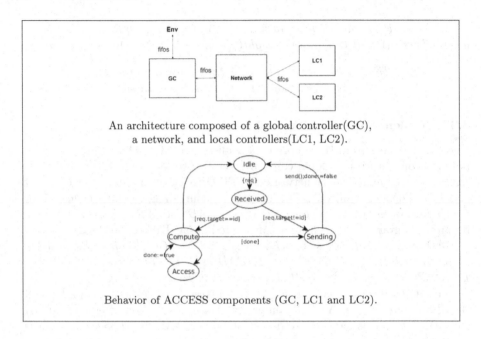

An architecture composed of a global controller(GC),
a network, and local controllers(LC1, LC2).

Behavior of ACCESS components (GC, LC1 and LC2).

Fig. 4. Description of the application extracted from [12]

3.3   Problem Decomposition

According to the method, the problem is decomposed into smaller subproblems.
A global solution is built with a combination of smaller solutions. The structure
of the properties *PRT1* and *PRT2* is similar to the structure of *PRTAuth1* and
PRTAuth2. Hence, the engineer selects the *AUTH problem case*.

3.4   Solution Design

The *AUTH problem case* is introduced in the solution building. The combination
strategy can be either a *composition* of self-contained and separated components,
an *application* of pattern, or a *ad hoc design* consistent with *problem case* properties.

Because the *AUTH problem case* is structured as a pattern, the most appropriate combination mechanism is the pattern application. Applying a pattern
requires that given hypotheses are respected. For instance, in order to apply the
authorization pattern we should have an *Access* state in the design, where the
authorization mechanism has to be introduced. The combination is realized in
two steps, first, hypotheses are checked, and second, transformations are applied
and verified. Let see how it works with the *AUTH problem case*. At the first
step, the following hypotheses must be respected: - *Hypothesis 1*, the reception
of a message is carried out by reading the input fifo. It happens in a transition
from the *Idle* state to the *Receive* state; *Hypothesis 2*, message sending is carried

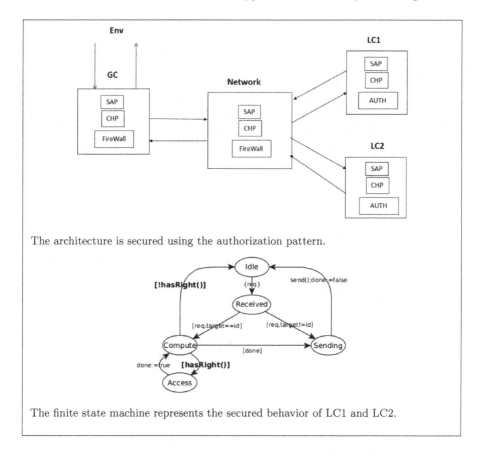

Fig. 5. Description of the secured application

out by a write into the output fifo, along a transition from the *Sending* state to the *Idle* state; - *Hypothesis 3*, each transition to the *Compute* state has a source state called *Receive*; - *Hypothesis 4*, the *Access* state has a single source state called *Compute*.

If hypotheses are respected, the second step applies the pattern transformation in order to produce a secured solution, as depicted in the Fig. 5. The transformation rules are not presented in the article, but can be found in [12].

3.5   Solution Verification and Diagnosis

Generally speaking, a security pattern aims to implement security policies in a system. According to Obeid, the set of formal properties materializes the security policy [13]. Properties verification is performed with a model-checker. Exploring the state space makes it possible to measure the effectiveness of the security patterns. Model-checking different designs allows the engineer to study the composition of different patterns in order to establish an optimal assembly.

3.6   Causes

Researchers [1,3,4,7] divide the diagnosis in two main tasks: isolation (localization) and causal analysis. Isolation extracts the subset of elements, part of models, that needs to be corrected. Causal analysis associates causes to the observed abnormalities. In our method, a *cause* can be a *model cause* or a *design cause*. A *model cause* happens when the selected problem is valid (for instance the *AUTH* pattern is the good choice), but its implementation is not valid (for instance the *AUTH* pattern is badly implemented). It locates the cause in the application of the pattern. Conversely, a *design cause* happens when the combination of the problem is valid (for instance the *AUTH* pattern is correctly implemented), but the combined problem case is not appropriated, or incomplete.

3.7   Iterating Through Problem and Solution Spaces

Assume that a new security policy is required for the same architecture, some counter-measures must be triggered in case of a security violation. According to the method, existing *problem cases* can be retrieved and combined. The checkpoint pattern (*CHP*) allows to apply specific regulations and defines properties that are closed to the new security constraints. The *CHP problem case* is selected and retrieved, and applied to the design already using the *AUTH problem case*.

Once *CHP problem case* has been applied and the solution verified, the resulting design gathers two *problem cases*, the checkpoint and the authorization. The *problem cases* combination can be stored in the knowledge base as a new reusable *problem case* named *SECACCESS*.

Let suppose that the architecture must evolve and a new local controller *LC3* added. The new problem can be solved by reusing the *SECACCESS problem case*. Note that *SECACCESS* is neither a pattern-based *problem case* but a component-based *problem case*, a kind of COTS easy to reuse.

4   Conclusion

Designing a solution for a given security problem and diagnosing eventual faults are tedious tasks. This is mainly due to a lack of domain knowledge and poorly managed information, that complicate diagnosis support and solution reuse. Security patterns capture basic problems and solutions of the domain, and make them available in a form usable by the community. Moreover, catalog of complementary, mutually-supporting patterns are available [14,15].

However, few research work address issues related to the progressive building of a suitable knowledge base. Our research hypothesis is that a method is required for analyzing the current problem, storing relevant information, and reusing known solutions as much as possible. The problem-oriented method that we propose follows a step-wise building of the solution, by reusing *problem cases*. In this paper, we highlighted the application of *problem cases* for the security domain, captured in a form of security patterns, and we discussed the possible combination mechanisms.

References

1. Ball, T., Naik, M., Rajamani, S.K.: From symptom to cause: localizing errors in counterexample traces. In: ACM SIGPLAN Notices, vol. 38. ACM (2003)
2. Basili, V.R., Caldiera, G.: Improve software quality by reusing knowledge and experience. MIT Sloan Manage. Rev. **37**(1), 55 (1995)
3. Clarke, E.M., Kurshan, R.P., Veith, H.: The localization reduction and counterexample-guided abstraction refinement. In: Manna, Z., Peled, D.A. (eds.) Time for Verification. LNCS, vol. 6200, pp. 61–71. Springer, Heidelberg (2010). https://doi.org/10.1007/978-3-642-13754-9_4
4. Cleve, H., Zeller, A.: Locating causes of program failures, p. 342. ACM Press (2005)
5. Fernandez, E.B., Larrondo-Petrie, M.M.: Designing secure SCADA systems using security patterns, pp. 1–8. IEEE (2010)
6. Gamma, E. (ed.): Design Patterns: Elements of Reusable Object-oriented Software. Addison-Wesley Professional Computing Series. Addison-Wesley, Reading (1995)
7. Groce, A., Visser, W.: What went wrong: explaining counterexamples. In: Ball, T., Rajamani, S.K. (eds.) SPIN 2003. LNCS, vol. 2648, pp. 121–136. Springer, Heidelberg (2003). https://doi.org/10.1007/3-540-44829-2_8
8. Hall, J., Jackson, M., Laney, R., Nuseibeh, B., Rapanotti, L.: Relating software requirements and architectures using problem frames. IEEE Computer Society (2002)
9. Leilde, V., Ribaud, V., Dhaussy, P.: An organizing system to perform and enable verification and diagnosis activities. In: Yin, H., et al. (eds.) IDEAL 2016. LNCS, vol. 9937, pp. 576–587. Springer, Cham (2016). https://doi.org/10.1007/978-3-319-46257-8_62
10. Leildé, V., Ribaud, V., Teodorov, C., Dhaussy, P.: A diagnosis framework for critical systems verification (short paper). In: Cimatti, A., Sirjani, M. (eds.) SEFM 2017. LNCS, vol. 10469, pp. 394–400. Springer, Cham (2017). https://doi.org/10.1007/978-3-319-66197-1_27
11. Leilde, V., Ribaud, V., Teodorov, C., Dhaussy, P.: Domain-oriented verification management. In: 8th International Conference on Model and Data Engineering (MEDI 2018), October 2018
12. Obeid, F.: Validation Formelle d Implantation de Patrons de Securite. Ph.D. thesis, ENSTA-Bretagne (2018)
13. Obeid, F., Dhaussy, P.: Validation formelle d'implementation des patrons de sécurité: application aux scada. In: Hurault, A., Stouls, N. (eds.) Actes des 15èmes journées sur les Approches Formelles dans l'Assistance au Développement de Logiciels, Besançon, France, pp. 13–18, June 2016
14. Schumacher, M., Fernandez-Buglioni, E., Hybertson, D., Buschmann, F., Sommerlad, P.: Security Patterns: Integrating Security and Systems Engineering. Wiley, Hoboken (2013)
15. Steel, C., Nagappan, R., Lai, R.: Core Security Patterns: Best Practices and Strategies for J2EE, Web Services, and Identity Management. Pearson Education, London (2012)

Formal Specification and Verification of Cloud Resource Allocation Using Timed Petri-Nets

Saoussen Cheikhrouhou[1][(✉)], Nesrine Chabouh[1], Slim Kallel[1],
and Zakaria Maamar[2]

[1] ReDCAD, University of Sfax, Sfax, Tunisia
{saoussen.cheikhrouhou,nesrine.chabouh,slim.kallel}@redcad.tn
[2] Zayed University, Dubai, United Arab Emirates
zakaria.maamar@zu.ac.ae

Abstract. Context: Known for its resource elasticity and pay-per-use model, more and more organizations are adopting cloud computing to support the execution of their business processes. To support organizations meet their financial restrictions, cloud providers offer different time-based pricing strategies.

Objective: The proposed approach aims at assisting business process designers identify necessary cloud resources with respect to temporal and financial restrictions on business processes. The former minimizes the search time for cloud resources while the latter minimizes the cost of leasing these resources.

Method: The proposed approach considers 2 inputs, a time-constrained business process specification and a list of allocated cloud resources, and then confirms whether this process has the necessary cloud resources, satisfies the temporal and financial restrictions, and is deadlock-free. To this end, the specification is automatically translated into a Temporal Petri-Net.

Results: The implementation on a real case study has shown that the proposed approach ensures a proper matching between process activities and cloud resources.

Keywords: Formal verification · Cloud resource · Business process Temporal properties

1 Introduction

With the rapid evolution of information and communication technologies, many organizations are taping into the world of cloud computing to reduce the operation costs associated with managing their Business Processes (BP). Among cloud benefits, we cite resource availability upon-request (*aka* elasticity) and pay-per-use model [12]. To cater to organizations' multiple needs, cloud providers offer different pricing strategies for their computation, storage, and communication resources. For instance, Amazon Web Services (AWS) offers on-demand,

© Springer Nature Switzerland AG 2018
E. H. Abdelwahed et al. (Eds.): MEDI 2018 Workshops, CCIS 929, pp. 40–49, 2018.
https://doi.org/10.1007/978-3-030-02852-7_4

reserved, and spot-instance prices. Although competition is a sign of any healthy marketplace, organizations should be made aware of the challenges associated with selecting the best providers, in our case providers of cloud resources. Indeed, the selection should permit to optimize first, the time of screening and selecting providers' offers and second, the cost of paying the selected providers' resources. In this paper, we raise the following question: how to assign organizations' BPs to cloud providers without violating temporal constraints (e.g., deadline) imposed on these organizations.

Satisfying organizations' temporal constraints with respect to cloud resources availabilities has been reported in the literature [2,8,11].

However, how to formally define this satisfaction for the sake of verification remains unexplored and handled on a case-by-case basis. This is, also, dependent on specific pricing strategies of cloud resources. Our previous work in [9] is one step towards a formal definition of time-constrained BPs. In this paper, we propose a formal specification of such BPs and their allocated cloud resources using Timed Petri Nets (TPN). To this end, we provide an automatic transformation of cloud resources, according to their pricing strategies, into TPN. In addition, we propose a formal verification that checks BP correctness along with meeting deadlines.

The remainder of this paper is organized as follows: Sect. 2 briefly defines some concepts upon which our approach is built. Section 3 introduces a motivating example. Section 4 details our approach for formal verification of cloud resource allocation. Transformation rules associated with this approach and the verification of this allocation correctness are presented. Prior to listing some related work in Sect. 6 and concluding in Sect. 7, some implementation details are discussed in Sect. 5.

2 Background

This section introduces the main concepts and definitions related to TPNs, time-constrained BPs, and cloud pricing models.

Time Petri Nets. A PN is formed upon a mathematical theory that uses automated tools to offer an accurate modeling and analysis of systems' behaviors [1]. Initially, PNs were a formal language without any reference to time or probability. However, for many practical applications, time is a must-have and designers should consider it when analyzing the correct behavior and performance of their applications. TPNs incorporate clocks and temporal constraints into transitions to help describe and analyze properly time-dependent systems. TPNs associate a firing time interval [a, b] with each transition (t), where a and b are rational numbers such that $0 \leq a \leq b$ and $a \neq \infty$.

Times a and b for t are relative to the moment at which t was enabled; a and b are referred to as earliest-firing-time and latest-firing-time of t, respectively. Formally, a TPN is a tuple Y = (P, T, Pre, Post, M_0, IS) where:

- (P, T, Pre, Post, M_0) is a PN [1].
- IS: $T \rightarrow Q^* * (Q^* \cup \{\infty\})$ is a static interval function that associates each t with a time interval IS(t)= [min, max], where Q^* is the set of positive rational numbers.

Cloud pricing models. Each cloud provider defines a proper model for selling its resources. For instance, Google offers per-minute billing strategy while others require the price of an hour. In our work, we adopt Amazon pricing strategies where:

- On-Demand-instances means pay for a resource by the hour with no long-term commitment.
- Reserved-instances means make a one-time, upfront payment for an instance of a resource that could be reserved for 1 or 3 year-terms. In return, the requestor receives a significant discount for each hour running that instance.
- Spot-instances means pay according to the supply and demand.

Time-constrained business process. In [4,5], we propose the formal specification of BPs' temporal constraints that can be relative and/or absolute. On the one hand, a relative constraint specifies requirements such as activity duration and temporal dependency. Activity duration corresponds to the minimum and maximum execution times of a given activity using a time interval [MinD; MaxD] with $0 \leq MinD \leq MaxD$. And, temporal dependency is a relationship between 2 activities in which one activity depends on either the start or the finish of another in order to either begin or end. 4 temporal dependencies exist: Start-to-Finish (SF), Start-to-Start (SS), Finish-to-Start (FS), and Finish-To-Finish (FF). On the other hand, an absolute constraint specifies the start and finish times of activities like an activity begins at a specific time or cannot finish later than a specific time.

3   Motivating Example

In Fig. 1, the service supervision BP is triggered when a signal is sent by a customer (request service trouble ticket) "a1" (a for activity). Then, necessary data are retrieved "a2" or the service test management is initiated "a3". Retrieving data can be performed automatically "a4" or via a script "a5". In parallel, the service test is performed by "a6" and "a7". The process ends by replying to the customer "a8" and initiating trouble shooting "a9".

Table 1 lists the time constraints on the service supervision BP. These constraints include duration of activities and temporal dependencies. For example, a1 and a5 have a minimum and maximum duration of 1h and 2h, respectively. A time interval is considered between the end of a7 and the beginning of a9, which must be between 2h and 5h. Furthermore, some activities need resources to run. For this, a1, a4, and a9 operate on 2 cloud Virtual Machines (VM1 and VM2). VM1 is shareable between a1 and a9 and VM2 is used by a4, only.

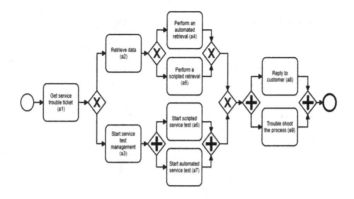

Fig. 1. Service supervision BP in BPMN

Table 1. Temporal constraints on process activities

	Activities								
Temporal Constraints	a1	a2	a3	a4	a5	a6	a7	a8	a9
Durations	[1h,2h]	[2h,3h]	[2h,10h]	[1h,4h]	[1h,2h]	[1h,4h]	[2h,5h]	[1h,1h]	[1h,2h]
Temporal dependency	TD(FS,a3,a7,2h,5h)								

4   Our Approach for Formal Specification and Verification of Cloud Resource Allocation

Our approach consists of 3 steps (Fig. 2): specification, transformation, and formal verification. The specification step handles BPs enriched with time constraints and cloud resources. More details about modeling BPs during this step are given in [9]. Then, the process models are transformed into TPNs during the transformation step. This latter uses a set of transformation rules and is implemented using a model-to-model transformation language, for instance XSLT. The objective of this step is to convert an extended BPMN process into a TPN model. Finally, the third step, formal verification, checks the correctness of the designed BPMN process thanks to the model checker TINA [1]. This correctness refers to specific properties written in S/E LTL [10] and means that matching each BP activity to a corresponding cloud resource meets temporal constraints. This is the main goal of the verification step.

4.1   Transformation Rules

We developed a set of rules that transform cloud and price enriched BPMN processes into TPN. This one is then checked to detect time violations that may occur while ensuring that the allocation of cloud resources is correct. We begin by transforming BPMN basic elements (e.g., start/end event, activities, and gateways) into TPN. Readers are referred to [3] for a complete description of the transformation rules. For illustration, an activity with a minimum value m

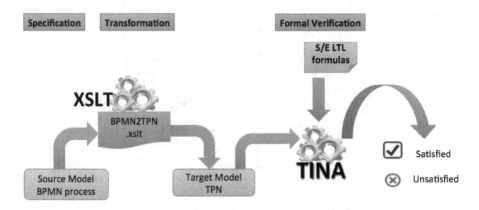

Fig. 2. General representation of our approach

and a maximum value M duration-constraint is transformed into 1 place and 2 transitions labeled with clocks depending on the activity's duration (Fig. 3).

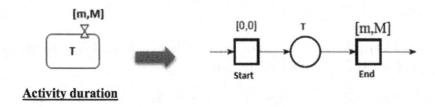

Fig. 3. Transformation of duration constraint on an activity into a TPN

We recall readers that 4 temporal dependencies (SF, SS, FS and FF) could exist between activities. For instance, SF denotes that activity a2 can only finish after a time interval [m,M] that a1 has started. Figure 4 shows SF transformation into a TPN.

For the rest of temporal dependencies, namely SS, FS and FF, we refer readers to [3].

Let's now tackle the transformation rules related to cloud pricing strategies of the allocated resources. The designer should choose one of the corresponding cloud strategies, namely on-demand, spot instance predefined-duration, spot instance non-predefined-duration, and reserved. Cloud pricing strategies have a direct impact on the total process cost, and thus, on the organisation revenue. First, the on-demand strategy does not need temporal constraint for cloud resources. Figure 5 shows the mapping of a1, with a duration constraint in [m, M] using a VM with on-demand strategy.

Reserved and spot-predefined duration pricing strategies require relative temporal constraints that indicate the time interval of resource availability [MinVM,

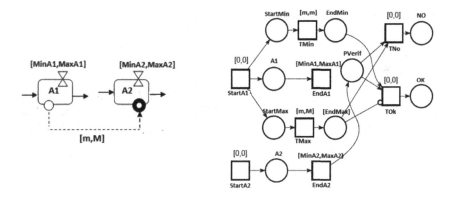

Fig. 4. Transformation of SF constraint between activities into a TPN

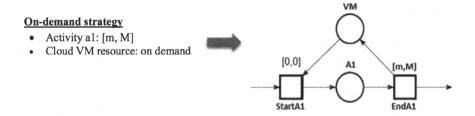

Fig. 5. Transformation of on-demand pricing strategy into a TPN

MaxVM]. Figure 6 shows the transformation of a1 with [n, M] as a duration constraint using a VM with reserved strategy. At the crossing of transition start of a1, a token is taken from UseVM place, which represents the cloud resource but without interruption of the interval [MinVM, MaxVM]. At the end of the allocation time of the cloud resource, a token is added to Pverif place to check the allocation of the cloud resource. If there is still a token in place a1 then the allocation of the cloud resource is declared invalid, otherwise the allocation is valid.

The transformation of spot instances with non-predefined durations is not considered in this work since it uses absolute temporal constraints attributes.

4.2 Formal Verification of BPs Using UPPAL

To formally verify a TPN against a set of properties, we use Tina model checker. Properties include deadlock freeness and user-defined properties such as process deadlines, and delays between activities.

- ◊ (- dead): to check the deadlock freeness of a process.
- ◊ (- dead_process): Permits to verify if the deadline x has been met. This means that dead_process place (associated with an observer for the deadline property) is false throughout the whole path leading to this place.

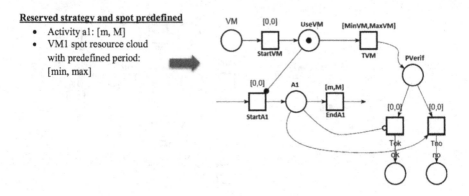

Fig. 6. Transformation of reserved pricing strategy into a TPN

5   Implementation

Our previous work [9] resulted in an Eclipse plug-in that extends BPMN 2.0.
Using this plug-in, a designer represents a BP's needs of cloud resources (VMs),
cloud pricing strategies, and time-constrained activities. This step helps generate
a source model, which is an XML document describing the BP. In this paper,
we discuss the rule-based implementation of BP transformation into TPN. This
transformation is executed by applying an XSLT file containing our transformation rules. Figure 7 exhibits an XSLT excerpt that transforms a SS temporal
dependency into 2 places and 1 transition with a delay of minFE and maxFE.
As a result, the output is an XML document that describes the generated TPN.
Figure 8 exhibits an excerpt of the automatic generation of the TPN document
of the motivating example (with focus on "a8" and "a9"). Finally, we formally
verify the matching between the activities, temporal constraints, and resource
temporal constraints. The generated TPNs are the inputs for the TINA model
checker. We check several properties using S/E LTL formulas such as deadline,
e.g., 17 hours, of the motivating example are met. The verification results show
that the resource allocation is correct (i.e., the S/E LTL property for deadlock
freeness is satisfied).

6   Related Work

Our related work consists of 2 parts. The first part is about BP formal specification. The second part is about BP allocation into clouds. Many works in the
literature address the issue of defining BP formal specification.

First, Dijkman et al. in [6] propose a formal BPMN semantics defined in terms
of a transformation to standard PN. The transformation has been implemented
as a tool that generates Petri Net Markup Language (PNML) code. But, the
authors do not consider any temporal dimension in their analysis.

Rachdi et al. [11], propose an approach that takes into account time concepts
in BPMN proposes. They present a formal semantics of BPMN defined in terms

```
<xsl:when test="$typeTD='StartToStart_ST_'">
    <xsl:element name="place">
    <xsl:element name="place">
    <xsl:element name="transition">
        <xsl:attribute name="id">
        <name>
        <delay>
            <interval closure="closed" xmlns="http://www.w3.org/1998/Math/MathML">
                <cn><xsl:value-of select="$minFE"/></cn>
                <cn><xsl:value-of select="$maxFE"/></cn>
            </interval>
            <graphics>
                <xsl:element name="offset">
                    <xsl:attribute name="x"><xsl:value-of select="0"/></xsl:attribute>
                    <xsl:attribute name="y"><xsl:value-of select="-10"/></xsl:attribute>
                </xsl:element>
            </graphics>
        </delay>
        <graphics>
    </xsl:element>
    <xsl:element name="arc">
    <xsl:element name="arc">
    <xsl:element name="arc">
    <xsl:element name="arc">
</xsl:when>
```

Fig. 7. XSLT excerpt (transformation rule for a SS temporal dependency)

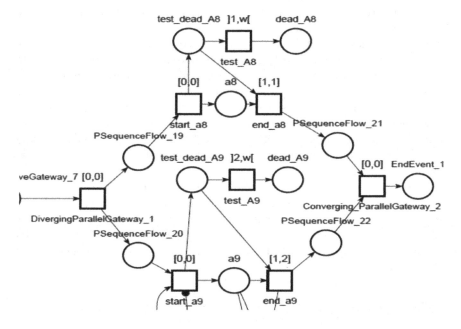

Fig. 8. An excerpt of the generated TPN

of transformation to TPN but without taking into consideration of temporal constraints as in our work nor the notion of resources.

Cheikhrouhou et al. [4,5] address the problem of formal specification and verification of temporal constraints of activities using timed automata. But, cloud resources were not considered.

Hachicha et al. [8] extend of the BPMN meta-model to optimally manage cloud resources. They formalize the resources consumed using a shared knowledge base. Therefore, the authors propose a semantic framework for BPs enriched by cloud resources. However, the temporal perspective for resources is out of reach. Several works have addressed the specification and formal verification of cloud resources in BPMN. Boubaker et al. [2] validate the consistency of the allocation of cloud resources using Event-B. The latter is used to formally specify cloud resource allocation policies in business process models and to verify its accuracy based on user requirements and resource properties. However, in this work, neither BPs nor cloud resources are enriched by time constraints. There are authors working on cloud pricing strategies in BPMN. Ben Halima et al. [9] formally specify temporal constraints on pricing strategies for cloud resources, especially virtual machines, and on BPMN activities. This specification is translated into timed automata to formally verify the correspondence between the time constraints of the business process and the cloud resources. But, this work does not support an automatic BPMN mapping to timed automata, which can lead to errors during the transformation.

Several searches extend BPMN with time constraints and cloud resource perspectives and use formal verification. Watahiki et al. [13] extend BPMN to handle time constraints. They also provide an automatic mapping of extended BPMN to timed automata. This approach aims to verify certain characteristics, such as deadlock. However, the scope of this article is limited to a small subset of BPMN elements. In addition, the extension proposed in this work gives specific temporal constraints to a single activity of the business process model and does not take into account time constraints related to a set of activities such as temporal dependency.

There is previous research that aims to check whether the selected cloud resource meets the time constraints of business processes. Du et al. [7] propose to dynamically verify the temporal constraints of multiple simultaneous business processes with resources. However, to our knowledge, the relative and absolute time constraints for cloud resources based on pricing strategies are not yet addressed.

7   Conclusion

In this paper, we addressed the concern of limited work on formal verification of matching BPs' activities to cloud resources taking into account temporal constraints on these activities and pricing strategies of cloud resources. We extended BPMN to enrich process activities with temporal constraints and needs of cloud resources. To achieve this verification, we proposed an automatic generation and conversion of the enriched BPs into TPNs using XSLT as a transformation language. Afterwards, we checked the BP using the TINA model checker. Finally, we implemented the proposed approach using a real use case. The adoption od accurate and efficient formal methods should help designers detect temporal inconsistencies of BP models. In term of future work, we would like to formally verify the correctness of the transformation rules.

References

1. Berthomieu, B., Vernadat, F.: Time Petri Nets analysis with TINA. In: Proceedings of the Third International Conference on the Quantitative Evaluation of Systems (QEST), pp. 123–124 (2006)
2. Boubaker, S., Gaaloul, W., Graiet, M., Hadj-Alouane, N.B.: Event-b based approach for verifying cloud resource allocation in business process. In: Proceedings of the 2015 IEEE International Conference on Services Computing, SCC, pp. 538–545 (2015)
3. Cheikhrouhou, S., Chabouh, N., Kallel, S., Maamar, Z.: Transformation of timed BPMN busines processes and cloud resources into timed Petri-Nets. Technical report (2018). http://www.redcad.tn/projects/bpmn2tpn/technicalreport-0618.pdf
4. Cheikhrouhou, S., Kallel, S., Guermouche, N., Jmaiel, M.: Toward a time-centric modeling of business processes in BPMN 2.0. In: The 15th International Conference on Information Integration and Web-based Applications and Services, IIWAS, p. 154 (2013)
5. Cheikhrouhou, S., Kallel, S., Guermouche, N., Jmaiel, M.: The temporal perspective in business process modeling: a survey and research challenges. Serv. Oriented Comput. Appl. **9**(1), 75–85 (2015)
6. Dijkman, R.M., Dumas, M., Ouyang, C.: Formal semantics and analysis of BPMN process models using Petri Nets. Technical report, Queensland University of Technology (2007)
7. Du, Y., Xiong, P., Fan, Y., Li, X.: Dynamic checking and solution to temporal violations in concurrent workflow processes. IEEE Trans. Syst. Man Cybern.-Part A: Syst. Hum. **41**(6), 1166–1181 (2011)
8. Hachicha, E., Gaaloul, W.: Towards resource-aware business process development in the cloud. In: Proceedings of the 29th IEEE International Conference on Advanced Information Networking and Applications, AINA, pp. 761–768 (2015)
9. Halima, R.B., Zouaghi, I., Kallel, S., Gaaloul, W., Jmaiel, M.: Formal verification of temporal constraints in business processes and allocated cloud resources. In: Proceedings of the 32nd IEEE International Conference on Advanced Information Networking and Applications, AINA (2018)
10. Mukund, M.: Linear-time temporal logic and büchi automata. Tutorial talk, Winter School on Logic and Computer Science, Indian Statistical Institute, Calcutta, p. 8 (1997)
11. Rachdi, A., En-Nouaary, A., Dahchour, M.: Liveness and reachability analysis of BPMN process models. CIT **24**(2), 195–207 (2016)
12. Van den Bossche, R., Vanmechelen, K., Broeckhove, J.: Cost-optimal scheduling in hybrid IaaS clouds for deadline constrained workloads. In: 2010 IEEE 3rd International Conference on Cloud Computing (CLOUD), pp. 228–235. IEEE (2010)
13. Watahiki, K., Ishikawa, F., Hiraishi, K.: Formal verification of business processes with temporal and resource constraints. In: Proceedings of the IEEE International Conference on Systems, Man and Cybernetics, Anchorage, Alaska, USA, 9–12 October 2011, pp. 1173–1180 (2011)

Petri Nets to Event-B: Handling Mathematical Sequences Through an ERTMS L3 Case

Zakaryae Boudi[1], Abderrahim Ait Wakrime[2]([☒]), Simon Collart-Dutilleul[3], and Mohamed Haloua[1]

[1] Ecole Mohammadia d'Ingénieurs, Med V University, Rabat, Morocco
zakaryae.boudi@gmail.com, haloua@emi.ac.ma
[2] Institut de Recherche Technologique Railenium, 59300 Famars, France
abderrahim.ait-wakrime@railenium.eu
[3] IFSTTAR-Lille, 20 Rue Elisée Reclus, BP 70317, 59666 Villeneuve d'Ascq Cedex, France
simon.collart-dutilleul@ifsttar.fr

Abstract. Mathematical techniques known as formal methods have demonstrated great value in building safe-by-design systems and processes. However, the booming industry automation and digitalization require sustained advances in engineering approaches to address the emerging control-command challenges, all with respect to the highest quality and safety standards. Our research suggests that combining different formal techniques can contribute in enriching the specification and verification phases of industrial systems design. In this paper, we show - and illustrate through an ERTMS (European Rail Traffic Management System) L3 case study addressing the calculation of Movement Authority - how the mapping of two specific features of Petri Nets (PNs) and Event-B, namely Lists and sequences, could fit in the model transformation of PNs to B-machines and be used both in modeling and verification.

Keywords: Colored Petri Nets · Event-B · ERTMS
Model transformation · Mathematical sequences

1 Introduction

Whether it is in transport, energy, healthcare, aerospace or industrial systems tend to involve increasing amounts of automation, data and connectivity. It is clear that this trend we can qualify as digital is not without bringing unprecedented sophistication and complex technical challenges, especially as the technology and use expectations evolve so quickly. While industrial systems' providers as well as end-users might positively welcome the disruption of artificial intelligence, IoT, big data or analytics, they are at the same time increasingly concerned about the technical implications of overseeing quality standards, safety and security.

© Springer Nature Switzerland AG 2018
E. H. Abdelwahed et al. (Eds.): MEDI 2018 Workshops, CCIS 929, pp. 50–62, 2018.
https://doi.org/10.1007/978-3-030-02852-7_5

It is true that advance in technology over the past decades, and particularly the transition from a hardware-driven automation to software-driven devices, brought the first use of mathematical and formal tools to produce safe-by-design automation. But among the many reasons which put mathematics in scope, besides technology, are changes in regulation requiring higher safety and quality demonstrations, such as certification and accreditation, bringing accordingly formal analysis in the core of system and software development. What's more, exploiting mathematical models implies the automation of a larger amount of development and validation work, and thus, reducing its provision costs. For example, the development of tools aiming to generate comprehensive test cases from formal specifications was one of the early interesting application of formal methods [1]. Also, another, more recent, cost saving and effective use of formal methods in the verification and validation process is theorem proving of systems meeting their specification [2]. At their heart, formal methods came not only to apply software based mathematical modeling on systems in order to help demonstrate they meet their specifications, quality and safety properties, but also to help build a sound understanding of systems' functioning and interactions, validate data before commissioning, generate test cases and reduce the overall development costs [2,3].

In this respect and after introducing related works, the used definitions of sequences, and qualifying general aspects surrounding the Petri net to Event-B transformation, the next sections will summarize the suggested Petri net modelling technique implementing the substring concept. On this basis, the following sections will provide further detail to the initial transformation definition, describing the way Lists are mapped into Event-B language, through a detailed case study. It will be explained how these formal methods and their transformation can be used in modeling and validating a railway ERTMS Level 3, especially with regards to the calculation of the Movement Authority (MA).

2   Focus and Related Works

This work falls in the research line aiming to bridge different formal techniques, and in particular, introduces an approach to broaden the features of the transformation of Petri nets to B-method, which is presented in [1,2]. For this purpose, this paper shows how capturing the concept of mathematical sequences, especially substrings, can be used as a mean to enhance modelling possibilities and the overall design, verification and validation process. As a reminder, the ultimate purpose of bridging Petri nets to Even-B is to open new ways of mathematically implement safety properties and prove they hold, in a direct, scalable and comprehensive setup.

Related Petri net to B transformation works are presented and qualified in [2] with regards to the proposed approach. In particular, it states that the transformation was developed in accordance with the mapping approach of Model Driven Engineering [3], using the colored Petri net (CPN) meta-model presented in [4], which is completely based on Jensen's formal definition. Besides, few works aiming at translating CPNs have been explored by the community. One is presented by Bon and Collart-Dutilleul in [5], where a set of transformation rules was introduced and applied to a railway signaling scenario. However, after careful consideration, we found that the resulting B-machines are not useable in practice within B tools. Indeed, those B-machines used a large amount of looping definitions, which are combined to other semantic errors. What is more, our analysis suggests that the theoretical aspects of this transformation can be very hard to apply on large CPN models due to the complexity of the rules. A recent research [6] attempted to correct and adapt these rules for a pattern of Petri net models, but still, the transformation has not proved easily scalable to large Petri net and B-method models.

It is also useful to mention the work in [7], where the authors presented a mapping from Place/Transition Petri nets to the B-language. This work can be seen as a simplified version of the authors' original contribution form Evaluative Petri Nets to B-machines. Although this mapping suggests a closer approach to our transformation, it does not cover colored Petri nets.

3   The Essentials of Sequences

3.1   Defining Finite Mathematical Sequences

A useful starting point is to clearly understand what definition it will be referred to when dealing with mathematical sequences all over this paper. Intuitively, a mathematical sequence is intended to represent an ordered list of the elements of a set, which might be infinite. In this paper, we will consider the following formal definition.

Definition 1. *A sequence is defined as a function whose domain is the set or a subset of natural numbers.*

We will use the symbol A_n to represent a sequence, where n is a natural number and an is the value of the function A_n on n. Let us note that this research considers only finite sequences, provided that a sequence may be finite or infinite. We will write $\{a_1, a_2, a_3, a_4, ..., a_n\}$ to represent the sequence.

3.2   From Subsequences to Substrings

Definition 2. *We define a subsequence in mathematics as a sequence which is derived from another sequence, by removing a number of elements without altering the order of the remaining ones. For example, the sequence $\{a_3, a_6, a_{11}\}$ is a subsequence of $\{a_1, a_2, a_3, a_4, ..., a_{20}\}$.*

The notion of subsequence brings us to what we call substrings, which is a refinement of the subsequence in a way that the remaining elements of the subsequence keep a successive order. As for the previous example, $\{a_2, a_3, a_4, a_5\}$ and $\{a_{20}, a_{21}, a_{22}, a_{23}\}$ are substrings of $\{a_1, a_2, a_3, a_4, ..., a_{40}\}$.

4 Capturing Sequences with Petri Nets

4.1 Petri Nets at a Glance

In brief, colored Petri nets are an extension of Petri nets where the main strength lies in the use of a functional language that is based on the notion of typing. They accordingly link each token to a type called "color" which differentiates tokens. Below Kurt Jensen's formal definition of a colored Petri net:

Definition 3. *A colored Petri net is a tuple $CPN = (\Sigma, P, T, A, N, C, G, E, I)$ satisfying the following requirements: Σ is a finite set of non-empty types, called color sets. P is a finite set of places. T is a finite set of transitions. A is a finite set of arcs such that: $P \cap T = P \cap A = T \cap A = \varnothing$. N is a node function. It is defined from A into $P \times T \cup T \times P$. C is a color function. It is defined from P into Σ. G is a guard function. It is defined from T into expressions such that $\forall t \in T : [Type(G(t)) = Bool \wedge Type(Var(G(t))) \subseteq \Sigma]$. E is an arc expression function. It is defined from A into expressions such that $\forall a \in A : [Type(E(a)) = C(p(a))_{MS} \wedge Type(Var(E(a))) \subseteq \Sigma]$; Where $p(a)$ is the place of $N(a)$. I is an initialization function. It is defined from P into closed expressions such that $\forall p \in P : [Type(I(p)) = C(p)_{MS}]$.*

4.2 CPN-tools: Lists in Focus

CPN-tools is one of the most advanced existing platforms for editing colored Petri nets. Architected by Kurt Jensen, Soren Christensen, Lars M. Kristensen, and Michael Westergaard [8,9], it combines colored Petri nets with the "Standard ML" functional programming language. Standard ML enables the definition of data (i.e. places, transitions, colors, variables, etc.) types as well as the corresponding algorithms. Many research projects have adopted CPN-tools for the availability of references and its common use in literature. CPN-tools ML environment allows the use of Lists and manipulating them via a number of functions.

Definition 4. *The List color is a variable-length color set, where values are a sequence whose elements type (color set) must be the same.*

The List structure provided by Standard ML gives a series of functions for manipulating mathematical sequences as defined earlier, knowing that it is traditionally an important datatype in functional programming [10]. Going forward, the next section will introduce the formal definitions of the Petri net to B-machines transformation, herby slightly adapted to Event-B.

5 Transforming Petri Nets to Event-B

5.1 Event-B in Brief

Confusion can arise from our use of Event-B as the transformation target formalism. For this reason, it is important to point out the distinction of classical

B (also called B for software) and Event-B. This distinction lays in the use of the clause "EVENTS" for the latter case rather than the traditional "OPERA-TIONS". The nuance between these two B-method features can be explained by the possibility to implement classical B "OPERATIONS" in the context of software development. Such a possibility is not allowed for "EVENTS", which are intended for system specification and can only be refined. An Event-B model uses two types of entities to describe a system: Machines and Contexts. A Machine represents the dynamic part of a model, namely, states and transitions. A Context contains the static part of the model. In this paper, we use Machine that includes both static and dynamic parts.

5.2   CPN to Event-B Formal Transformation

The formal transformation we further in this research is the one introduced in [1,2], which finds its roots on Jensen's formal definition already recalled in Sect. 2. Accordingly, the structure of CPN models is described as a tuple $CPN = (S, P, T, A, N, C, G, E, I)$ that satisfies a number of given requirements. Let $CPN2B : CPNs \rightarrow EventBMCH$ be a mapping between colored Petri nets and Event-B machines. $EventBMCH$ is the image of $CPNs$ through $CPN2B$. The formal definitions of the transformation are provided hereafter. Note that these definitions use the concepts of Jensen's formal definition of colored Petri nets.

Definition 5 (Structural transformation). Let $cpn = (S, P, T, A, N, C, G, E, I)$ be a colored Petri net such that $cpn \in CPNs$. Then the image $EventBmch = CPN2B(cpn)$ has the structure shown in Listing 1.

The structural transformation is captured by Listing 1 where: $\forall i \in \{1..k\} \, \forall j \in \{1..p\}$; the sets $color_i$ and the definitions $color_{k+j}$ correspond to the elements of S, the finite set of non-empty types, called color sets. $\forall i \in \{1..k\}$; the variables $state_{Idplace_i}$ correspond to the elements of P, the finite set of places. $\forall i \in \{1..k\}$; the variables $Enabled\_Idtransition_i$ correspond to the elements of T, the finite set of transitions. $\forall i \in \{1..k\}$; the variables $color_{Idplace_i}$ correspond to $Col = C(pl)$, where pl is the place corresponding to the variable $state_{Idplace_i}$. $Ms(ss) == ss \rightarrow NAT$ is a multiset based on ss defined as a total function from ss to all natural numbers. $Ms\_empty(ss) == \{elt | elt : ss \times \{0\}\}$ is the empty multiset, based on ss, is composed of pairs of elements of the support set related to 0. Thus, it is a total function, which for each element of the starting set combines the integer 0.

Note 1. A multiset is specified as a relationship between a set known as "base set" of the multiset and natural numbers. The elements of a multiset are pairs $(ee \mapsto nn)$ where ee belongs to the base set and nn is an integer representing the coefficient (number of occurrences) of the element in the multiset.

```
MACHINE Bmch
SETS
Color₁ = {elt1_{C1}, ..., eltN_{C1}}  ∧ ... ∧  Color_k = {elt1_{Ck}, ..., eltN_{Ck}}
DEFINITIONS
Ms(ss) == ss → NAT  ∧  Ms_empty(ss) == {elt|elt : ss × {0}}  ∧
Color_{k+1} = {elt|elt ∈ ENS}  ∧ ... ∧  Color_{k+p} = {elt|elt ∈ ENS}
VARIABLES
state_{Idplace₁}  ∧ ... ∧  state_{Idplace_k}  ∧
occ_elt1_C1_{Idplace}  ∧ ... ∧  occ_eltN_C1_{Idplace}  ∧ ... ∧
occ_elt1_Ck_{Idplace}  ∧ ... ∧  occ_eltN_Ck_{Idplace}  ∧
Enabled_Idtransition₁  ∧ ... ∧  Enabled_Idtransition_k  ∧
INVARIANT
state_{Idplace₁} ∈ Ms(color_{Idplace₁})  ∧ ... ∧  state_{Idplace_k} ∈ Ms(color_{Idplace_k})  ∧
occ_elt1_C1_{Idplace} ∈ NATURAL  ∧ ... ∧  occ_eltN_C1_{Idplace} ∈ NATURAL  ∧ ... ∧
occ_elt1_Ck_{Idplace} ∈ NATURAL  ∧ ... ∧  occ_eltN_Ck_{Idplace} ∈ NATURAL  ∧
Enabled_Idtransition₁ ∈ BOOL  ∧ ... ∧  Enabled_Idtransition_k ∈ BOOL
```

Listing 1. Structural transformation.

Definition 6 (Behavioral transformation). *Let $cpn = (S, P, T, A, N, C, G, E, I)$ be a colored Petri net such that $cpn \in CPNs$. Then the image $EventBmch = CPN2B(cpn)$ has an initialization and operations shown in Listing 2.*

The behavioral transformation is captured by Listing 2 where: $\forall i \in \{1..k\}$ $\forall j \in \{1..p\}$; the elements $eltj\_color_{Idplace_i}$ correspond to the elements of the variables $color_{Idplace_i}$. (refer to Definition 1). $\forall i \in \{1..p\}; nat_i \in NATURAL$. $\forall i \in \{1..k\}; bool_i \in BOOL$. $\forall i \in NATURAl$; the predicates $predicate_i$ correspond to $Exp = (G(transition\_i) \wedge E(arc_1) \wedge ... \wedge E(arc_p))$ where $\forall j \in \{1..p\} : arc_j \in A$ and $(N(arc_j) = (x, transition_i))$. $\forall i \in \{1..k\}$; the substitutions $substitution_i$ correspond to $Exp = (G(transition_i) \wedge E(arc_1) \wedge ... \wedge E(arc_p))$ where $\forall j \in \{1..p\} : arc_j \in A$ and $(N(arc_j) = (transition_i, x))$.

Note 2. Although the behavioral transformation is characterized by the use of two events for each transition, the use of only one event ($Ev\_Fired\_Idtransition$) can be sufficient in many practical cases. The main idea behind the introduction of the other one is to leave open possibilities for the use of the Boolean variables *enabled_Idtransition* in expressing property invariants related to transitions. In fact, sometimes, it is hard to establish those invariants using variables corresponding to places. Further, the predicates in the target Event-B machine could be enriched in order to facilitate the proving process.

```
INITIALISATION
state_Idplace_1 := Ms(color_Idplace_1) ⊲ {(elt1_color_Idplace_1 ↦ n_1) ∧ ...∧
              (eltp_color_Idplace_1 ↦ n_p)} ∧ ...∧
state_Idplqce_k := Ms(color_Idplace_k) ⊲ {(elt1_color_Idplace_k ↦ n_1) ∧ ...∧
              (eltp_color_Idplace_k ↦ n_p)}∧
occ_elt1_C1_Idplace := nat_1 ∧ ...∧ occ_eltN_C1_Idplace := nat_p ∧ ...∧
occ_elt1_Ck_Idplace := nat_1 ∧ ...∧ occ_eltN_Ck_Idplace := nat_p ∧
Enabled_Idtransition_1 := bool_1 ∧ ...∧ Enabled_Idtransition_k := bool_k
EVENTS
Ev_Enabled_Idtransition_1 =
PRE predicate_1
THEN Enabled_Idtransition_1 := TRUE
END;
...
Ev_Enabled_Idtransition_k =
PRE predicate_k
THEN Enabled_Idtransition_k := TRUE
END;
Ev_Fired_Idtransition_1 =
SELECT predicate_1
THEN substitution_1
...
WHEN predicate_n
THEN substitution_n
END;
...
Ev_Fired_Idtransition_k =
SELECT predicate_1
THEN substitution_1
...
WHEN predicate_n
THEN substitution_n
END;
END
```

Listing 2. Behavioral transformation.

In addition, it is also convenient to recall that the use of "SELECT" in the *Ev_Fired_Idtransition* is justified by the fact that the firing of the transition may involve different tokens (colors) choices according to the elements of the "color set" related to the incoming and outgoing places.

6   Moving to Sequences: The ERTMS L3 Movement Authority Case Study

6.1   Description and CPN Modeling

Autonomous train driving and ERTMS are certainly part of the most topical trends in rail transportation technology. In the present example, the purpose is to specify a safe by design MA computation solution in an ERTMS L3 equipped line. Before going further, let us remind that ERTMS, the European Rail Traffic Management System, is composed of ETCS (European Train Control System) and GSM-R. It is a railway signalling and traffic management system intended to control and command rail traffic safely, based on interoperable technology and operating rules, in such way to guarantee uninterrupted movement across European countries.

It is important to note that when we talk about ERTMS in this paper, we refer to ETCS. The general architecture of ETCS is outlined in the System Requirement Specification (SRS) developed by the European Union Agency for Railways [11]. For information, GSM-R is a radio system used for communication between trackside equipment and on-board computer. This system may however be replaced by a more relevant protocol in the next few years. In the case of ERTMS level 3, the transmission of information is carried out by the radio. The detection and verification of the train integrity are performed at Radio Block Center (RBC), along with the train computer which sends position and integrity information [11]. Train detection and integrity functions are performed on-board, and the MA is calculated without track-side signals or physical circuits.

As we consider particularly the MA calculation in our study, and more precisely the Virtual Blocks type of ERTMS L3 where train detection circuits can be divided into several virtual blocks we call Virtual Sub-Sections (VSSs), we define an MA as the ordered set of free VSSs ahead of the train, upon which the train can move. The 'occupied' and 'free' status of a VSS is based on both reported train position and trackside train detection. Of course, note that real life MA computation is undoubtedly more complex and requires highly sophisticated algorithms, for additional details see [12]. The present simplified case can be of practical interest to showcase CPN's modeling and transformation to Event-B (Fig. 1).

Fig. 1. Virtual block ERTMS L3 case description

First, we assume that two trains circulate above a six virtual blocks track. The system requires a safe software function that allows Train 1's on-board computer to compute the MA. It is also assumed both train can only advance by one VSS distance (step) for each cycle, if the MA is not empty, and for each cycle, Train 1 can measure its position as well as receive the position of Train 2. Mathematically speaking, we can consider that the MA is a substring of the sequence:

$$\{VSS1, VSS2, VSS3, VSS4, VSS5, VSS6\}$$

where the elements have orders between the VSS occupied by the head of Train 1 and the VSS occupied by the tail of Train 2. For example, if we consider the initial state in Fig. 1, the MA should be obtained by excluding $VSS1$, $VSS2$, $VSS4$, $VSS5$ and $VSS6$ from the overall sequence $\{VSS1, VSS2, VSS3, VSS4, VSS5, VSS6\}$, leaving the $MA = \{VSS3\}$.

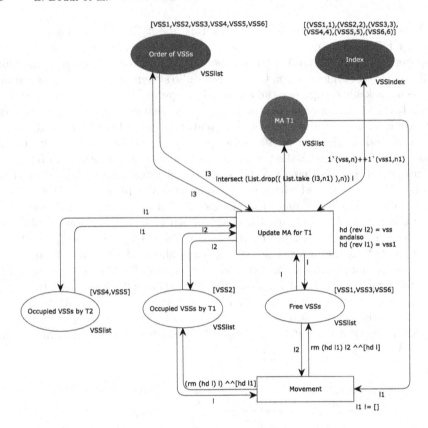

Fig. 2. MA function Petri net

At this stage, we will design a Petri net command system using the Lists type as a way to handle mathematical sequences, which provides a safe-by-design MA at each cycle. We will then demonstrate that it can make the right decisions in all configurations. Unlike the other programmatic techniques, Petri net models make it easier to carry the specification of our solution on a graphical system representation (inputs and outputs). In effect, the present model in Fig. 2 contains three "places" representing the inputs of the MA algorithm, namely, state of occupation of VSSs by Train 1 and Train 2, as well as free VSSs. As an output, the transition "Update MA for T1" and system of "arcs" calculates the set of VSSs representing the MA, and fills it accordingly in the green place "MA T1". We notice that the set of MA should contain ordered VSSs, which is explaining the recourse to Lists and the two monitoring place "Order" and "Index" we detail in the next section. The order of occupied VSSs is also important for capturing the information about which VSS is occupied by the head or tail of trains. Ultimately, the transition "Movement" implements a one-step movement, i.e. Train 1 moving by a distance of one VSS.

6.2   Computing the MA Using the CPN Model

Two monitoring places intended for increasing Petri net sequence manipulability are the "Order" and "Index" places (Fig. 3). Those places help to identify which parts of input Lists are relevant to the construction of the target substring standing for the MA. This technique considers that the output sequence is a substring of the sequence in the "Order" place, which stands for the overall List. In order to fine-tune the calculation of MA and exploit the ML functions, the "Index" place provides the pair $(VSSn, n)$, where n is an integer equal to the order of $VSSn$ in the list of the place "Order". In this respect, the model visualizes those pieces of input data that the calculator needs to consider as it determines the MA list.

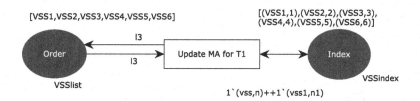

Fig. 3. Sequence structure of colored Petri net

Let us note that such an approach is approximating a generalized structure that can be applied in multiple problems. In future works, we will further assess the suitability of the same structure for different modeling and application cases.

Inputs: $l, l1, l2$ and $l3$, variables of type $VSSlist$ corresponding respectively to the free VSSs, VSSs occupied by Train 2, VSSs occupied by Train 1 and the overall VSS sequence. $1`(vss, n) + +1`(vss1, n1)$, two elements from the Index Place which will be precised in the transition guard.

Transition Guard: $hd (rev\ l2) = vss$ and also $hd (rev\ l1) = vss1$.

Output Arc (MA): $intersect (List.drop((List.take(l3, n1)), n))\ l$.

6.3   Transforming List Manipulations into B Language

It has already been shown, in [1,2] and earlier sections in this paper, that the structural and behavioural parts of the Petri net model can be transformed into B-machines. The current rules of the transformation, however, require that the designer implements Petri net Guards and Arcs inscriptions directly in the EVENTS clause of the B-machine. A critical step is to fit the most common algorithmic patterns in Petri nets to the mathematical programming features provided by Event-B. In this regard, capturing mathematical sequences, represented by Lists, call for a specific mapping into sequence structures in the B language and, in this case, a slightly different use of B-machine clauses.

Among our findings, the color set of type "List" in the Petri net model is mapped to the type "$NATURAL \mapsto Color$", i.e., a partial function from the set of naturals to the set of the elements contained in the list (expressed in ASCII). In the present case, the Petri net declaration: $colsetVSS = with\ VSS1|VSS2|VSS3|VSS4|VSS5|VSS6$; $colsetVSSlist = list\ VSS$; will correspond to the B-machine set: $colorVSS = \{VSS1, VSS2, VSS3, VSS4, VSS5, VSS6\}$ where state variables are of type $NATURAL \mapsto colorVSS$. The sequence structure will be found in the "DEFINITIONS" clause of the B-machine (Listing 3).

```
MACHINE
ERTMS_L3_Target_Mch
SETS
colorVSS = {VSS1, VSS2, VSS3, VSS4, VSS5}
ABSTRACT_VARIABLES
State_Free_VSSs   ∧   State_Occupied_VSSs_by_T1   ∧
State_Occupiedvᵥ SSs_by_T2   ∧   State_MA_T1   ∧
enabled_Update_MA_for_T1   ∧   enabled_Movement
DEFINITIONS
color_VSSlist == [VSS1, VSS2, VSS3, VSS4, VSS5]   ∧
Ms(ss) == ss → NAT   ∧   Ms_empty(ss) == {elt|elt : ss × {0}}
INVARIANT
State_Free_VSSs : NATURAL ↦ color_VSS   ∧
State_Occupied_VSSs_by_T1 : NATURAL ↦ color_VSS   ∧
State_Occupied_VSSs_by_T2 : NATURAL ↦ color_VSS   ∧
State_MA_T1 : NATURAL ↦ color_VSS   ∧
enabled_Update_MA_for_T1 : BOOL   ∧
enabled_Movement : BOOL   ∧
\\Safety Invariant : the VSS of the MA are all obligatorily free
ran(State_MA_T1) ∩ (ran(State_Occupied_VSSs_by_T1) ∪
                    ran(State_Occupied_VSSs_by_T2)) = ∅
```

Listing 3. Transformation of sequence structure.

The mapping of MA calculations, that uses Standard ML list functions from the Petri net sid is done through the manipulation of sequences from the Event-B side as presented in Listing 4.

```
EVENTS
Ev_enabled_Update_MA_for_T1 =
  SELECT  State_Free_VSSs ≠ ∅ ∧ State_Occupied_VSSs_by_T1 ≠ ∅ ∧
          State_Occupied_VSSs_by_T2 ≠ ∅
  THEN  enabled_Update_MA_for_T1 := TRUE
  END;
Ev_fired_Update_MA_for_T1 =
  SELECT  State_Free_VSSs ≠ ∅ ∧ State_Occupied_VSSs_by_T1 ≠ ∅ ∧
          State_Occupied_VSSs_by_T2 ≠ ∅ ∧ enabled_Update_MA_for_T1 = TRUE
  THEN  State_MA_T1 := Seq_VSS ↑ (Seq_VSS (last(State_Occupied_VSSs_by_T2))
                                  − card(State_Occupied_VSSs_by_T2)) ↓
                      Seq_VSS (last(State_Occupied_VSSs_by_T1)) ∧
                      enabled_Update_MA_for_T1 := FALSE
  END;
```

Listing 4. Events to manipulate the sequences.

6.4   Verifying Properties Using Event-B Tools

The ultimate purpose of bridging Petri nets to Even-B is to mathematically implement safety properties and prove they hold. For this reason we run the obtained Event-B model using the semi-supervised simulation and verification environments of ProB and Atelier-B, two tools which complete each other towards validating and refining the understanding of the specification model. To recognize whether the MA the model calculates is safe for the train, we run for this example the ProB model checker from the desired initial state. This rigorous analysis reveals that the safety invariant (expressed in red in Listing 3) is not violated (Fig. 4).

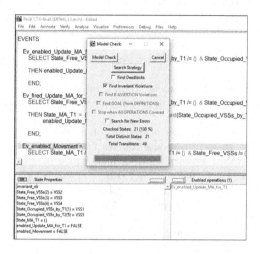

Fig. 4. Model-checking and scenario animation using ProB.

7   Conclusion and Perspectives

In the evolution towards more automation and connectivity, development of safe systems and use of mathematical approaches will become even more imperative. Certainly, combining formal methods is not a totally new practice for safe-by-design systems, but the fact remains that it has shown so little development with regards to the rapid advance of systems' connectivity and multiplicity of interactions, which has given rise both to more diverse and sophisticated applications and more complexity in design stages. Larger and more complex interactions make it hard to rely on only few and disconnected techniques for engineering systems, while respecting high quality and safety standards. This is one reason this research opted for bridging formal methods, taking the specific case of Petri nets and Event-B.

Therefore, this contribution addressed the way the transformation of Petri net models into Event-B machines handles mathematical sequences, showing in the meantime where such features could be applied in a real life railway ERTMS use case. Today, this research and its applications are only in their early stages.

Future work will attempt to expand and generalize Petri net applications for sequences, and formalize their mapping into Event-B, all across multiple case studies.

References

1. Boudi, Z., Ben-Ayed, R., Collart-Dutilleul, S., Nolasco, T., Haloua, M.: A CPN/B method transformation framework for railway safety rules formal validation. Eur. Transp. Res. Rev. **9**(2), 13 (2017)
2. Boudi, Z., Collart-Dutilleul, S., et al.: Colored Petri nets formal transformation to B machines for safety critical software development. In: 2015 International Conference on Industrial Engineering and Systems Management (IESM), pp. 12–18. IEEE (2015)
3. Combemale, B., Crégut, X., Garoche, P.L., Thirioux, X.: Essay on semantics definition in MDE. An instrumented approach for model verification. J. Softw. (JSW) **4**(9), 943–958 (2009)
4. Istoan, P.: Methodology for the derivation of product behaviour in a software product line. Ph.D. thesis, Université Rennes 1 (2013)
5. Bon, P., Dutilleul, S.C.: From a solution model to a B model for verification of safety properties. J. UCS **19**(1), 2–24 (2013)
6. Sun, P., Bon, P., Collart-Dutilleul, S.: A joint development of coloured petri nets and the b method in critical systems. J. Univ. Comput. Sci. **21**(12), 1654–1683 (2015)
7. Korečko, Š., Sobota, B.: Petri Nets to B-language transformation in software development. Acta Polytech. Hung. **11**(6), 187–206 (2014)
8. Jensen, K.: Coloured Petri Nets: Basic Concepts, Analysis Methods and Practical Use, vol. 1. Springer, Heidelberg (2013)
9. Jensen, K., Kristensen, L.M., Wells, L.: Coloured petri nets and cpn tools for modelling and validation of concurrent systems. International Journal on Software Tools for Technology Transfer **9**(3–4), 213–254 (2007)
10. Ratzer, A.V., et al.: CPN tools for editing, simulating, and analysing coloured Petri Nets. In: van der Aalst, W.M.P., Best, E. (eds.) ICATPN 2003. LNCS, vol. 2679, pp. 450–462. Springer, Heidelberg (2003). https://doi.org/10.1007/3-540-44919-1_28
11. Abrial, J.R.: The B-Book: Assigning Programs to Meanings. Cambridge University Press, Cambridge (2005)
12. Eurasian Economic Union Group: Hybrid ERTMS/ETCS Level 3: Principles, Brussels, Belgium (July 2017)

Model-Based Verification and Testing Methodology for Safety-Critical Airborne Systems

Mounia Elqortobi[✉], Warda El-Khouly, Amine Rahj,
Jamal Bentahar, and Rachida Dssouli

Concordia University, Montreal, QC, Canada
m_elqort@mail.concordia.ca, w_elkh@encs.concordia.ca,
{amine.rahj,jamal.bentahar,
rachida.dssouli}@concordia.ca

Abstract. In this paper, we address the issue of safety-critical software verification and testing that are key requirements for achieving DO-331 and DO-178C regulatory compliance for airborne systems. Formal verification and testing are considered two different activities within the airborne standards and they belong to two different levels in avionics software development cycle. The objective is to integrate model-based verification and model-based testing within one framework and to capture the benefits of their cross-fertilization. It is achieved by proposing a methodology for the verification and testing of parallel communicating agents based on formal models. The results of formal verification and testing can be used as evidence for certification.

Keywords: Model-based verification · Model checking
Communication graph · Methodology · Model-based testing
Partial reachability graph · MC/DC (Modified Condition/Decision Coverage)

1 Introduction

Developing safety-critical software requires rigorous processes. To prevent catastrophic events, the avionics industry has introduced a rigorous certification process described in the RTCA [1, 2] standard. The DO-178C standard [1] includes a supplement on formal methods called DO-333. In DO-333, a formal method is defined as "a formal model combined with a formal analysis". DO-178C and its supplement have been successfully applied into a production of software systems at Dassault-Aviation and Airbus [3]. The motivation of this work is to increase software dependability by integrating formal verification techniques with testing and to capture the benefits of their cross-fertilization. In addition, formal verification and test results can be used as evidence for certification. Although model-based testing [5, 16] and verification activities [3–5, 19] are natural approaches to the certification of avionics software, the

---

Sponsored by NSERC/CRD CMC CS Canada. Project CRIAQ AVIO 604, CRDPJ 463076-14.

E. H. Abdelwahed et al. (Eds.): MEDI 2018 Workshops, CCIS 929, pp. 63–74, 2018.
https://doi.org/10.1007/978-3-030-02852-7_6

integrated model-based engineering approach is not yet well studied in the literature and several challenges need to be addressed [17, 18].

In this paper, we propose a model-driven approach that encompasses two main levels: verification/design and validation/implementation. As per Fig. 1, in the first level, we adopt model checking, a formal and fully automatic technique for model-based verification. It is a natural choice for a rigorous verification of avionics systems against desirable properties including safety and liveness. In the second level, we transform the finite state machines (FSM) verification model [11–13] to an Extended Finite State Machine (EFSM) testing model using graph rewriting [20]. We generate both local test cases for each EFSM agent in its context and global test cases for Communicating EFSM (CEFSM) model. The test generation methods satisfy the Modified Condition/Decision Coverage (MC/DC) criteria, all DU paths, and ensure

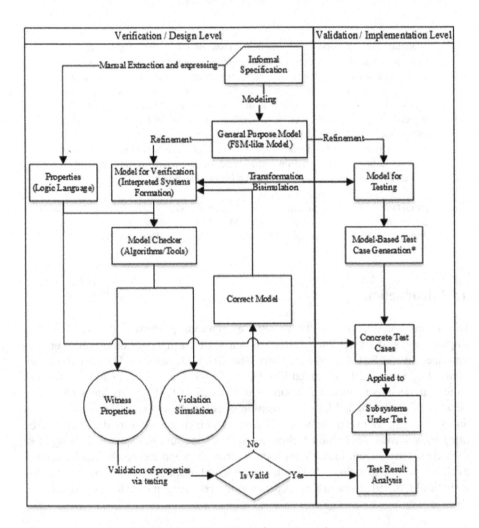

Fig. 1. An overview of our approach

that the verified properties hold in the implementation. The selection of coverage criteria are based on the satisfaction of DO 178C for MC/DC and a use of middle ground structural coverage for all DU paths. Better structural coverage criteria such as all paths is impractical.

Section 2 presents an overview of the proposed approach and the case study called landing gear system [9]. Section 3 introduces our model-based testing approach and shows how to automatically generate test cases. Section 4 concludes and identifies future work.

2   The Proposed Framework and Case Study

In this section, we introduce the proposed verification and testing framework. The methodology begins with formally modeling the safety-critical airborne system from the given informal requirement specification. Then, the obtained model is encoded using ISPL+ (an extended version of the input language of the symbolic model checker MCMAS+ introduced in [10]). We extract and express the system requirements in the form of temporal properties using Computation Tree Logic (CTL) [8]. MCMAS+ automatically checks whether the model satisfies the intended properties and graphically produces witness-examples or counter-examples. The produced witness-examples help the designer identify a successful execution, and in the case of existential properties claiming the existence of a successful path, these examples prove the satisfaction of properties, while the produced counter-examples guide designers to detect and repair design errors in the formal system model. In the validation/implementation part, we use model transformation that automatically produces a reduced CEFSM that is the input to our test generation tool. We use an approach that automatically generates abstract local and global test cases from EFSM and CEFSM. The test generation environment addresses the conformity of the implementation to low level requirements and the satisfaction of the avionics standards such as DO-178C. The test case generation algorithms take MC/DC and all DU paths as coverage criteria. Finally, our approach analyzes the obtained test results and compares them with the produced witness-examples to validate our properties via testing (see Fig. 1 for overview of the approach).

2.1   Case Study: Landing Gear System

Frédéric Boniol and Virginie Wiels proposed a case study of a landing gear system for an aircraft [9]. It is a representative scenario for complex industrial needs. We adopt it as our use case study. The landing system is responsible for maneuvering landing gears and attached doors. It specifically consists of three landing packages situated in the front, right, and left part of the aircraft. The landing system can be controlled by a software and can be in two modes: normal and emergency. In the outgoing and retraction situations, the normal mode is the default one. The emergency mode is deployed to handle the failure situation. This work considers only the outgoing sequence and its normal and emergency modes. The architecture of the system consists of three parts: (1) a pilot part; (2) a mechanical part that incorporates the mechanical devices and three landing packages; and (3) a digital part that includes the control unit software.

Regarding the pilot part, a pilot has a button switch at his disposal with two positions: UP and DOWN. When the button switch is going from UP to DOWN, the outgoing sequence is initialized. The pilot has three lights in the cockpit, which reflect the current status of the gears and doors. These lights are as follows:

- One green light meaning that "gears are locked down".
- One orange light meaning that "gears maneuvering".
- One red light meaning that "landing gear system failure".

Before initializing the outgoing sequence, all the gears are locked up and all the lights are off. In case of failure (i.e., the red light is on), the pilot manually pulls the mechanical handle to deploy the emergency hydraulic system. When all the gears are successfully extended and all accompanying sensors are valid, the green light must be lit. Regarding the mechanical part, the motion of landing gears and doors is performed by a set of hydraulic cylinders such that the cylinder position basically corresponds to the door or landing gear location. The digital part is in charge of sending an electrical order to activate each electro-valve. The digital part plays an intermediate role between the pilot part and the mechanical part. Specifically, the software embedded in the digital part is responsible for controlling gears and doors, detecting anomalies, and informing the pilot through a set of lights about the status of the system. It also generates commands directed to the hydraulic system to open or close the doors and extend or retract the gears with respect to the values of employed sensors and it captures the pilot orders.

2.2 Modeling the Landing Gear System

In this section, we show how our model M can formally model the landing gear system. In our modeling, we specifically consider the normal and emergency modes of the landing gear system without going into low-level details regarding the mechanical devices of sensors and electro-valves. To achieve this aim, we introduce three agent machine models: M_p for pilot, M_c for control unit, and M_e for emergency. Specifically, the pilot agent machine model M_p models the behavior of the pilot part and the control unit agent machine model M_c models the behavior of the digital part. The emergency agent machine model M_e models the behavior of the emergency system. Instead of adding another agent machine to model the behavior of the hydraulic cylinders, we depend on the status of doors and gears to directly represent the status of the employed cylinders.

Figures 2, 3, and 4 show the models of the pilot, control unit, and emergency agent machines respectively. In each figure, we introduce the input and output of each transition in a tabular form where the symbols "?" and "!" refer to the process of receiving and sending an action. Moreover, the output of a transition can be directly assigned by the shared and unshared variables when there is no explicit output action. Given that, it is easy to define the Boolean predicate of each transition using the conjunction operator between its input and output. The communication graph, as shown in Fig. 5, shows the communication between the 3 agents. The obtained models need experts' validation.

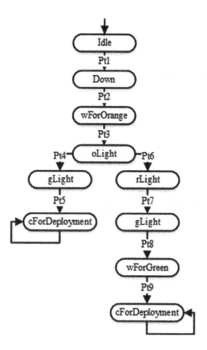

	Input, Ouput, Predicate
Pt1	?Landing_Specs(speed,distance) !Press_Down_Button
Pt2	?Press_Down_Button_Ack !Wait_For_Orange_Light
Pt3	?Orange_Light_On !Orange_Light_On_Ack
Pt4	?Green_Light_On !Green_Light_On_Ack
Pt5	?Confirm_Gear_Deployment !Deployment_Status:=Success
Pt6	?Red_Light_On !Red_Light_On_Ack
Pt7	?Confirm_Gear_Deployment_Error !Initialize_Emergency_System
Pt8	?Green_Light_OnMe !Green_Light_OnMe_Ack
Pt9	?Confirm_Gear_DeployemtMe !Deployment_Status:=Success

Fig. 2. Pilot agent Mp

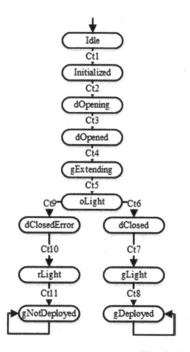

	Input, Ouput, Predicate
Ct1	?Press_Down_Button !Press_Down_Button_Ack
Ct2	?Process_Received_Command !Open_Gear_Doors
Ct3	?Open_Gear_Doors_Ack !Outgoing_Gears
Ct4	?Outgoing_Gears_Ack !Orange_Light_On
Ct5	?Orange_Light_On_Ack !Close_Gear_Doors
Ct6	?Close_Gear_Doors_Ack !Doors_Close_Success
Ct7	?Gears_Extended !Green_Light_On
Ct8	?Green_Light_On_Ack !ControlUnig_Disconnected
Ct9	?Close_Gear_Doors_Error !Doors_Close_Error
Ct10	?Gears_Nonextended !Red_Light:=On
Ct11	?Red_Light_On_Ack !ControlUnit_Disconnected

Fig. 3. Controller agent Mc

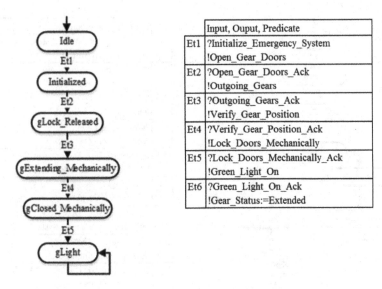

		Input, Ouput, Predicate
	Et1	?Initialize_Emergency_System
		!Open_Gear_Doors
	Et2	?Open_Gear_Doors_Ack
		!Outgoing_Gears
	Et3	?Outgoing_Gears_Ack
		!Verify_Gear_Position
	Et4	?Verify_Gear_Position_Ack
		!Lock_Doors_Mechanically
	Et5	?Lock_Doors_Mechanically_Ack
		!Green_Light_On
	Et6	?Green_Light_On_Ack
		!Gear_Status:=Extended

Fig. 4. Emergency agent Me

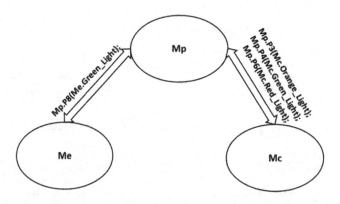

Fig. 5. Communication graph

2.3 Model Checking

To validate our model M (a combination of M_p, M_c and M_e), we need to perform the review and tracing activities. By tracing activity, we will be able to track the behavior of the encoded model using the possibility released in the MCMAS + tool called Explicit Interactive Mode. According to the model checking technique, we have to formally: (1) model the system underlying the verification process; and (2) express the requirements. The correctness of these requirements has been proven on the modeled system using MCMAS+. So far, we completed the first activity. For the second activity, we used the computation tree logic (CTL) [8] supported by the MCMAS+ model checker tool to express the following requirements:

$$\phi_1 = AG(PressedDown) \rightarrow AF(GearsExtended \wedge DoorsClosed))$$

$$\phi_2 = EG(E(PressedDown\ U\ PressedDown \wedge GearsExtended \wedge DoorsClosed))$$

$$\phi_3 = AF\neg E(\neg PressedDown\ U\ (GearsExtended \wedge DoorsClosed))$$

$$\phi_4 = AG\ \neg(PressedDown \wedge AG(\neg GreenLight))$$

$$\phi_5 = AF(GreenLight)$$

In [9], a set of requirements is presented with respect to the normal mode. The requirement called R11bis states that "when the command line is working (normal mode), if the landing gear command handle has been pushed DOWN and stays DOWN, then eventually the gears will be locked down and the doors will be seen closed". We expressed this requirement in the three different CTL formulae ϕ_1, ϕ_2 and ϕ_3. The CTL formula ϕ_4 expresses the safety requirement. Finally, the CTL formula ϕ_5 expresses the liveness requirement. The quantifier ranging over all computation paths ("A") enables us to check the status of both normal and emergency modes. For example, the liveness formula ϕ_5 allows us to check the status of the 'green light' that will eventually happen in each mode. All these formulas are evaluated to true on the model M using MCMAS+. Therefore, our design model is error-free and at the same time it is strong as it achieves the safety and liveness requirements urgently needed in both modes. Moreover, we report on some statistical results such as the execution time of verifying these formulas is 0.298 s and the memory consumed is 6 Megabytes.

3   Model-Based Test Generation Approach

The objectives of the proposed approach are to complement formal verification with testing to increase software dependability (such as safety), and to offer both formal verification and testing results as evidence for software certification. The main idea is to demonstrate that the verified properties are properly propagated from the design level to the implementation level and that they hold within the implementation under test (IUT). Test cases are generated to satisfy both MC/DC and all DU paths criteria. In addition, witness test cases from the verification model are covered by more refined and concrete test cases that we apply to the implementation under test, and analyze the test results.

Despite all published works on EFSM based test generation as described in recent survey papers [6, 7, 14, 15], there are still a lot of challenges to address. We modified the algorithms [11–13] to address MC/DC and all DU paths coverage criteria, and implemented them with up to date research outcomes. In our approach, the generation of test sequences starts with the verification model that is transformed/refined to a testing model using graph rewriting technique that insures equivalence both ways [20]. From the testing model, the technique generates local test sequences for each EFSM agent in its context and creates a list of transitions used for communication between a pair of agents. A transition-marking algorithm marks every transition involved in the communication between agents. A composition algorithm that is guided by a communication graph of the EFSMs, builds a partial reachability graph of CEFSM. Local

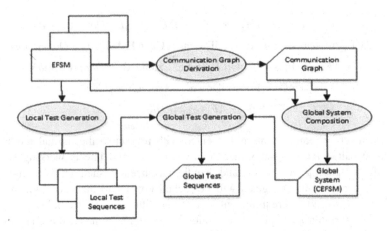

Fig. 6. Test generation process

test cases generation is important since not all transitions are involved in the communication. It also serves the purpose of standalone testing of an EFSM agent (Fig. 6).

3.1 Test Generation Process for the Case Study

In this case study, and for the sake of readability, the EFSMs are only a partial representation of a landing gear system. Following the DO-178C standards, the satisfaction of the MC/DC is mandatory, and it is used as a criterion in this paper for test sequences generation. The steps of test generation process are: (1) derive the local test sequences from each EFSM; (2) obtain the abstract communication graph of all EFSMs; (3) following the communication graph, obtain the global system as a partial reachability graph of CEFSMs; (4) from the local tests sequences and the CEFSM, generate the global test sequences. Figure 7 represents the obtained system model with the communication points, labels, transitions, and the input and output lists. We can see that the M_c and M_P agents are started at the same time. It is in fact a parallel communicating system. The transitions representing the communication between agents are described as orange, green, and red to represent the landing gear system lights of the same color.

The test generation approaches, that satisfy MC/DC and all DU-paths, are applied to the landing gear system case study. To generate feasible test sequences, we use the transformed model with all aforementioned information, the local test sequences, as well as the communication graph. To generate def-use feasible test sequences, 4 different elements are defined for each transition in the EFSM: assignment-use (A-usage), input-use (I-usage), computational-use (C-usage), and predicate-use (P-usage). These elements enable the links between the test sequences of each machine, which will render the test sequences feasible. The proposed algorithms provide a full set of feasible and non-feasible test sequences that will go through all possible transitions existing in the system under test. For every property being validated, there will always be feasible

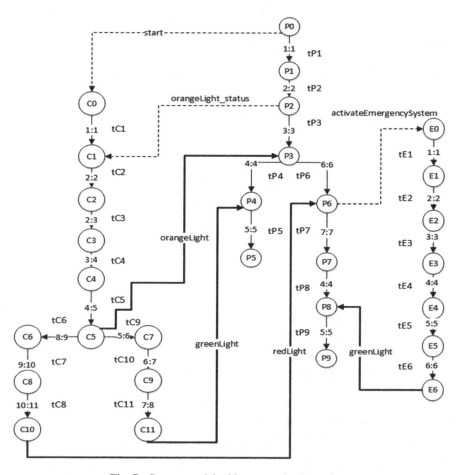

Fig. 7. System model with communication points

test sequences. We generate the paths linking two states from different machines by marking them as synchronization points.

For the landing gear system, the communication variables are: start, activateEmergencySystem, orangeLight(on, off), greenLight(on,off), redLight(on,off). These variables indicate the possible communication between the agents. For example, if activeEmergencySystem is on, it means that the redLight variable is also on. Then, communication points are identified, the input and output list for each transition is defined. The communication points for the pilot, controller and emergency agents can be seen respectively at P0, P2, P3, P4, P6, P8 - C0, C1, C5, C10, C11 - E0, and E6. Table 1 shows examples of the application of the algorithm using the landing gear case study. It identifies the different variable usage lists enabling the definition of feasible test sequences. Table 2 shows examples of test sequences to reach specific transitions in the system model. The chosen transitions represent a case of parallelism as shown in Table 3.

Table 1. Example of usage lists

Trans.	A-usage	I-usage	P-usage	Preamble
tP2	Orange light	–	–	tP1
tP4	–	Green light tC11	Green light on	tP1, tP2, tP3, [tC11]
tC11	–	Green light on Orange light off	Green light on	tC1, tC2, tC3, tC4, tC5, tC9, tC10

Table 2. Test sequences of the landing gear system

Transition	Tests sequences from a transition
tP5 Feasible	tP1, tP2, tP3, tC1, tC2, tC3, tC4, tC5, tC9, tC10, tC11, tP4, **tP5**
tP5 Non-feasible	tP1, tP2, tP3, tP4, **tP5**
tP9 Feasible	tP1, tP2, tP3, tC1, tC2, tC3, tC4, tC5, tC6, tC7, tC8, tP6, tE1, tE2, tE3, tE4, tE5, tE6, tP7, tP8, **tP9**

Table 3. Parallelism shown for feasible test sequences tP5 of the landing gear system

	Feasible test sequences – tP5		
Mp	tP1, tP2, tP3		tP4, **tP5**
Mc	tC1, tC2, tC3, tC4, tC5	tC9, tC10, tC11	

3.2 Witness Properties Verification

Table 4 below shows specific feasible test sequences for a selection of witness properties for liveness. The feasible test sequences are given by the input and output information, as well as the transition for which those input and output prove the witness example to be true. These tests sequences represent the transition in which the witness

Table 4. Feasible test sequences for witness example for liveness properties

#	Witness example for liveness properties	Feasible test sequences
1	EF GreenLight	Sequences leading to transitions: Mp: tP4 – tP5 – tP8 Mc: tC10 – tC11 Me: tE5 – tE6
2	EF (RedLight && EF GreenLight)	Sequences leading to transitions: Mp: tP8 – tP9 Me: tE5 – tE6
3	EF (PressedDown && EF GreenLight)	Sequences leading to transitions: Mp: tP4 – tP5 – tP8 – tP9 Mc: tC10 – tC11 Me: tE5 – tE6

example holds. Hence, all the possible transitions forming a path need to render a feasible test sequence up to the mentioned transition. For example, *EF GreenLight* holds true when a sequence executes up to transition tp5 (refer to Table 2 for the complete feasible test sequence).

3.3 Properties Verification

Several properties are defined below to verify whether the used algorithm validates the properties. The two feasible test sequences shown in Table 2 were analyzed with regards to those properties. Both feasible test sequences for transitions tP5 and tP9 verify all the properties identified so far.

$$\text{AG} \, (\, \text{PRESSED\_DOWN} \, \rightarrow \, \text{AF} \, (\, \text{EXTENDED} \, \&\& \, \text{CLOSED\_GEAR\_DOORS}))$$
$$\text{AG} \, \text{EF} \, (\, !\text{PRESSED\_DOWN} \, || \, \text{AF} (\, \text{EXTENDED} \, \&\& \, \text{CLOSED\_GEAR\_DOORS}))$$
$$\text{AF} \, (\, !\text{E} \, (!\text{PRESSED\_DOWN} \, \text{U} \, (\text{EXTENDED} \, \&\& \, \text{CLOSED\_GEAR\_DOORS}))$$
$$\text{AG} \, (\, !(\text{PRESSED\_DOWN} \, \&\& \, \text{AG} \, (!\text{GREEN\_LIGHT})))$$
$$\text{AF} \, \text{GREEN\_LIGHT}$$

The satisfaction of MC/DC criterion will lead to the generation of several non-feasible paths. It is necessary to ensure that these paths are handled correctly, which will control both the satisfaction of the properties and the alternatives triggered by glitches or possible malfunctions. Table 5 shows examples of tests cases generated to satisfy MC/DC criterion. Some test cases for a specific transition are not feasible and will either end in an error or be idle.

Table 5. Examples of test cases for MC/DC satisfaction

Transition	Test case	Status
tP5	tP1, tP2, tP3, tP4 –	Error: green light is on
tP5	tP1, tP2, tP3, tP4 –	Error: red light is on

4 Conclusion and Future Work

The proposed methodology and its application show that the integration of verification and testing activities is important to improve software dependability and achieve software certification in airborne industry. For future work, we plan to address the following challenging issues such as testing continuous and hybrid systems need more research and innovation to address them properly. The oracle problem needs more data mining and intelligence for analyzing and correlating outputs and searching in artifact such as specifications, logs and test architectures.

References

1. http://www.rtca.org. RTCA/DO-178C: Software Considerations in Airborne Systems and Equipment Certification, Supplement to DO-178C and DO-278A: DO-332 Object-Oriented Technology and Related Techniques, DO-331 Model-Based Development and Verification, DO-333 Formal Methods (2011)
2. Zoughbi, G., Briand, L., Labiche, Y.: Modeling safety and airworthiness (RTCA DO-178B) information: conceptual model and UML profile. J. Softw. Syst. Model. **10**(3), 337–367 (2011)
3. Moy, Y., Ledinot, E., Delseny, H., Wiels, V., Monate, B.: Testing or formal verification: DO-178C alternatives and industrial experience. J. IEEE Softw. **30**(3), 50–57 (2013)
4. Peleska, J., Siegel, M.: Test automation of safety-critical reactive systems. S. Afr. Comput. J. **19**, 53–77 (1997)
5. Peleska, J.: Industrial-strength model-based testing - state of the art and current challenges. MBT **2013**, 3–28 (2013)
6. Yang, R., Chen, Z., Zhang, Z., Xu, B.: EFSM-based test case generation: sequence, data, and oracle. Int. J. Softw. Eng. Knowl. Eng. **25**(4), 633–667 (2015)
7. Dssouli, R., Khoumsi, A., Elqortobi, M., Bentahar, J.: Testing the control-flow, data-flow, and time aspects of communication systems: a survey. Adv. Comput. **107**, 95–155 (2017)
8. Clarke, E., Grumberg, O., Peled, D.: Model Checking. The MIT Press, Massachusetts (1999)
9. Boniol, F., Wiels, V.: The landing gear system case study. In: Boniol, F., Wiels, V., Ait Ameur, Y., Schewe, K.-D. (eds.) ABZ 2014. CCIS, vol. 433, pp. 1–18. Springer, Cham (2014). https://doi.org/10.1007/978-3-319-07512-9_1
10. El-Kholy, W., Bentahar, J., El-Menshawy, M., Qu, H., Dssouli, R.: Conditional commitments: reasoning and model checking. ACM Trans. Soft. Eng. Methodol. **24**(2), 9:1–9:49 (2014)
11. Bourhfir, C., Aboulhamid, E., Dssouli, R., Rico, N.: A test case generation approach for conformance testing of SDL systems. Comput. Commun. **24**(3–4), 319–333 (2001)
12. Bourhfir, C., Dssouli, R., Aboulhamid, E., Rico, N.: Automatic executable test case generation for extended finite state machine protocols. In: Kim, M., Kang, S., Hong, K. (eds.) Testing of Communicating Systems. ITIFIP, pp. 75–90. Springer, Boston, MA (1997). https://doi.org/10.1007/978-0-387-35198-8_6
13. Bourhfir, C., Dssouli, R., Aboulhamid, E., Rico, N.: A guided incremental test case generation procedure for conformance testing for CEFSM specified protocols. In: Petrenko, A., Yevtushenko, N. (eds.) Testing of Communicating Systems. ITIFIP, vol. 3, pp. 279–294. Springer, Boston, MA (1998). https://doi.org/10.1007/978-0-387-35381-4_17
14. Ammann, P.E., Black, P.E., Majurski. W.: Using model checking to generate tests from Specifications. In: Proceedings of the Second IEEE International Conference on Formal Engineering Methods (ICFEM 1998), pp. 46–54. IEEE Computer Society (1998)
15. Yin, X., Jiangyuan, Y., Wang, Z., Shi, X., Wu, J.: Modeling and testing of network protocols with parallel state machines. IEICE Trans. Inf. Syst. **98**(12), 2091–2104 (2015)
16. Utting, M., Pretschner, A., Legeard, B.: A Taxonomy on Model-Based Testing. University of Waikato, Hamilton (2006)
17. Miller, S., Whalen, M., Cofer, D.: Software model checking takes off. Commun. ACM **53** (2), 58–64 (2010)
18. Fraser, G., Wotawa, F., Ammann, P.E.: Testing with model checkers: a survey. Softw. Test., Verif. Reliabil. **19**(3), 215–261 (2009)
19. Ouhammou, Y., et al.: A model-based process for the modelling and the analysis of avionic architectures. IJIIDS **10**(1/2), 117–144 (2017)
20. Habel, A., Heckel, R., Taentzer, G.: Graph grammars with negative application conditions. Fundam. Inf. **26**(3/4), 287–313 (1996)

MEDI4SG 2018 Workshop

Introduction to the International Workshop on Models and Data Engineering for Social Good (MEDI4SG 2018)

The MEDI International Workshop on Models and Data Engineering for Social Good (MEDI4SG) was chaired by Prof. Essaid El Bachari, Prof. Mohammed El Adnani, and Prof. Jihad Zahir from Cadi Ayyad University Morocco.

In September 2015, countries around the world adopted 17 sustainable development goals (SDGs) to end poverty, protect the planet, ensure prosperity for all, and achieve inclusive development by leaving no one behind. In fact, digital footprint, user-generated content (UGC), sensors, and other new sources of data today offer an unprecedented opportunity to dive into an ocean of structured and unstructured data. These data allow for the development of new approaches to better inform policies, to support effective decision-making, and to enhance quality of life for millions of humans around the globe and in Africa, specifically, which will therefore increase chances to achieve SDGs.

MEDI4SG fosters sound research using models and data engineering on real and challenging problems that are related, but not limited, to health and well-being, education, climate change, sustainable tourism, and sustainable cities. The workshop also promotes south–north and junior–senior cooperation between researchers committed to sustainable and inclusive development.

To encourage and promote the results and outcome of the MEDI4SG workshop, we are pleased to inform authors that some of the best papers were accepted in special issues of *Computer Science and Information Systems* (CSIS). All accepted papers for the workshop are published by Springer in *Communications in Computer and Information Science*.

We accepted three papers that tackle topics related to the overall orientations of the workshop.

1. "Gamification and Serious Games-Based Learning for Early Childhood in Rural Areas," by Rachid Lamrani, El Hassan Abdelwahed, Souad Chraibi, Sara Qassimi, and Meriem Hafidi. This paper proposes a Montessori method based on a serious games solution. The authors developed several serious games according to an agile method. They aim to test and to evaluate the user's experience and assess the children's acceptance and usefulness of the proposed system in rural preschools near Marrakech city in Morocco.
2. Context-Based Sentiment Analysis: A Survey, by Oumayma El Ansari, Jihad Zahir and Hajar Mousannif. This paper is a short survey on context-based sentiment analysis for English content. Different approaches from the literature and interpretations of the notion of context are presented, and the challenges posed by Arabic content are discussed. The paper is relevant to the topic of the workshop in the sense that tracking perception of social phenomena on social media and

monitoring the online discussions on controversial issues, especially those related to sustainable development, leads to an interesting set of evidence and knowledge.

3. "A Multi-Agent System-Based Distributed Intrusion Detection System for a Cloud Environment," by Omar Achbarou and My Ahmed El Kiram. This paper presents a new distributed intrusion detection system based on a multi-agent system to identify and prevent known and unknown attacks in this environment. Experiments demonstrated the performance and efficiency of the proposed system integrated with multi-agent technology.

The great success of the workshop is due to the hard work of all Program Committee members and external reviewers. We also thank all the authors for their contributions.

October 2018

Essaid El Bachari
Mohammed El Adnani
Jihad Zahir

MEDI4SG 2018 Workshop Chairs

Essaid El Bachari   Cadi Ayyad University, Morocco
Mohammed El Adnani   Cadi Ayyad University, Morocco
Jihad Zahir   Cadi Ayyad University, Morocco

MEDI4SG 2018 Program Committee

Witold Kinsner	University of Manitoba, Canada
Esteban Vázquez Cano	National University of Distance Education, Spain
Abdelaziz Khadraoui	University of Geneva, Switzerland
Abdelila Maach	University Mohammed V, Morocco
Lahcen Oubahssi	Université du Maine, France
Rachid LATIF	University Ibn Zohr, Morocco
Eric Leclercq	University of Burgundy, France
Agouti tarik	Cadi Ayyad University, Morocco
Sebastián Ventura	University of Cordoba, Spain
Richard Chbeir	Université UPPA, France
Chraibi Souad	Cadi Ayyad University, Morocco
Bubacarr Bah	African Institute for Mathematical Sciences, South Africa
Jelmam Yassine	National Engineering School of Tunis, Tunisia
Issam Qaffou	Cadi Ayyad University, Morocco
Martin Gordon Mubangizi	Pulse Lab Kampala, Uganda
My Ahmed El Kiram	Cadi Ayyad University, Morocco
Sana Nouzri	Cadi Ayyad University, Morocco

Gamification and Serious Games Based Learning for Early Childhood in Rural Areas

Rachid Lamrani$^{(\boxtimes)}$, El Hassan Abdelwahed, Souad Chraibi,
Sara Qassimi, and Meriem Hafidi

Computer Systems Engineering Laboratory (LISI), Cadi Ayyad University,
Marrakech, Morocco
rachid.lamrani@ced.uca.ac.ma,
{abdelwahed,chraibi}@uca.ac.ma,
{sara.qassimi,meriem.hafidi}@ced.uca.ma

Abstract. Early childhood education has a high impact on the success of higher education. Besides, it allows a sustainable social and economic development of the country. It enables a relevant upbringing and education of future generations by providing the necessary skills and competencies. This is especially regarding African developing countries and rural areas in particular. Therefore, it is necessary to support the development of the early childhood education in terms of apprehending the knowledge and improving the children's skills. Actually, recent pedagogical and neuroscience researches show that the best way to teach children is through playing, getting their attention, their engagement, receiving feedback and consolidating their skills. In fact, playing represents a natural and privileged method for children's learning. Correspondingly, our approach integrates all aspects mentioned above to develop a playful and creative learning. The proposed approach is a play-based learning using the Montessori pedagogical principal as a core of the method that is implanted in several types of serious games. This paper proposes a Montessori's Method based on serious games solution. We developed several serious games according to an agile method. Future works will focus on deploying and validating this solution in a real context, precisely in rural preschools near Marrakech. Our aim is to evaluate the user's experience and assess the children's acceptance and usefulness of our system.

Keywords: Preschool learning · Serious games · Gamification
Montessori · The play power · Early childhood education

1 Introduction

Education is an essential right that must be accessible to all people without any discrimination and it has an essential effect on promoting gender equality and empowering women. It is one of the basic pillars of economic and national development [1, 2]. Poor education practices are among the main factors affecting the social and cultural development of the society. Education is crucial to give people capabilities such as literacy, confidence, and attitudes [3]. Furthermore, education is crucial to foster tolerance between people and it contributes to forming more peaceful societies.

© Springer Nature Switzerland AG 2018
E. H. Abdelwahed et al. (Eds.): MEDI 2018 Workshops, CCIS 929, pp. 79–90, 2018.
https://doi.org/10.1007/978-3-030-02852-7_7

However, it remains a challenge in some parts of the world, particularly in developing countries that have a significant number of dropping out of school. This is due to several reasons, such as poverty, tuition fees, or associated costs (uniforms, supplies) as well as the lack of security. All those causes might create barriers pushing some parents to keep their children away from school. An example of the inequality in the matter of education is the lack of opportunities affording education for girls in rural areas. As a solution, it is essential for gathering all efforts to find innovative approaches to deliver an accessible education allowing a gapless learning. So we should assess individuals' needs and elaborate strategies defining targeted objectives of the educational system that meet their specific expectations. The usage of the emergent digital technologies offers promising solutions and efficient approaches to achieve good education goals.

Besides, the family is the first source of learning and supportive relationships to children, especially the parents who are considered as the first and the most important teachers and who have the biggest part of the education responsibility [7]. For the good upbringing of their children, the parents have to set up intellectual and emotional life bases, to give suitable and valuable attitudes in order to ensure an active participation for a good preschool departure [8, 9]. Children are curious from the moment they are born and they want to learn about their world and understand it. Learning starts at birth, and the first six years are for discovering and exploring. So, a strong beginning in the early years provides them with the best and fairest chance to reach their fullest potential [10]. Children's early learning is the main factor for school success and helps their brains develop well.

Playing is the natural way for children to improve their future skills from the moment they are born [4, 5]. When they play, they use plenty of their senses to capture and acquire diverse information and extend their knowledge about their environment. Moreover, through the fun playthings, children will develop new skills and their ability to talk, think, act, feel and learn about themselves. Otherwise, playing provides children with the opportunity to boost their attention span, learn to get along with others, cultivate their creativity and address their social, emotional and cognitive needs. It also develops children's main academic skills (language, mathematics, etc.) that are the base for later learning, without forgetting that it is an innate human behavior, which goes with us along our lives. It also has a vital role in the healthy development of the children enabling them an open and ludic way of developing, learning, and socializing [11–13]. In fact, whether it is a toddler, teenager, or even a retired person, playing is a fantastic way of learning and development [14]. Allowing children to choose their activities and establish their own ways of doing things, give them the feeling of controlling their learning and the opportunity to make new challenges. Furthermore, providing an adapted solution gives children the opportunity to reach their goals which increase their confidence and motivations.

The rapid widespread of Information and communications technologies (ICT) reached and involved in children's daily life provides learners with better learning opportunities. It has also changed teaching methods and makes access to high-quality educational content easier, such as textbooks, videos, and distance education with a lower price. ICT have paved the way for personalized learning, adapted to the pace of each learner. Serious games, IoT, Virtual reality, cloud computing and many other emerging technologies offer the possibility to develop innovative learning solutions like the mobile and pervasive learning systems. Those new technologies can be considered as promising ways to perform the objectives and needs cited above and used to improve the existing educational methods in order to reduce the gap between technologies, gamification, and learning approaches.

This paper presents a methodological approach that underlines serious games and the cognitive of playing based on new technologies in order to offer a research-based solution that makes playtime more stimulating and educational for children.

2 The Benefits of Early Childhood Education

The preschool prepares young children for the elementary education and it's considered as an instructive period in the formation of concepts and constant ideas [35]. The preschool is an important step in life that ensures children, from birth to age six, the best possible departure in life. It helps the children starting strong and being prepared for lifelong learning and success. The inequalities begin in the first six years and on the other side the early childhood education promotes the better intellectual development of individuals. So, the role of pre-school education is vital in preventing school failure. In fact, a child is not a vase that needs to be filled in, but a source that we leave unleashing, based on good education practices.

The preschool must be a linguistic gateway allowing the children to develop their mother tongue strengthening their emotional and social development, promoting the early acquisition of behaviors and attitudes, while imbuing the new languages. Also, it allows children to live in the community preparing for the social relationships which make them aware that there are rules to respect and constraints to accept.

Most of the time, the child is asked to do activities that are neither a decision nor a personal motivation on his part but just imposed by the teacher whatever the activity is. Therefore, the child does not pay close attention and is not really engaged. Also, the child has often the difficulty to consolidate what he learned because he does not have the possibility to repeat the same activity when it's necessary. While making mistakes during his activities, the signal of error that the child could detect is insufficient, that is because the teacher doesn't have the possibility to give individual and immediate feedback to each child. Thereby, we should reconsider the preschool's teaching methods in order to fit the real needs of the children improving their motivation and confidence.

3 Pillars of Learning: When Neuroscience Explore the Enigma of Education

Neuroscience synergizes with other disciplines, have broadened our understanding of the brain in a way that is highly relevant to educational practices [37]. Cognitive science has identified at least four key factors as pillars of learning processes and pedagogical strategies [15]. Actually, good learning involves attention, active engagement, feedback and consolidation (see Fig. 1).

Fig. 1. Foundations of the proposed approach

Indeed, mobilizing children's *attention* is a priority goal. The teacher must create attractive materials that do not distract the child from his primary task. Therefore, given the sensitivity of their brain to social cues, the educational counseling attitude is essential: he must focus the child's attention through visual and verbal contact.

Moreover, the active *engagement* role underscores how important it is for the child to be maximally attentive, active, and predictive, and in this respect, to maximize curiosity in order to have a total engagement. Thus, a care must be taken in order to introduce to the child learning situations that are neither easy nor difficult, adequate to his context. As a matter of fact, preserving commitment means that the teacher must avoid giving a long lecture, but involve the children, test them frequently, guide them while allowing them to discover certain aspects by themselves, and reward systematically their curiosity rather than discourage it.

Withal, the importance of the *feedback* underlines the educational status of the error. The educational accompanist should realize that from the point of view of cognitive neuroscience, far from being a fault or a weakness, the error is normal, inevitable even, and in any case indispensable for learning. Better an active child who is wrong and learns from his mistakes, than a passive child.

Further, the *consolidation* considered as the knowledge automation. Automation is the act of passing from conscious treatment with an effort, to an automated unconscious treatment.

Correspondingly, the child learns by his emotional intelligence [16, 17], then develops a link with his mistress, which makes him learn more words and operations.

As soon as it grew, he should be initiated at the intelligence logic, which must be implemented by single organizations and visual methods.

4 Learning Through Play

Outdoor Games and playing are very important for every child, considered as a legitimate right of the child; it represents a crucial aspect of the physical, intellectual and social child development. It's fundamental to their well-being.

While playing, the children develop their skills on several aspects: reflection, problem solving, expression, moves, cooperation, and exercise of moral conscience [19, 20, 24]. That's how their development unconsciously improves [21]. When tackling the brain development, scientists have proved that many of the fundamental tasks children must achieve can be most effectively learned through play. They also confirm that play is essential to healthy and even exceptional to the brain development [22, 23].

Moreover, all kinds of play and games can be specified by means of different components. The first component is the rule or gameplay, which creates the pattern defined through the game rules that connect the player and the game. The second is the challenge, which determines the bonuses to reward the good actions or the obstruction and barriers that avoid the player reaching the game goal easily. Challenges are used to create the different difficulty levels of the game in order to encourage enjoyment and motivate the player to spend more time with the game. The third component is the interaction which represents the way the player communicates with the game. Interaction refers to any action that is done by to start some activity, it can be visual, listening, physical (typing, mouse, touchpad, button pressing), dialogue exchange, etc. And the last component is the objective which is defined as something that one's efforts or actions are intended to attain or accomplish.

Nowadays, the children have the ability to manipulate brilliantly different technological devices (computers, console games, smartphones, etc.) which play a significant formative role in their personal development [18]. Moreover, the usage of technologies contributes to reducing the distance and offering access to pedagogical resources, especially when it comes to the rural areas. Furthermore, that enables access to other ways to learn and offers innovative methods to develop our skills. So, it will be fascinating to conceive ludic and funny products and services based on the new technologies and the concept of the four learning pillars by making the child in the center of the educational act. Wrapping up the learning activities by games is what makes learning through playing more fun and consequently more motivating for students.

5 Gamification in Learning and Serious Games

Gamification is generally considered as the application of game elements in conventional contexts aiming to change and enhance individuals' behaviors and attitudes. Gamification techniques are benefiting from advances in ICT. Applications of gamification span a wide range including healthcare, marketing, management and recruitment, as well as learning and teaching. The relation between gamification and education is on the rise and learning activities are an important context that can be subject to gamification.

A serious game is a computer application that combines with consistency, both serious aspects such as learning, or communication intent, with playful springs from the video game like collaboration, competition and strategy [25, 26]. Actually, their main use aims to improve users' skills, engagements and performances [27, 33].

Relevant serious games applications, have recently been developed in different domains, including education, training, well-being, advertisement, cultural heritage, interpersonal communication, and healthcare [28]. Advances in gaming technologies allow the real-time interactive visualization and simulation of realistic virtual heritage scenarios, such as reconstructions of ancient sites and virtual museums [29]. Many research contributions are directed towards taking advantage of the success of video games and using them to benefit the educational domain, such as [30].

Also, there are a few research and project using serious games in the context of preschool to develop the children's abilities and academic skills in mathematics and languages [31, 32].

6   Proposed Approach: Gamification and Serious Games Based Learning for Early Childhood

As it was mentioned above, one of the motivating challenges is to elaborate pertinent solutions addressing the problem of the growth of the number of dropping out of school in early childhood especially. In this context, we have initialized a project aiming to develop innovative solutions to deliver an accessible early childhood education. Our goal is to eliminate the inequality in the matter of education and create real opportunities for children, in particular young girls, in rural areas to have access to education.

The pedagogical method we adopted within our project is based on Montessori approach [6, 36, 38]. It stated that the purpose of the early childhood education wasn't to fill the child by predetermined studies, but rather, to cultivate her own desire to learn. This approach proposes to organize the main learning activities around children playing activities. It distinguishes five categories of activities and skills to develop (see Fig. 2). Also, it assumes that during learning activities, the individual should be autonomous and be mainly motivated by its natural curiosity and its love of knowledge. Two fundamental principles of this approach are, first, allows each child to learn by doing according to its own choice and rhythm without no obligation, and secondly, to help him to refine its natural learning tools when it's needed.

All the serious games that we have developed within our project are aligned to the Montessori approach and with respect to the pillars of learning reflecting the educational cognitive science point of view (see Fig. 1). Indeed, errors are considered as phases of the game and do not prevent children's to continue. Also, immediate feedback ensures the checking of the quality of what we have learned, that is a very important factor for effective learning. We aim to deliver and to introduce some games and apps with purpose (serious games), allowing a gamification integration, to manage behaviors or learning, such, mathematics improving and science skills, languages progression (see Fig. 2).

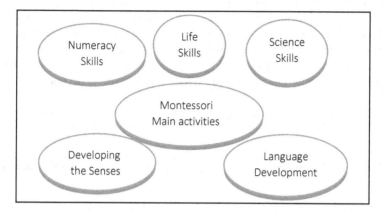

Fig. 2. The montessori approach main activities and skills

7 Realization and Deployment

All the serious games we have developed could be used within group of children in the context of an online learning or a blended learning that combines them with traditional classroom methods. They are accessible using a mobile device like a smartphone or a desktop (see Fig. 3).

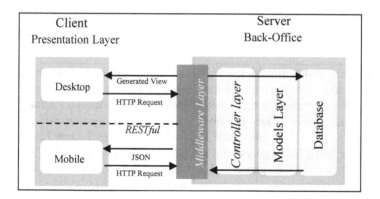

Fig. 3. System architecture

Montessori Method's materials, physical or digital (serious games), would enrich the universe surrounds children to enhance and promote a playfully and creative learning. An adult can supervise and assess the children's learning activities reminding them with benevolence the dangers, prohibitions, respect and without too much intervention or leadership.

Presently, we have implemented more than twelve serious games spread between different Montessori Approach main activities and skills (see Fig. 3). While continuing agile development of other games, we project to deploy, as quickly as possible, and conduct tests of our approach in a real context in rural preschools near Marrakech. Our aim is to get feedback as earlier as possible relative to user experience and assess the children's acceptance and usefulness of our system. The goal is to evaluate each step in the chain of the learning process including its technical aspects according to an agile method.

Below, we present some examples of serious games that we have already developed (Tables 1, 2 and 3).

Table 1. Some serious games developed concerning the language and the numeracy skills development

Activities and skills : Language development	**Activities and skills** : Numeracy skills
Game goal and Guidelines: This game help kids recognizing a letter, numbers shapes, associate them with phonic sounds, and put their alphabet knowledge to use in fun exercises. It has the same pedagogical goal and it is aligned with the entitled games "The phonetic alphabet" and "Identifying alphabets" in [38].	**Game goal and Guidelines:** This game is about numbers and how to use them and apply some basic mathematical operations with quantities (using fruits). This game has the same pedagogical goal and it is aligned with the entitled game "Addition using numerals" in [38]

Table 2. Some serious games developed concerning the senses and the life skills improvement

Activities and skills : Developing the senses	**Activities and skills** : Life skills

Game goal and Guidelines: This game teaches the kid the colors, their spelling and their phonetic sound. This game has the same pedagogical goal and it is aligned with the entitled game "Discovering colors" in [38]	**Game goal and Guidelines:** This game shows the child the importance of brushing teeth. This game has the same pedagogical goal and it is aligned with the entitled game "Cleaning teeth" in [38]

Table 3. Some serious games developed concerning the science skills development

Activities and skills : Science skills	**Activities and skills** : Science skills
	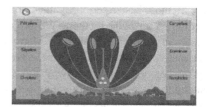
Game goal and Guidelines: This game teaches the child the continents, the countries and their location by making his first experience of geography as concrete & as fun as possible. This game has the same pedagogical goal and it is aligned with the entitled game "Introducing a globe and map " in [38]	**Game goal and Guidelines:** This activity serves double purposes. While the child is making and constructing a puzzle of a flower, he is learning about the parts of a flower and their names. This game has the same pedagogical goal and it is aligned with the entitled game "Make a flower puzzle " in [38]

8 Conclusion and Perspectives

Playing is the main children's source of pleasure whether on its emotional, social, physical, language or cognitive development. Covering up learning activities with games is what makes learning through playing more fun and consequently more motivating for students. Through play, the child would feel more confident, autonomous and have more pleasure to acquire new academic skills (mathematics, language, etc.) and social aptitudes (confidence, communication, etc.). While playing and doing fun actions, he would be more motivated and curious to discover the world around him while adopting a positive attitude towards action.

Gamification is generally considered as the application of game elements in conventional contexts aiming to enhance individuals' behaviors and to improve their skills. A serious game is a computer application that combines with consistency, both serious aspects such as learning, or communication intent, with fun and ludic video game's features.

Nowadays, African countries present a significant number of dropping out of school, in particular in preschool. This is due to several reasons, such as poverty, growth tuition fees as well as the lack of security. Learning starts at birth, and the first six years are for discovering and exploring. Indeed, a strong beginning in the early years provides individuals with the best and fairest chance to reach their fullest potential. Therefore, it would be essential for gathering all efforts to find innovative solutions to deliver an accessible education allowing a gapless learning.

A part of our actual research studies deals with the above problems and challenges. In this paper, we have presented our propositions and contributions to assure the development of the children's early learning, in particular in rural areas. In fact, access to preschool is the main factor for individuals' school success and thus social and economic development of the countries. For early childhood, we propose a Montessori's Method based serious games solution. We developed several serious games according to an agile method. We project to deploy this solution in a real context, precisely in rural preschools near Marrakech. Our aim is to evaluate the user's experience and assess the children's acceptance and usefulness of our system.

It's a beginning of a long way and a rewarding challenge. Many questions remain open and there are many motivating perspectives to address. For example, one of them is how to enable the teachers to track and analyze students' activities and progress during the educational games session. Another challenge that we try to face is about the youth unemployment problem in Northern Africa. To treat the scourge of youth unemployment, we project to capitalize on the outcomes of the actual project to develop a pervasive collaborative system to enhance Northern African youth entrepreneurship through gamification [34].

Acknowledgment. The development of some serious games reported here was conducted in fulfillment of the requirements of the degree of Bachelor in Computing Sciences in Cadi Ayyad University. The authors would like to kindly thank the students Outhmane Lagnaoui, Ilyass Moummad, Yousra El Messoussi and Imane Messak.

References

1. Every child has the right to an education. https://www.unicef.org/crc/index_73893.html. Accessed 18 June 2018
2. Monteiro, A.: The right of the child to education: what right to what education? Procedia - Soc. Behav. Sci. **9**, 1988–1992 (2010)
3. Sen, A.: Development as Freedom. Anchor Books, New York (2013)
4. Sheridan, M., Howard, J., Alderson, D.: Play in Early Childhood. Routledge, London (2011)
5. Cutter-Mackenzie, A., Edwards, S., Moore, D., Boyd, W.: Young Children's Play and Environmental Education in Early Childhood Education. Springer, Heidelberg (2014). https://doi.org/10.1007/978-3-319-03740-0
6. Lillard, A.: Preschool children's development in classic montessori, supplemented montessori, and conventional programs. J. Sch. Psychol. **50**, 379–401 (2012)
7. Landry, S.H.: The role of parents in early childhood learning. In: Tremblay, R.E. (ed.) Encyclopedia on Early Childhood Development (2014)
8. Erola, J., Jalonen, S., Lehti, H.: Parental education, class and income over early life course and children's achievement. Res. Soc. Strat. Mobil. **44**, 33–43 (2016)
9. Grindal, T., et al.: The added impact of parenting education in early childhood education programs: a meta-analysis. Child Youth Serv. Rev. **70**, 238–249 (2016)
10. Alexander, K., Entwisle, D., Olson, L.: Lasting consequences of the summer learning gap. Am. Sociol. Rev. **72**, 167–180 (2007)
11. Yilmaz, R.: Educational magic toys developed with augmented reality technology for early childhood education. Comput. Hum. Behav. **54**, 240–248 (2016)
12. Moreno, M.: Supporting child play. JAMA Pediatr. **170**, 184 (2016)
13. Milteer, R., Ginsburg, K., Mulligan, D.: The importance of play in promoting healthy child development and maintaining strong parent-child bond: focus on children in poverty. Pediatrics **129**, e204–e213 (2011)
14. Miller, J., Kocurek, C.: Principles for educational game development for young children. J. Child. Media **11**, 314–329 (2017)
15. Dehaene, S.: Cognitive foundations of learning in school-aged children. Collège de France. https://www.college-de-france.fr/site/en-stanislas-dehaene/course-2014-2015.htm. Accessed 19 June 2018
16. Raver, C., Garner, P., Smith, D.: The roles of emotion regulation and emotion knowledge for children's academic readiness: are the links causal? In: Planta, B., Snow, K., Cox, M. (eds.) School Readiness and the Transition to Kindergarten in the Era of Accountability, pp. 121–147. Paul H Brookes Publishing, Baltimore (2007)
17. Eggum, N., et al.: Emotion understanding, theory of mind, and prosocial orientation: relations over time in early childhood. J. Posit. Psychol. **6**, 4–16 (2011)
18. Plowman, L.: Researching young children's everyday uses of technology in the family home. Interact. Comput. **27**, 36–46 (2014)
19. Hughes, F.: Children, Play, and Development. Sage Publications, Los Angeles (2010)
20. Berk, L.: Child Development. Pearson, Boston (2013)
21. Catron, C.: Early Childhood Curriculum: A Creative Play Model. Pearson, Boston (2008)
22. Diamond, M.: Response of the brain to enrichment. An. Acad. Bras. Ciênc. **73**, 211–220 (2001)
23. Diamond, M., Krech, D., Rosenzweig, M.: The effects of an enriched environment on the histology of the rat cerebral cortex. J. Comp. Neurol. **123**, 111–119 (1964)
24. Vaughan, C., Brown, S.: Play. Avery, New York (2014)

25. Djaouti, D.: Serious Games pour l'éducation: utiliser, créer, faire créer? Tréma **44**, 51–64 (2016)

26. Wattanasoontorn, V., Boada, I., García, R., Sbert, M.: Serious games for health. Entertain. Comput. **4**, 231–247 (2013)

27. Giessen, H.: Serious games effects: an overview. Procedia - Soc. Behav. Sci. **174**, 2240–2244 (2015)

28. Davis, S., Moar, M., Jacobs, R., Watkins, M., Riddoch, C., Cooke, K.: 'Ere Be Dragons: heartfelt gaming. Digit. Creat. **17**, 157–162 (2006)

29. Neto, J., Silva, R., Neto, J., Pereira, J., Fernandes, J.: Solis'Curse - a cultural heritage game using voice interaction with a virtual agent. In: 2011 Third International Conference on Games and Virtual Worlds for Serious Applications (2011)

30. Muratet, M., Torguet, P., Jessel, J., Viallet, F.: Towards a serious game to help students learn computer programming. Int. J. Comput. Games Technol. **2009**, 1–12 (2009)

31. Nikiforidou, Z., Pange, J.: Shoes and squares: a computer-based probabilistic game for preschoolers. In: Procedia - Social and Behavioral Sciences, vol. 2, pp. 3150–3154 (2010)

32. Schuurs, U.: Serious gaming and vocabulary growth. In: De Wannemacker, S., Vandercruysse, S., Clarebout, G. (eds.) ITEC/CIP/T 2011. CCIS, vol. 280, pp. 40–46. Springer, Heidelberg (2012). https://doi.org/10.1007/978-3-642-33814-4_5

33. Lamrani, R., Abdelwahed, E.H.: Learning through play in pervasive context: a survey. In: IEEE/ACS 12th International Conference of Computer Systems and Applications (AICCSA), Marrakech, pp. 1–8 (2015)

34. Lamrani, R., Abdelwahed, E.H., Chraibi, S., Qassimi, S., Hafidi, M., El Amrani, A.: Serious game to enhance and promote youth entrepreneurship. In: Rocha, Á., Serrhini, M., Felgueiras, C. (eds.) Europe and MENA Cooperation Advances in Information and Communication Technologies. Advances in Intelligent Systems and Computing, vol. 520, pp. 77–85. Springer, Cham (2017). https://doi.org/10.1007/978-3-319-46568-5_8

35. Arbianingsih, Rustina, Y., Krianto, T., Ayubi, D.: Developing a health education game for preschoolers: what should we consider? Enfermería Clínica, **28**, 1–4 (2018)

36. Alvarez, C.: Les lois naturelles de l'enfant. Les Arènes (2016)

37. Sigman, M., Peña, M., Goldin, A., Ribeiro, S.: Neuroscience and education: prime time to build the bridge. Nat. Neurosci. **17**, 497–502 (2014)

38. Pitamic, M.: Teach Me to Do it Myself: Montessori Activities for You and Your Child. Barron's Educational Series (2004)

Context-Based Sentiment Analysis: A Survey

Oumayma El Ansari[✉], Jihad Zahir, and Hajar Mousannif

LISI Laboratory, Faculty of Sciences Semlalia, Cadi Ayyad University,
Marrakech, Morocco
ansari.oumaima@gmail.com,
{j.zahir,mousannif}@uca.ac.ma

Abstract. Social Networks became the most important source of information. User-generated content is constantly increasing which provides unprecedented opportunities to support decision-making processes and advocacy efforts. This paper is a short survey on context based sentiment analysis for English content; we present different approaches from the literature and interpretations of the notion of context. Moreover, we explain the challenges posed by Arabic content and discuss an approach that could be implemented for context based sentiment analysis for Arab language.

Keywords: Sentiment analysis · Context-based sentiment analysis
Arabic language

1 Introduction

Nowadays, people are more connected to internet and especially social networks (e.g. 330 million of Twitter users are monthly active [1]). This huge amount of the generated data triggered the desire of exploring the useful information in order to determine how the crowds think and feel. Tracking perception of social phenomena on social media and monitoring the online discussions on controversial issues, especially those related to sustainable development, would lead to a new set of evidence and knowledge. Hence, it's not surprising that the analysis of opinions and feelings expressed in social networks became one of the most vital fields in NLP, presented as Sentiment Analysis (SA) [2, 3]. As opposed to traditional surveys and data collection and analysis methods, the main advantage of SA lies in the fact that it's both a low-cost and a quick approach to picture public opinion in a given timeframe.

The main task in SA is subjectivity and polarity classification, it consists of identifying whether the text is subjective or objective and determining the degree of subjectivity: Positive (e.g. COP 23 recommendations rock), negative (e.g. It's a big failure!), neutral (e.g. I will watch it tomorrow), mixed (e.g. I loved the scenario but the actors sucks) [4].

Many Sentiment Analysis techniques were described in the literature, generally these could be divided into two types [5]: Dictionary based techniques [2, 4, 6], where a lexicon is used to label the words with the polarity, and Machine Learning based methods [2, 3] that consist of using training data and classification features to classify the text.

E. H. Abdelwahed et al. (Eds.): MEDI 2018 Workshops, CCIS 929, pp. 91–97, 2018.
https://doi.org/10.1007/978-3-030-02852-7_8

In a text, the global representation of a sentence could influence the meaning of each lexical item. As a result, the same word could change its polarity in different contexts. This particularity represents one of the main challenges in sentiment analysis [5].

Generally, SA systems that handle polarity presented by one single word give ambiguous results, in order to improve their approaches, researchers try to focus more on Context Based Sentiment Analysis.

In this paper we present a short survey on CBSA for English language and expose the challenges that stand against the development of CBSA for Arabic content. The remainder of this paper is organized as follow: We start by providing a background in Sect. 2, then, a general process flow of a typical CBSA system is presented in Sect. 3. We introduce, in Sect. 4, different types of context modeling for English content. Finally, before we conclude, we present different challenges in CBSA for Arabic content in the last section.

2 Background

Context in Sentiment Analysis is defined as the set of lexical items that precede or follow a word or a passage that could influence its valence.

It's important to assimilate the difference between the polarity and valence. The polarity of a word could be one of three: positive, negative or neutral, generally it's given by a lexicon. While the valence represent the attitude that is communicated by the word in a particular context, it's called also the contextual polarity [9]. This contextual polarity is influenced by different valence shifters: a lexical phenomena that can shift the valence of a lexical item from one pole to the other or, influence it's perlocutionary force to increase or decrease, e.g.: 'not' 'strongly' 'possibly'… . These influencers exist in the sentence level such as negation or topic level.

3 General Process Flow of a CBSA System

In general, a context based sentiment analysis process starts first with the preprocessing of the dataset in order to eliminate all the ambiguities that could influence the treatment. The second step is the most vital, it consists of defining the context's level and collecting all the related terms or features. Finally the classification phase which combines and analyses the influence of the context and the key words in order to detect the polarity (Fig. 1).

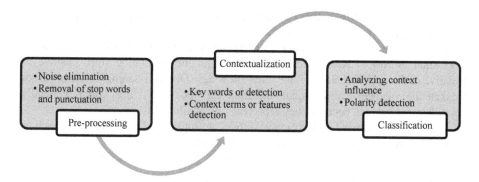

Fig. 1. General context based sentiment analysis process

4 Modeling Context

Several research paths have emerged in context based sentiment analysis, the difference between the works done in this field is the interpretation of the 'context'. In [7] and [13] the authors presented the sentence-based context while the work in [10] presents the valence shifters that are the relevant influencers in sentence-based context, the papers [8] and [12] focus on defining the context in twitter and [11] focused on developing a context-based lexicon.

4.1 Sentence-Based Context

In [7] the authors presented a method that takes into account the context embeddded by neighboring words on each word of the sentence, it's the sentence-based context.

This method suggests that a word doesn't always carry the same annotation in a specific domain, e.g.: in the same camera's description the word 'long' could be positive (*long battery life*) and negative (*long time to focus*).

The described algorithm applied to 500 hotel reviews uses the *Influence Function*, which calculates the score of each word in the basis of its relevance and also with taking in consideration the features of the text that surrounds it. Thus, the scores of the neighboring lexical items could increase or decrease the positivity/negativity of each word.

Authors of [13] present an effective new approach for sentiment analysis for both regular long text and noisy long text. This method takes into consideration the sentence based-context, it consists of two phases. (a) The learning phase: identification of key terms that indicate the presence of a sentiment and context terms for each key term in order to generate features for supervised learning.

(b) The detection phase: the goal of this phase is to use a classifier in order to give a score that indicates the probability of the existence of a given sentiment and generate the polarity.

[10] describes how the context could affect, strengthen, weaken or switch the individual valence of each lexical item.

All the different shifters that could improve the interactions between lexical items in a text are represented in the two types of context.

In sentence-based context many valence shifters are represented: First, the *negatives* such as 'not', 'none', 'never' could change the annotation from positive to negative or the opposite. Second, the intensifiers e.g. 'Deeply', 'strongly' strengthen or weaken the valence. Third, modal operators e.g. 'possibly', 'if', 'could' generally neutralize the valence because they represent unreal situations.

For the domain-based context many shifters are introduced e.g. connectors such as 'althought', reported speech, the existence of subtopics.

4.2   Topical Context

In [8] the concept of 'context' is interpreted under another angle. The authors introduce a rich context-sensitive model for tweets.

This work addresses the ambiguity in the process of analyzing one single tweet at a time, and gives a new approach of determining the polarity of a tweet according to the conversation where it belongs.

This method treated two types of contexts: a. Conversations: sequences of tweets that reply each one to the previous. b. Topic: based on hashtags. The work is based on a learning machine approach that implements the Markovian formulation of Support Vector Machine (learning algorithm that labels collectively the tweets in a sequence).

In the same orientation, [12] sheds lights on target dependent twitter sentiment classification. In addition to taking into consideration the related tweets to a single tweet, authors incorporate target dependent features.

This method consists of three steps: The first and the second are subjectivity and polarity classification depending on the target, these steps include the pre-processing, determining target-dependency features and target extensions (synonyms and aspects that are related to the target), and finally the classification which is based on a binary SVM classifier. The third step is the graph-based optimization that relies on representing the related tweets of each tweet in a tree in order to evaluate the context and boost the performance of the classification.

4.3   Conversional Context

The work in [11], authors developed a context dependent lexicon that's defined as:

A dictionary of opinion words conditioned on different aspects of the given domain. The purpose of this lexicon is to assign a score to each pair of aspect and opinion word e.g. score (bad, battery). Many useful sources are combined to create the context dependent lexicon: a. General-purpose lexicon that is context-independent. b. Thesaurus: Wordnet. c. Linguistic heuristics ('and', 'but' and negation rules).

Using two data sets from two different domains; hotel reviews and printers feedback, the candidate lexicon entries were first generated, then the author presented the method as an optimization problem to solve based on an objective function, for this purpose many constraints are proposed to form the function. The final step is to transform the problem into a linear programming problem (Table 1).

Table 1. Summary of the methods done in context-based sentiment analysis

Reference	Context interpretation	Description	Source of data	Technique
[7]	Sentence-based	The influence of neighboring lexical items on a word	Hotel reviews from TripAdvisor	Genetic algorithm
[8]	Conversional	The influence of related tweets on a single tweet	SemEval-2013 tweets corpus	Machine learning
[10]	Sentence based	Describes the valence shifters that could influence a word	–	Describing the valence shifters
[11]	Aspect-based context	Develop a context-based lexicon	TripAdvisor reviews, printers feedbacks	Machine learning,
[12]	Conversional target dependent context	The influence of related tweet on a single tweet and the influence of target	Created a target-dependent dataset of tweets	Machine learning
[13]	Sentence based	This method is more effective on noisy texts and takes in consideration the context in the sentence level	Hotel reviews from TripAdvisor, twitter, automatically transcribed phone calls	Supervised learning

The different methods and approaches presented above show that the context could be interpreted in different ways, this could depend on the nature of the data source (tweets, comments, reviews…), the objective of the sentiment analysis work and also the specification level of the context (domain, sentence …).

5 CBSA in Arabic: Challenges and Opportunities

5.1 Challenges

The main challenges in Arabic Sentiment Analysis are the language itself. In the top of the list comes the diversity of Arabic dialects used in social media; each Arab country speak at least one dialect. Second, one of the main characteristics of Arabic is that a word with the same spelling could have different meaning due to the Arabic punctuation. e.g. 'علم' could mean 'science' or' a flag'. Moreover, the Arabic punctuation is usually absent in the social media content. These properties constitute the major difficulties when analyzing an Arabic text, especially dealing with the context in the sentiment analysis process.

5.2   Opportunities

As presented in the works focusing on English context based sentiment analysis, several approaches were introduced in this regard. Therefore, these approaches could be developed and extended in order to deal with all the properties of the Arabic language. As exposed in reference [14], the best methods that could deal with context treatment are the lexicon based methods because they take into consideration the influence of the domain and the valence-shifters. This method is represented in [11].

6   Conclusion and Perspectives

Social media offers a lot of valuable information in decision-making, and its content is constantly increasing. As far as we know there's no work done in context based sentiment analysis in Arabic, which offers important opportunities in this field. This paper surveys the works done in CBSA in English and exposed the challenges that limit researches for Arabic content. Taking into account the very limited number of corpuses that are available in Arabic language, the next step in our research is to develop an adapted CBSA system for Arabic content using a lexicon based approach.

References

1. https://www.omnicoreagency.com/twitter-statistics/. Accessed 14 May 2018
2. Birjali, M., Beni-Hssane, A., Erritali, M.: Machine learning and semantic sentiment analysis based algorithms for suicide sentiment prediction in social networks. Procedia Comput. Sci. **113**, 65–72 (2017)
3. Al-Twairesh, N., Al-Khalifa, H., Al-Salman, A., Al-Ohali, Y.: AraSenTi-Tweet: a corpus for Arabic sentiment analysis of Saudi tweets. Procedia Comput. Sci. **117**, 63–72 (2017)
4. Abdul-Mageed, M., Diab, M. T.: AWATIF: a multi-genre corpus for modern standard Arabic subjectivity and sentiment analysis. In: LREC, pp. 3907–3914, May 2012
5. Context Assisted Sentiment Analysis Paper Identification Number: IAR-168
6. Tartir, S., Abdul-Nabi, I.: Semantic sentiment analysis in Arabic social media. J. King Saud Univ.-Comput. Inf. Sci. **29**(2), 229–233 (2017)
7. Sharma, S., Chakraverty, S., Sharma, A., Kaur, J.: A context-based algorithm for sentiment analysis. Int. J. Comput. Vis. Robot. **7**(5), 558–573 (2017)
8. Vanzo, A., Croce, D., Basili, R.: A context-based model for sentiment analysis in twitter. In: Proceedings of COLING 2014, The 25th International Conference on Computational Linguistics: Technical Papers, pp. 2345–2354 (2014)
9. Wilson, T., Wiebe, J., Hoffmann, P.: Recognizing contextual polarity: an exploration of features for phrase-level sentiment analysis. Comput. Linguist. **35**(3), 399–433 (2009)
10. Polanyi, L., Zaenen, A.: Contextual valence shifters. In: Shanahan, J.G., Qu, Y., Wiebe, J. (eds.) Computing attitude and affect in text: Theory and applications, pp. 1–10. Springer, Dordrecht (2006). https://doi.org/10.1007/1-4020-4102-0_1
11. Lu, Y., Castellanos, M., Dayal, U., Zhai, C.: Automatic construction of a context-aware sentiment lexicon: an optimization approach. In: Proceedings of the 20th International Conference on World Wide Web, pp. 347–356. ACM, March 2011

12. Jiang, L., Yu, M., Zhou, M., Liu, X., Zhao, T.: Target-dependent twitter sentiment classification. In: Proceedings of the 49th Annual Meeting of the Association for Computational Linguistics: Human Language Technologies-Volume 1, pp. 151–160. Association for Computational Linguistics, June 2011

13. Katz, G., Ofek, N., Shapira, B.: ConSent: context-based sentiment analysis. Knowl. -Based Syst. **84**, 162–178 (2015)

14. Taboada, M., Brooke, J., Tofiloski, M., Voll, K., Stede, M.: Lexicon-based methods for sentiment analysis. Comput. Linguist. **37**(2), 267–307 (2011)

A Multi-agent System-Based Distributed Intrusion Detection System for a Cloud Computing

Omar Achbarou[✉], My Ahmed El Kiram, Outmane Bourkoukou,
and Salim Elbouanani

Computer Science Department, Laboratory ISI, Cadi Ayyad University,
Marrakech, Morocco
omar.achbarou@gmail.com

Abstract. The Cloud security is one of the major obstacles to the adoption of cloud computing services. It requires some solutions such as Intrusion Detection Systems (IDSs) for protecting each user against all malicious. Existing IDS because of lower detection rate and higher false positive rate couldn't be suitable for a distributed environment such as the cloud. To tackle this problem, we propose a new distributed intrusion detection system based on a multi-agent system to identify and prevent known and unknown attacks in this environment. Carried out experiments demonstrated the performance and efficiency of our proposed system integrated with multi-agent technology.

Keywords: Cloud computing · Intrusion detection system · Distributed system
Multi-agent systems

1 Introduction

Cloud computing is based on the logic of consumption of service, implying that responsibility for the deployment, control, management and maintenance of the infrastructure, platform or software is the responsibility of the cloud service provider (CSP) [1]. Despite the enormous technical and commercial benefits of the cloud environment, security and privacy concerns are the main obstacles to its widespread adoption around the world, and particular attention should be paid to security when choosing a cloud service. In view of these security concerns, the integration of an IDS can be important for detecting attacks or other activity that can be considered suspicious or illegal.

Existing IDS solutions have been developed for conventional networks and systems, but are not easily adaptable to a dynamic environment such as cloud computing. Thus, it is necessary to develop a flexible, secure solution that is adapted to the changing and complex evolution of the cloud environment. Although IDS models have been proposed in the research literature, IDS components alone are not able to parse all of the large reports generated. Thus, these proposed solutions remain limited due to their insulation; in other words, they are not able to collaborate or cooperate with each other. Their detection results are therefore isolated, and cannot be collected and

© Springer Nature Switzerland AG 2018
E. H. Abdelwahed et al. (Eds.): MEDI 2018 Workshops, CCIS 929, pp. 98–107, 2018.
https://doi.org/10.1007/978-3-030-02852-7_9

analyzed systematically. Thus, there is a need for IDS solutions based on the concepts of collaboration, cooperation, autonomy and dynamism; these concepts are needed to detect attacks effectively and to respond to intrusions by reducing response time.

In this work, we propose a solution that meets these requirements in the form of a multi-agent system-based distributed IDS (MAS-DIDS) that can identify and prevent all anomalies in a cloud environment. This system is based on a distributed architecture of IDSs that work in collaboration and communicate with each other, in order to adapt to the complexity of cloud networks. Each IDS is composed of a group of dynamic, responsive, and cooperating agents which work together to make the IDS more autonomous and flexible. The main objective of our research work is to implement a MAS-DIDS that combines the two techniques of signature-based and anomaly-based intrusion detection, in order to block both known and unknown attacks within a complex, dynamic and changing environment. Finally, the efficiency and performance of the proposed model are studied in terms of different metrics: detection rate (DR), false positive rate (FPR), and response time.

The rest of the paper is organized as follows. The next section presents a theoretical background, in which we describe the main concepts of cloud computing, IDS and our types, and multi-agent systems (MAS). We discuss several related works in the area of multi-agent IDSs in Sect. 3. Section 4 forms the core of this paper, and explains and describes our proposed model in detail. Section 5 presents the details of a performance evaluation and the effectiveness of our proposed model based on an experimental study. The final section summarizes the main contributions of this work.

2 Theoretical Background

2.1 Cloud Computing

Cloud Computing is a flexible, reliable and cost-effective environment that offers a set of services in the form of on-demand services, accessible from anywhere, anytime and by anyone. Cloud computing builds on established trends to reduce the cost of delivering services while increasing the speed and agility with which services are deployed regardless of the location of users or equipment [2].

Beyond the proposed definitions, NIST has defined a cloud computing model with five essential characteristics, three service models and three deployment models [2], as shown in Fig. 1.

In general, the architecture of a cloud computing can be divided into three layers: the infrastructure layer (IaaS: Infrastructure as a Service) application layer (SaaS: Software as a Service) and Platform layer (PaaS: Platform as a Service). Each layer represents a different part of the cloud computing stack [3].

- IaaS: The most basic cloud-service model is that of providers offering computing infrastructure, machines and other resources. In the case of IaaS, resources and hardware are virtualized.
- PaaS: To provide a platform allowing customers to run, develop, and manage applications without the complexity of building and maintaining the infrastructure typically associated with developing and launching an application.

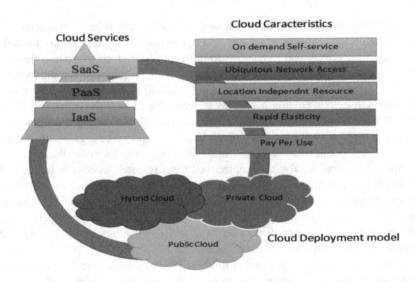

Fig. 1. Cloud computing architecture

- SaaS: To use provider software running on a cloud infrastructure and accessed from various client devices via a client interface.

  There are three common deployment models to consider [4, 5]:

- The private cloud is designed for exclusive use by a single organization;
- In a public cloud, the cloud provider offers their resources as a service to the general public;
- A hybrid cloud is a combination of cloud deployment models (public and private) that attempts to address the limitations of each approach.

2.2   Intrusion Detection Systems

As detailed in previous section, there are different types of attacks in cloud environment. Intrusion Detection System is effective solution to detect and resist these attacks. IDSs are software or hardware systems that realize intrusion detection, log detected information, alert or perform predefined procedures [6]. They can be either hardware or software that includes whole observed computing entities.

An HIDS is an agent that monitors and analyzes any action, internal or external, that bypasses the system security policy, while an NIDS attempts to detect unauthorized access to a network by analyzing the network traffic for signs of malicious activity and anomalous events [7]. A distributed IDS consists of a several IDSs in the cloud network communicating with each other, or with a central point that manages that system. By distributing these cooperative IDSs on this environment to process and to analyze the collected events [8].

An IDS increases the security level of a cloud by using two main intrusion detection techniques [9]; the first is based on signatures (signature-based detection or misuse detection) and the second on behaviors (anomaly detection).

- A signature-based detection technique detects attacks by verifying that observations match known attacks. This technique therefore uses a knowledge base for the different existing attacks [10]. This principle of intrusion detection is reactive and meets several constraints; the IDS only detects attacks that have been defined.
- An anomaly detection technique is based on research on abnormal behavior, and anything that deviates from normal conditions triggers an alarm [8]. This type of detection is effective on unknown attacks but can generate a large number of false positives.

Some IDSs combine both techniques to achieve better results. This is approach used in our proposal, which incorporates both techniques.

2.3 Multi-agent Systems

A Multi-Agent system has a group of intelligent agents interacting with the environment and with themselves [11]. An agent is a computer system located in an environment that acts autonomously and flexibly to achieve the objectives for which it was designed [12]. Agents can be described with different characteristics:

- **Flexibility:** The agent is able to carry out actions in an autonomous and reflexive way in order to achieve the objectives set for it. Flexibility in this case means **reactivity** and **pro-activity**;
- **Autonomous:** The agent is able to act without any intervention, that is to say, the agent decides himself which action to undertake among those that are possible;
- **Social:** The agent must be able to interact with other agents when the situation so requires to complete his tasks or to help these agents perform their tasks.

3 Related Works

In the literature, there are many works that use an IDS with the agent approach to secure systems against attacks. However, most of these studies have developed solutions for well-defined networks and systems, and are not suitable for dynamic and complex environments such as the cloud environment. Agent-based IDS implementation is one of the new paradigms for intrusion detection in this environment, and this approach has been examined by several researchers.

In their article, Venkataramana and Padmavathamma [13] introduced a multi-agent intrusion detection and prevention system using agents for the detection of attacks in the cloud. In [14, 15], the authors proposed a trust model that used mobile agent technology. In this work, mobile agents can dynamically move across the cloud network to perform certain tasks, such as accounting and monitoring the integrity and authenticity of virtual machines. Depren et al. [16] have proposed an intelligent intrusion detection system using both anomaly and misuse detection techniques, to enable a computer networks to handle attacks. Wang and Zhou [17] presented the concept of a cloud alliance, involving communication between agents and the exchange of mutual alerts, primarily to resist DoS and DDoS attacks. In [18], an IDS based on mobile agent technology and cryptographic mechanisms has proposed by Idrissi et al. This proposal consists on elaborating detection mechanisms, based on cryptographic traces generated by mobile agent to secure CC architecture against insider threats. Authors Seresht and Azmi [19] proposed a hybrid IDS that analyzes the network traffic in the system environment, this analysis is performed by using virtual machines. Indeed, each instance is composed by intelligent agents to perform a defined selection algorithm. These agents communicate and cooperate with others to detect anomalies. A thorough study of security solutions based on agent technology reveals IDS solutions that use the different properties of intelligent agents to detect attacks and respond to intrusions. Existing solutions are poorly suited to the growing complexity of cloud networks; they use centralized and non-collaborative IDSs and are not suitable for dynamic environments. Thus, they are not able to cooperate and communicate with each other to detect complex attacks. For example, if an IDS detects a new attack, it does not share this result with other IDSs in its environment.

In the next section, we therefore propose a secure solution that meets all these requirements in the form of a DIDS based on a multi-agent approach, which can identify and prevent all attacks in a cloud environment.

4   Proposed MAS-DIDS System

We propose a Multi-Agent System-Based Distributed Intrusion Detection System, as shown in Fig. 2, with a distribution and cooperation mode, which detects known or unknown attacks in a distributed environment. This system is composed of a group of intelligent agents with mobility and responsiveness, which can communicate and cooperate with each other in order to effectively detect coordinated and distributed attacks in this environment.

First, as the network administrator, the cloud service provider (CSP) receives the packets from different users. The CSP transfers these packets to the Management Agent (MA), which also checks and analyzes the packets before sending them to the available IDSs (IDS-1, IDS-2,..., IDS-n) in the system. The IDSs use Sniffing Agent (SA) as a network capture and analysis tool, allowing the capture results to be saved in a file entitled "ResultsFile.cap" for analysis by the Filter Agent (FA). The FA also communicates with the SA to parse and filter the list of packets using signatures (fingerprint attack). Then, the FA routes the hashed packets to a Misuse Detection Agent (MDA). This node is responsible for checking each signature in the local database, coordinating with the Basic Agent (BA). Two results are possible after checking a signature with BA: either the signature exists or it does not. When a signature exists in the local database, the MDA concludes that this is proof of an ongoing known attack, and an alert is generated to initiate a response. However, when a signature does not exist in a local database that is currently synchronized with the global database, the current packet is transmitted to the anomaly intelligent agent (AIA). The goal of the AIA is to detect anomalies through an analysis of possible abnormal behaviors; on this basis, it

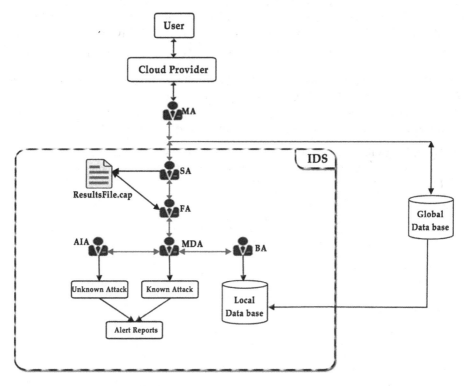

Fig. 2. Proposed MAS-DIDS architecture

can classify a current packet as an unknown attack or a false positive. In order to avoid false positives, the AIA communicates the alert triggered to the MA, which classifies the alert by applying the following formula:

#number of IDSs sending the same alert/#number of IDSs in the system > 0.5   (1)

If the result is greater than 0.5, the packet is classified as a new type of attack to block. On this basis, the MA allows the rules obtained to be automatically added to the global database, and communicates the alert to the CSP via the central console, in order to block the source of the detected attack.

5   Experimental Results

In this paper, several experiments have been made to verify the performance of our approach. This Proposed model has been implemented using some tools and libraries such as the Java language, the JADE framework, the JPCAP platform and the Aglets platform that has been configured on an Eclipse IDE.

JADE (Java Agent DEvelopment Framework) is a software Framework, which simplifies the implementation of multi-agent systems [20]. The Aglets platform can be distributed by moving agents from one machine to another one [21]. In addition, JPCAP is an open source framework for capturing and sending network packets [22]. It provides facilities to capture raw packets live from the wire and save captured packets to an off-line file [23].

Indeed, the Sniffer Agent based on the JPCAP library collects the network events using the "*CaptureTool*" class and saves them into a sniffing file.

As a matter of fact, two interesting measures were used to validate the performance of our Proposed system: false positive rate (FR) and detection rate (DR).

- DR refers to the amount of attacks detected among all detections (2);
- FR refers to the number of instances falsely detected as attacks among all detections (3).

$$DR = \frac{TP}{TP + FN} \tag{2}$$

$$FR = \frac{FP}{TN + FP} \tag{3}$$

TP: true positive
FP: false positive
FN: false negative.

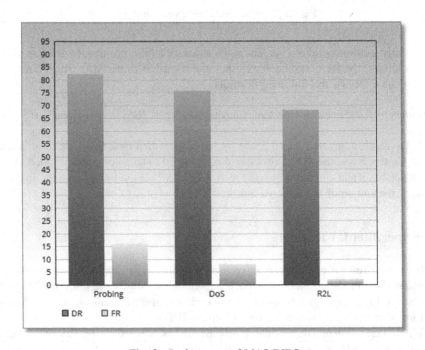

Fig. 3. Performance of MAS-DIDS.

Based on these concepts, Fig. 3 shows the detection performance of our model based on the results given in Table 1, which proves the increase in DR and the decrease in FPR in our simulated cloud environment.

Table 1. Experimental results

Attack type	DR	FR
Probing	82%	16%
DoS	75.5%	8%
R2L	68%	2.3%

The experiment results of our proposed model prove that it has a detection rate higher than 80% and a false alarm rate lower than 8% are reached. So R2L attacks have the best performance. Consequently, we can conclude that the results indicate that our proposed system provides many favorable characteristics, such as high detection rate and low false positive rate and good response time for detection.

The proposed system was compared with similar systems where there was IDS model which was not based on multi-agent systems. The results of this comparison are proved in Fig. 4 based on the data given in Table 2. It demonstrates that our proposition worked not only better in term of efficiency but also in term of response time.

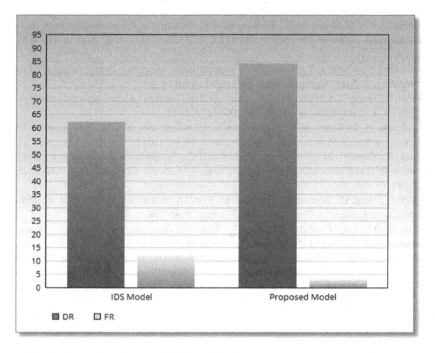

Fig. 4. Comparison between IDS model without agent and our proposed system.

Table 2. Experimental data

Simulation system	DR	FR
IDS model	62%	12%
Proposed model	84%	3.2%

6 Conclusions

Distributed IDS based on multi-agent system has been the important of research direction in the field of intrusion detection, and has the advantages of detecting distrusted attacks and balancing the load in a cloud environment. On the basis of analyzing the existing IDS models based on multi-agent system, this paper presented a new distributed IDS based on intelligent agent technology. Experiments proved that our proposal is efficient and valuable for detecting all intrusions in cloud computing. In future, we plan to experiment our proposed system in real cloud environment.

References

1. Ramachandran, M., Chang, V.: Towards performance evaluation of cloud service providers for cloud data security. Int. J. Inf. Manag. **36**(4), 618–625 (2016)
2. Mell, P., Grance, T.: The NIST Definition of Cloud Computing. Recommendations of the National Institute of Standards· and Technology, vol. 145, p. 7. NIST Special Publication (2011)
3. Achbarou, O., El kiram, M.A., El Bouanani, S.: Securing cloud computing from different attacks using intrusion detection systems. Int. J. Interact. Multimed. Artif. Intell. **4**(3), 61 (2017)
4. Subashini, S., Kavitha, V.: A survey on security issues in service delivery models of cloud computing. J. Netw. Comput. Appl. **34**(1), 1–11 (2011)
5. Singh, S., Jeong, Y.S., Park, J.H.: A survey on cloud computing security: issues, threats, and solutions. J. Netw. Comput. Appl. **75**, 200–222 (2016)
6. Achbarou, O., El Kiram, M.A., Elbouanani, S.: Cloud security: a multi agent approach based intrusion detection system. Ind. J. Sci. Technol. **10**(18) (2017)
7. Patel, A., Taghavi, M., Bakhtiyari, K., Júnior, J.C.: An intrusion detection and prevention system in cloud computing: a systematic review. J. Netw. Comput. Appl. **36**(1), 25–41 (2013)
8. Modi, C., Patel, D., Borisaniya, B., Patel, H., Patel, A., Rajarajan, M.: A survey of intrusion detection techniques in Cloud. J. Netw. Comput. Appl. **36**(1), 42–57 (2013)
9. Liao, H.-J., Lin, C.-H.R., Lin, Y.-C., Tung, K.-Y.: Intrusion detection system: a comprehensive review. J. Netw. Comput. Appl. **36**, 16–24 (2012)
10. Keegan, N., Ji, S.-Y., Chaudhary, A., Concolato, C., Yu, B., Jeong, D.H.: A survey of cloud-based network intrusion detection analysis. Hum.-Cent. Comput. Inf. Sci. **6**(1), 19 (2016)
11. Cavalcante, R.C., Bittencourt, I.I., Da Silva, A.P., Silva, M., Costa, E., Santos, R.: A survey of security in multi-agent systems. Expert Syst. Appl. **39**(5), 4835–4846 (2012)
12. Baig, Z.A.: Multi-agent systems for protecting critical infrastructures: a survey. J. Netw. Comput. Appl. **35**(3), 1151–1161 (2012)

13. Venkataramana, K., Padmavathamma, M.: Multi-agent intrusion detection and prevention system for cloud environment. Int. J. Comput. Appl. **49**(20), 24–29 (2012)
14. Hada, P.S., Singh, R., Manmohan Meghwal, M.: Security agents: a mobile agent-based trust model for cloud computing. Int. J. Comput. Appl. **36**(12), 975–8887 (2011)
15. Saadi, C., Chaoui, H.: Cloud computing security using IDS-AM-Clust, Honeyd, Honeywall and Honeycomb. Proc. Comput. Sci. **85**, 433–442 (2016)
16. Depren, O., Topallar, M., Anarim, E., Ciliz, M.K.: An intelligent intrusion detection system (IDS) for anomaly and misuse detection in computer networks. Expert Syst. Appl. **29**(4), 713–722 (2005)
17. Wang, H., Zhou, H., Wang, C.: Virtual machine-based intrusion detection system framework in cloud computing environment. J. Comput. **7**(10), 2397–2403 (2012)
18. Idrissi, H., Ennahbaoui, M., Souidi, E.M., El Hajji, S.: Mobile agents with cryptographic traces for intrusion detection in the cloud computing. Proc. Comput. Sci. **73**, 179–186 (2015)
19. Seresht, N.A., Azmi, R.: MAIS-IDS: a distributed intrusion detection system using multi-agent AIS approach. Eng. Appl. Artif. Intell. **35**, 286–298 (2014)
20. Bellifemine, F., Caire, G., Poggi, A., Rimassa, G.: JADE: a software framework for developing multi-agent applications. Lessons learned. Inf. Softw. Technol. **50**(1–2), 10–21 (2008)
21. Shinde, P., Parvat, T.J.: DDoS attack analyzer: using JPCAP and WinCap. Proc. Comput. Sci. **79**, 781–784 (2016)
22. Su, C.J.: Mobile multi-agent based, distributed information platform (MADIP) for wide-area e-health monitoring. Comput. Ind. **59**(1), 55–68 (2008)
23. Fortino, G., Garro, A., Russo, W.: Achieving mobile agent systems interoperability through software layering. Inf. Softw. Technol. **50**(4), 322–341 (2008)

IWCFS 2018 Workshop

Introduction to the Second International Workshop on Cybersecurity and Functional Safety in Cyber-Physical Systems (IWCFS 2018)

This section contains invited and contributed papers presented at the Second International Workshop on Cybersecurity and Functional Safety (IWCFS 2018), held on October 24, 2018, in Marrakesh, Morocco.

In response to the call for papers, IWCFS 2018 received ten submissions by 30 authors from eight different countries. After a detailed reviewing process, with about three reviews per paper, a careful selection procedure was carried out using EasyChair for the electronic discussion. Following strict criteria of quality and originality, six papers were selected for presentation. Additionally, Prof. Alexander Egyed from Johannes Kepler University Linz was invited for an exclusive talk on the subject, "A Roadmap for Engineering Safe and Secure Cyber-Physical Systems."

We are greatly indebted to many colleagues who contributed to the scientific program of the workshop, especially the invited speaker and all authors of the submitted papers. We also thank the authors of the accepted papers for their prompt responses to our editorial requests. We would like to express our special thanks to the members of the IWCFS 2018 Program Committee and all external reviewers for their precise, detailed, and timely reviewing of the submissions. We want to thank the Organizing Committee of the 8th International Conference on Model and Data Engineering (MEDI 2018) – where IWCFS 2018 was a collocated workshop – for their support and guidance. Finally, we would like to express our gratitude to our institutes, i.e., Software Competence Center Hagenberg GmbH, Johannes Kepler University Linz, and Tecnalia, for their cooperation.

October 2018

Atif Mashkoor
Johannes Sametinger
Xabier Larrucea

IWCFS 2018 Workshop Chairs

Atif Mashkoor   Software Competence Center Hagenberg GmbH
Johannes Sametinger Johannes Kepler University Linz, Austria
Xabier Larrucea   Tecnalia Research & Innovation, Spain

IWCFS 2018 Program Committee

Yamine Ait Ameur	IRIT, France
Paolo Arcaini	National Institute of Informatics, Japan
Richard Banach	University of Manchester, UK
Ladjel Bellatreche	ENSMA, France
Miklos Biro	Software Competence Center Hagenberg GmbH, Austria
Jorge Cuellar	Siemens, Germany
Angelo Gargantini	University of Bergamo, Italy
Osman Hasan	National University of Science and Technology, Pakistan
Jean-Pierre Jacquot	University of Lorraine, France
Muhammad Taimoor Khan	Alpen-Adria-Universität, Austria
Bernhard Moser	Software Competence Center Hagenberg GmbH, Austria
Muhammad Muaaz	Johannes Kepler University, Austria
Elvinia Riccobene	University of Milan, Italy
Martin Ochoa Ronderos	Universidad del Rosario, Colombia
Jerzy W. Rozenblit	University of Arizona, USA
Neeraj Kumar Singh	IRIT, France
Edgar Weippl	SBA Research, Austria

Invited Talk: A Roadmap for Engineering Safe and Secure Cyber-Physical Systems

Alexander Egyed$^{(\boxtimes)}$ (iD)

Institute for Software Systems Engineering, Johannes Kepler University, Linz, Austria
alexander.egyed@jku.at
http://www.alexander-egyed.com/

Extended Abstract. Safety and Security cannot simply be added to systems. Neither does an architectural choice or design pattern inherently guarantee safety and security. Nor does a safe and secure part of a system make the whole system safe and secure. Ensuring safety and security is an engineering process. This is especially true for Cyber-Physical Systems (CPS) where safety and security concerns transcend hardware and software across different disciplines and across hardware/software subsystems [1].

From an engineering perspective, safety and security reflect functionalities that a given CPS must satisfy. Unfortunately, CPS requirements merely reflect goals that engineers must satisfy without revealing how to satisfy them. The implementation of safety and security concerns is thus a discovery process during engineering – much like how engineering unfolds in general. As engineers define and refine the structure and behavior of CPS – the design – they continuously validate this design structure and behavior against security and safety concerns [6]. For the most part, this implies that:

- Safety and security concerns are discovered incrementally during the engineering process as engineers make design decisions (i.e., changing/augmenting the structure and behavior). This discovery process is reactive and it is not obvious to engineers when they fail to discover a safety or security concern.
- Safety and security concerns are resolved by adapting the design of the CPS. Safety and security concerns thus cause design changes that need to be propagated to all affected engineering disciplines and system/subsystems boundaries [5]. Often, this resolution process is ad hoc and it is not obvious to engineers if they propagated the changes completely and correctly.

In CPS, the discovery and resolution process of safety and security concerns tends to be done separately by every engineering discipline. While not all resolutions affect all these engineering disciplines, many do. Resolving safety and security concerns thus tends to be a multi-disciplinary problem that requires coordinated changes and augmentations to the existing design [2]. This poses a range of challenges to the engineering process.

- Focus on collaboration: for CPS, safety and security concerns may be detectable by individual engineers but their resolution tends to require a coordinated set of changes across different engineering disciplines (co-evolution).

© Springer Nature Switzerland AG 2018
E. H. Abdelwahed et al. (Eds.): MEDI 2018 Workshops, CCIS 929, pp. 113–114, 2018.
https://doi.org/10.1007/978-3-030-02852-7_10

This not only crosses engineering discipline boundaries but also tool boundaries as different disciplines tend to use different kinds of engineering tools [4]. Today, it is not understood how, say, a software change affects the electrical circuitry of a CPS [3].

– Focus on variability: CPS are inherently configurable system – often customizable to specific customer requirements. Here, safety and security concerns transcend variations of CPS. Changes to one variant may affect others [7]. More significantly, we must distinguish how safety and security affect the engineering of a single CPS variant vs. how they restrict a customer from reconfiguring a CPS during runtime – the latter being increasingly vital for self-adaptable, self-healing or self-optimizing systems where customers want increasing control over CPS with unknown effects onto safety and security.

– Focus on modularization: While a safe and secure subsystem of a CPS does not guarantee a safe and secure CPS, a safe and secure CPS cannot be built on unsafe or insecure subsystems. Most companies see modularization as the key to combine software and hardware in smaller, more manageable parts – rather than developing large, monolithic software systems. The safety and security of the system is then the cumulative safety and security of its parts [8]. This relationship is not yet fully understood.

References

1. Biró, M., Mashkoor, A., Sametinger, J., Seker, R.: Software safety and security risk mitigation in cyber-physical systems. IEEE Softw. **35**(1), 24–29 (2018)
2. Clerc, V., Lago, P., van Vliet, H.: The usefulness of architectural knowledge management practices in GSD. In: 2009 Fourth IEEE International Conference on Global Software Engineering, pp. 73–82, July 2009
3. Demuth, A., Kretschmer, R., Egyed, A., Maes, D.: Introducing traceability and consistency checking for change impact analysis across engineering tools in an automation solution company: an experience report. In: 2016 IEEE International Conference on Software Maintenance and Evolution, ICSME 2016, Raleigh, NC, USA, 2–7 October 2016, pp. 529–538 (2016)
4. Demuth, A., Riedl-Ehrenleitner, M., Kretschmer, R., Hehenberger, P., Zeman, K., Egyed, A.: Towards flexible and efficient process and workflow support in enterprise modeling. In: Persson, A., Stirna, J. (eds.) CAiSE 2015. LNBIP, vol. 215, pp. 270–281. Springer, Cham (2015). https://doi.org/10.1007/978-3-319-19243-7_26
5. Demuth, A., Riedl-Ehrenleitner, M., Lopez-Herrejon, R.E., Egyed, A.: Co-evolution of metamodels and models through consistent change propagation. J. Syst. Softw. **111**, 281–297 (2016)
6. Egyed, A., Zeman, K., Hehenberger, P., Demuth, A.: Maintaining consistency across engineering artifacts. IEEE Comput. **51**(2), 28–35 (2018)
7. Linsbauer, L., Lopez-Herrejon, R.E., Egyed, A.: Variability extraction and modeling for product variants. Softw. Syst. Model. **16**(4), 1179–1199 (2017)
8. Trubiani, C., Ghabi, A., Egyed, A.: Exploiting traceability uncertainty between software architectural models and extra-functional results. J. Syst. Softw. **125**, 15–34 (2017)

Towards a Requirements Engineering Approach for Capturing Uncertainty in Cyber-Physical Systems Environment

Manzoor Ahmad[1]([⊠]), Christophe Gnaho[2], Jean-Michel Bruel[3], and Régine Laleau[4]

[1] Univ Pau and Pays Adour/E2S UPPA, LIUPPA, EA3000, 64000 Pau, France
manzoor.ahmad@univ-pau.fr
[2] LACL University Paris Descartes, Paris, France
christophe.gnaho@parisdescartes.fr
[3] University of Toulouse, 31000 Toulouse, France
bruel@irit.fr
[4] LACL University Paris-Est Créteil, 94000 Créteil, France
laleau@u-pec.fr

Abstract. By nature, Cyber-physical systems are very often subjected to uncertainty events that can occur in their environment. This paper presents the first results of our work on how to deal with environment uncertainty in goal-based requirements engineering. This work is motivated by the fact that current goal-based approaches do not natively allow for unanticipated adaptations. To do so, we explore the introduction of RELAX concepts into SysMLKaos. RELAX is a Requirements Engineering language for Dynamically Adaptive Systems that includes explicit constructs to handle the inherent uncertainty in these systems. On the other hand, SysMLKaos is a Goal Based Requirements Engineering approach that takes into account Non-Functional Requirements at the same level of abstraction as Functional Requirements and models the impact of Non-Functional Requirements on Functional Requirements. We use an extract of a Landing Gear System case study to illustrate the proposed approach.

Keywords: Critical systems · Cyber-physical systems
Goal oriented requirements modeling · Unanticipated adaptations

1 Introduction

Cyber-physical systems are very often subjected to uncertainty events that can occur in their environment [17, 18]. For these systems, the software may need to be reconfigured at run-time in order to handle new environmental conditions. We believe that the success of their implementation depends, to a large extent, on Requirements Engineering (RE) approaches that are able to explicitly capture, from the early RE phase, the adaptability in requirements and to take into account the environmental uncertainty. However, there has been little work on Cyber-physical systems in the field of RE languages, but many works have been done on design and architecture issues [8].

© Springer Nature Switzerland AG 2018
E. H. Abdelwahed et al. (Eds.): MEDI 2018 Workshops, CCIS 929, pp. 115–129, 2018.
https://doi.org/10.1007/978-3-030-02852-7_11

One potential way to address this issue consists of using Goal Oriented Requirement Engineering (GORE) [9] approaches because they are well suited to explore alternative requirements and can then be used to represent possible alternative behaviors when the system environment changes. However, GORE approaches would not natively allow for unanticipated adaptations because possible behaviors are only those predefined by the set of enumerations. Thus, the question is how can we extend GORE with unanticipated adaptations and environmental uncertainty modeling capability?

On the other side, RELAX language [11] is a textual RE language that deals explicitly with uncertainty. In contrast to GORE approaches, RELAX supports the explicit expression of environmental uncertainty in requirements. However, it lacks some interesting features that are found in GORE approaches, such as:

- To provide support for reasoning about alternative system configurations where different solutions can be explored and compared
- To handle the way of operationalizing/realizing the (RELAX-ed[1]) requirements.

Consequently, we think that it would be interesting to benefit from both GORE and RELAX approaches by integrating them.

We have proposed in a previous work SysMLKaos [5], a GORE approach to manage Functional Requirements (FRs) and Non-Functional Requirements (NFRs) in critical systems. The objective of this paper is to present the current results of the investigation on how to incorporate RELAX [11] concepts into SysMLKaos [5] and how to ensure that the RELAX-ed requirements will be realized and later on verified (out of the scope of this paper). In a previous work [1], we have defined a general framework in which the present work fits. It completes the previous work with new contributions such as the improvement and extension of the mapping rules and taking into account both FRs and NFRs. The blue color part in Fig. 2 shows those contributions.

This work resides at the early RE phase. It focuses on requirements elicitation and modeling and does not deal with the development of the underlying adaptation mechanisms. We illustrate the proposed approach by applying it on the requirements of the Landing Gear System (LGS) [2] of an aircraft.

The remainder of the paper is organized as follows. Section 2 presents the background of the proposed work, Sect. 3 describes the proposed approach, Sect. 4 illustrates the proposed approach, Sect. 5 surveys the related work and Sect. 6 concludes the paper and provides directions for future work.

2   Background

This section briefly introduces the background of the proposed work. It respectively presents an overview of RELAX and SysMLKaos approach.

---

[1] We use the RELAX name as a verb to indicate the insertion of RELAX operators into a requirement.

2.1   Relax

RELAX is an RE language which provides explicit constructs to handle uncertainty [11]. This uncertainty can be due to changing environmental conditions, such as sensor failures, noisy networks, malicious threats, and unexpected (human) input.

Table 1 shows the vocabulary provided by RELAX to enable the analysts to identify the requirements that may be RELAX-ed, when the environment changes. It includes a set of operators organized into modal, temporal, ordinal and uncertainty factors. Each of the RELAX-ation operators defines constraints on how a requirement may be RELAX-ed at run-time. In addition, it is important to indicate what uncertainty factors warrant a RELAX-ation of these requirements, thereby requiring adaptive behavior. This information is specified using the MON (monitor), ENV (environment), REL (relationship), and DEP (dependency) keywords. The ENV properties capture the "state of the world" – i.e., they are characteristics of the operating context of the system. Often, however, environmental properties cannot be monitored directly because they are not observable. The MON keyword is used to identify properties that are directly observable and contribute information towards determining the state of the environment. RELAX is intended to be used at the software requirements phase once hardware constraints have already been defined. In particular, physical sensors (denoted by MON) are assumed to be known. The REL keyword is used to specify in what way the observables (given by MON) can be used to derive information about the environment (given by ENV). The distinction between ENV and MON comes from the field of control theory wherein parameters to be estimated cannot necessarily be directly observed [11]. For example, an aircraft equipped only with direction finding equipment cannot directly estimate its position. Rather, it can observe its distance from a set of known waypoints and must compute its position from these measurements. In our parlance, the aircraft position is a property of the environment, whereas the distances from waypoints are monitorable. REL would be used to define how to compute the position from the distance measurements. Finally, requirements dependencies are delimited by DEP, as it is important to assess the impact on dependent requirements after RELAX-ing a given requirement.

In RELAX, the conventional modal verb *SHALL* is retained for expressing a requirement while RELAX operators provide more flexibility in how and when that functionality may be delivered. Once the requirements engineer determines that indeed a certain level of flexibility can be tolerated, then the downstream developers, including the designers and programmers, have the flexibility to incorporate the most suitable adaptive mechanisms to support the desired functionality. These decisions may be made at design time and/or run-time [4, 16]. RELAX expressions are defined by a grammar and the semantics of RELAX expressions is defined in terms of Fuzzy Branching Temporal Logic (FBTL) [15]. FBTL can describe a branching temporal model with uncertain temporal and logical information. It is the representation of uncertainty in FBTL that makes it suitable as a formalism for RELAX. RELAX also outlines a process to transform traditional requirements in the form of SHALL statements into invariant (those that cannot be changed) and RELAX-ed requirements (those that are adaptable).

Table 1. RELAX vocabulary

RELAX operators	Description
Modal operators	
SHALL	A requirement must hold
MAY...OR	A requirement specifies one or more alternatives
Temporal operators	
EVENTUALLY	A requirement must hold eventually
UNTIL	A requirement must hold until a future position
BEFORE, AFTER	A requirement must hold before or after a particular event
IN	A requirement must hold during a particular time interval
AS EARLY, LATE AS POSSIBLE	A requirement specifies something that should hold as soon as possible or should be delayed as long as possible
AS CLOSE AS POSSIBLE TO [frequency]	A requirement specifies something that happens repeatedly but the frequency may be relaxed
Ordinal operators	
AS CLOSE AS POSSIBLE TO [quantity]	A requirement specifies a countable quantity but the exact count may be relaxed
AS MANY, FEW AS POSSIBLE	A requirement specifies a countable quantity but the exact count may be relaxed
Uncertainty factors	
ENV	Defines a set of properties that define the system's environment
MON	Defines a set of properties that can be monitored by the system
REL	Defines the relationship between the ENV and MON properties
DEP	Identifies the dependency between the (relaxed and invariant) requirements

2.2   SysMLKaos

SysMLKaos [5] approach is based on KAOS [9] and the NFR Framework [3]. It is founded on two main ideas: To integrate NFRs from the early requirements engineering phase i.e., at the same level of abstraction as FRs and to emphasize the impact of NFRs on FRs. Figure 1 shows an extract of the SysMLKaos meta-model. Functional and non-functional requirements are modelled as abstract goals, which are recursively refined into sub-goals, thanks to the AND/OR refinement mechanism.

A Functional Goal (FG) that cannot be further refined into sub-goals is called Elementary Functional Goal (EFG). A Non-Functional Goal (NFG) that cannot be further refined is called an Elementary Non-Functional Goal (ENFG). When all the abstract NFGs are refined into a set of ENFGs, we need to find and express solutions that satisfied them. To do so, we use the concept of contribution. Thus, a contribution (meta-class Contribution) captures a possible solution to satisfy an ENFG. It expresses the way by which an ENFG could be achieved.

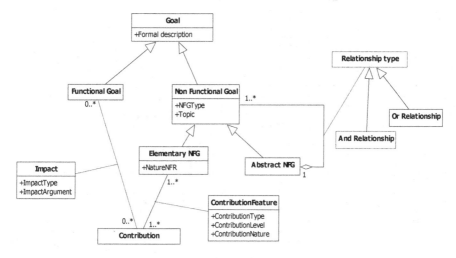

Fig. 1. SysMLKaos meta-model [5]

The characteristics of contribution are captured in Fig. 1 by the association class ContributionFeature which provides three properties: ContributionNature, ContributionType, and ContributionLevel. The first one specifies whether the contribution is positive or negative, the second one specifies whether the contribution is direct or indirect and the third allows us to associate to the type of contribution (positive or negative), a level that can range from very high to low. A positive (resp. negative) contribution helps positively (resp. negatively) to the satisfaction of an ENFG. A direct contribution describes an explicit contribution to the ENFG. An indirect contribution describes a kind of contribution that is a direct contribution to a given goal but induces an unexpected contribution to another goal. Finally, the concept of Impact is used to express the impact of NFGs on FGs, it captures the fact that a contribution has an effect on FGs. Indeed, the specificity of the SysMLKaos approach is the analysis and modelling of the impact of NFGs on FGs, which can be expressed in different manners. We have shown that NFGs may have an impact on the choices and decisions that are taken when refining FGs and when transforming them into target systems. In addition, analysing NFGs can lead to the identification of new FGs, which must be integrated with the existing FG hierarchy. The analysis and modelling of the impact of NFGs on FGs lead to a new goal model that we call integrated goal model as shown in Sect. 4.

3   The Proposed Approach

As shown in Fig. 2, the proposed approach consists of three main steps that are respectively supported by three processes. The parts in blue color show the new contributions.

- Identifying and expressing RELAX-ed requirements
- Mapping RELAX-ed requirements to SysMLKaos concepts
- Applying the SysMLKaos process.

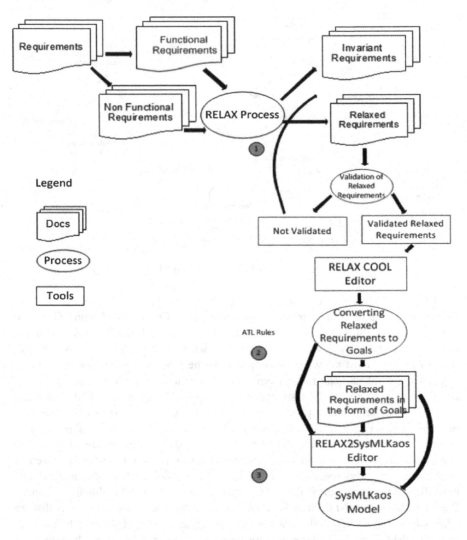

Fig. 2. The proposed approach (Color figure online)

3.1 Identifying and Expressing RELAX-ed Requirements

During this step, we take requirements (FRs or NFRs) as input in the form of SHALL statements and apply RELAX process [11] to get those that are associated with the adaptability features called RELAX-ed requirements and those that are fixed called invariant requirements. Then we validate the RELAX-ed requirements with the help of an expert. If the RELAX-ed expression is acceptable then we proceed with the next step, if it is not acceptable, we propose two options: cancel the RELAX-ation (i.e., declare the requirements as invariant) or complement the RELAX-ed property with an additional invariant (e.g., a max or min boundary that constraint the RELAX-ed expression).

The resulting RELAX-ed requirements are then formalized using an editor that we developed called RELAX COOL editor [1] that takes into account the uncertainty factors associated with each RELAX-ed requirement. We have used Xtext[2] for the development of the RELAX COOL editor. We then use a process based on the mapping rules explained in the next section for the conversion of RELAX requirements (RELAX-ed and invariant) into SysMLKaos goal concepts.

3.2   Mapping RELAX-ed Requirements to SysMLKaos Concepts

To support the mapping process, we have developed a tool called RELAX2-SysMLKaos editor [1], which is based on Atlas Transformation Language (ATL) transformations. The implemented mapping rules are briefly explained in this section (see Table 2).

In SysMLKaos, requirements are in the form of *Abstract Goals* while RELAX requirements are in the form of *RELAX-ed (or invariant) requirements*. In SysMLKaos the concept of *EFG* refers to a goal that cannot be further refined into sub-goals. For the purpose of defining the mapping rules, we propose to express an *EFG* thanks to the following format: *Verb + Object* where *Object* is related to properties that define the system's environment and *Verb* represents an action over this environment. For example: EFG1: Push (the verb) command (the object) to up, EFG2: Close (the verb) the doors (the object). In RELAX, the concept of *ENV* (environment) refers to properties that capture the operating context of the system. Therefore, the *ENV* concept of RELAX can be mapped to the *Object* concept of SysMLKaos.

In SysMLKaos, an *EFG* is placed under the responsibility of an *agent*, a human being or automated component that are responsible for achieving the goal. An agent can be a part of the system or a part of the system environment. For example: EFG1 is placed under the responsibility of the Pilot, EFG2 is placed under the responsibility of electro-valves. In RELAX, the concept of *MON* (monitor) is used to identify properties that are directly observable and contribute information towards determining the state of the environment. For example: sensors, calculator, pilot etc. Therefore, we argue that the *MON* concept of RELAX can be mapped to the *Agent* concept of SysMLKaos.

In RELAX, the concept of *REL* (relationship) is used to specify in what way the observables (given by *MON*) can be used to derive information about the environment (given by *ENV*). For example: Pilot push command up, Calculator treat the order. Therefore, this concept can be mapped to the *Agent + EFG (verb + object)* concept of SysMLKaos.

For Dependency/Impact, SysMLKaos describes it as an impact of an NFG on an FG; it captures the fact that a Contribution has an impact on an FG, which in turn shows the Impact of an NFG on an FG. RELAX has positive and negative dependency which shows the dependency of a RELAX-ed requirement on another requirement.

---

[2] https://www.eclipse.org/Xtext/.

Table 2. Mapping between RELAX and SysMLKaos

Concept	RELAX	SysMLKaos
Requirements description	RELAX requirements	Abstract goal
Environment	ENV	Object
Monitoring	MON	Agent
Relationship	REL	Agent + Elementary functional goal
Dependency	Positive/negative	Impact/Conflict (from KAOS)

As we said, ATL is used to support the mapping process; it provides a model transformation language together with a toolkit. An ATL transformation program is composed of rules that define how source model elements are matched and navigated to create and initialize the elements of the target models. The generation of target model elements is achieved through the specification of transformation rules. The RELAX abstract syntax is defined in the RELAX meta-model (source) and the SysMLKaos abstract syntax is defined in the SysMLKaos meta-model (target). An example of an ATL transformation rule is shown in Fig. 3. It describes the mapping of RELAX-ed requirement to SysMLKaos Abstract Goal.

```
rule RelaxedRequirement2AbstractGoal {
    from
            relaxedRequirement : RelaxMetaModel!RelaxedRequirementDeclaration
    to
            abstractGoal : SysMLKAOSMetaModel!AbstractGoal (name <- relaxedRequirement.name)
}
```

Fig. 3. An example of the ATL transformation rule

3.3 Applying the SysMLKaos Process

Thanks to the SysMLKaos process, the resulting goals (from the second step) are recursively refined into sub-goals and the impact of NFGs on FGs are analyzed and modeled and finally integrated. This step is illustrated in the next section. For more details on SysMLKaos process, see [5].

4 Illustration of the Approach

This section illustrates with an excerpt of the LGS case study [2], the proposed approach.

4.1   Landing Gear System Overview

The LGS of an aircraft is in charge of maneuvering landing gears and associated doors. It is composed of 3 landing sets: front, left and right. Each landing set contains a door, a landing gear and associated hydraulic cylinders. The action to be done at each time depends on the state of all the physical devices and on their temporal behavior. It is composed of three main parts: a mechanical part which contains all the mechanical devices and the three landing sets, a digital part including the control software, and a pilot interface.

The only human input to the system is the pilot handle: when pulled up it orders the gears to retract, and when pulled down it orders the gears to extend. The signal from the pilot handle is fed both to the replicated computer system and to the analogical switch. The purpose of the analogical switch is to protect the system against abnormal behavior of the digital part. In order to prevent inadvertent order to the electro-valves, the general electro-valve can be stimulated only if this switch is closed. A set of discrete sensors informs the digital part about the state of the equipment. In order to prevent sensor failures, each of them is triplicated (i.e. each sensor is divided into three independent micro-sensors). The architecture and the requirements of the LGS are presented in [2].

4.2   An Illustrative Example

Step 1: Identifying and expressing RELAX-ed requirements

Let us consider one of the main FRs of the LGS: "Retract Landing Gear". According to the LGS document [2], the retraction of the landing gear is subject to time-relative requirements, which can risk lives if violated. Therefore, we also consider the NFR "timed response". These two requirements are expressed as follows (the italic part of the sentence corresponds to the NFR).

FR "Retract Landing Gear" and NFR "Timed Response of the Landing Gear": When the command line is working (normal mode), if the landing gear command handle has been pushed UP and stays UP then the gears shall be locked UP *before a maximum delay of 5 s after the handle position has been pushed up and the doors shall be seen closed before a maximum delay of 10 s after the gears locked up.*

Once the requirements have been formulated, the requirements engineer must examine them to determine the sources of environmental uncertainty that may compromise their satisfaction. For example, one of the electro-valves may fail, but since retracting the landing gear is a critical requirement, the LGS should be able to achieve this requirement in some other way. The identified environmental uncertainty is then documented using the RELAX uncertainty factors. They are summarized in Table 3.

Based on the documented environmental uncertainty factors, the requirements engineer must identify requirements (or the part of the requirements) that may be RELAX-ed at run-time when the environment changes. For example, it may be acceptable to temporarily RELAX the closing of doors that can be considered as a non-critical requirement in an emergency situation in order to ensure that the retraction of the gears, which is considered as critical for the flight safety, can still be met. For that,

Table 3. Retract landing gear

Uncertainty factors	Description
ENV	Command, order, doors, gears
MON	Pilot, Calculator, Electro-valves, Cylinder
REL	Pilot pushes the command to up
	Calculator treat the order
	Electro-valves handle the command of the gears retraction
	Cylinder do the gears retraction
	Cylinder do the doors closing
	Cylinder do the doors opening

the RELAX-ed requirements are augmented with RELAX vocabulary in order to declaratively specify where flexibility in the behavior is tolerated. The RELAX-ed version of the above requirement is given below:

Relax-ed version of FR "Retract Landing Gear" and NFR "Timed Response of the Landing Gear": When the command line is working (normal mode), if the landing gear command handle has been pushed UP and stays UP then the gears shall be locked UP *before a maximum delay of 5 s after the handle position has been pushed up* and the doors shall be seen closed *AS SOON AS POSSIBLE after the gears locked up.*

Step 2 and Step 3: Mapping RELAX requirements to SysMLKaos concepts and applying the SysMLKaos process

The next step consists of applying the RELAXToSysMLKaos mapping rules in order to convert the RELAX requirements into SysMLKaos goal concepts. Thus, the above requirement is first transformed to the following two abstract goals:

- *Functional Goal* [Retract Landing Gear]: *InformalDef*: When the command line is working (normal mode), if the landing gear command handle has been pushed UP and stays UP then the gears will be locked UP and the doors will be seen closed
- *Non-Functional Goal* [TimedResponse (Landing Gear)] *InformalDef*: The gears shall be locked up *BEFORE* a maximum delay of 5 s after the handle position has been pushed up and the doors shall be closed AS SOON AS POSSIBLE after the gears locked up.

Thanks to the SysMLKaos process, the two abstracts goals are then refined in parallel, in two distinct goal models. It is important to note that the refinement of these goals is partly guided by the documented environmental uncertainty information and by the RELAX-ed expressions. For example, thanks to the correspondence rules, the MON and REL are particularly useful to identify SysMLKaos elementary FGs along with their related agents. The RELAX-ed expressions are useful to identify temporal constraints on some sub-goals. Figure 4 presents an overview of the two goal models. The FG "Retract landing gear" is refined using the "AND refinement" into five sub-goals: Push command to Up, Treat the order, Open the doors, Lock up the gears and Close the doors. The NFG "TimedResponse [Landing Gear]" is "AND refined" into the following two sub-goals: *TimedResponse [Gears]:* "Globally the gears must occur (locked up) *before a maximum delay of 5 s* after the handle position has been pushed up" and *TimedResponse [Doors]:* "Globally, the doors must occur (close) *as soon as possible* after the gears locked up".

As shown in Fig. 4, the contribution "Ensure timed order control" represents an alternative way to contribute positively to the satisfaction of the two sub-goals. In addition, this contribution has an impact on the FGs "Lock up the gears" and "Close the doors". This impact should be reflected in the FG model that thereby needs some changes that result in a new FG.

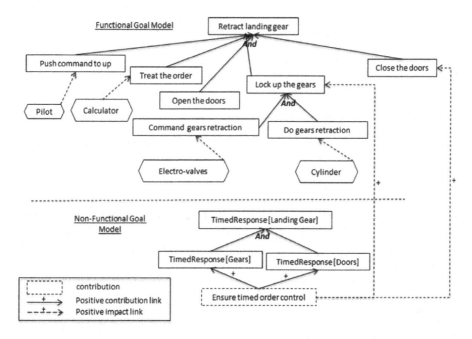

Fig. 4. An excerpt of the SysMLKaos model of the FG and NFG

Figure 5 shows the new FG goal model where the two goals "Lock up the gears" and "Close the doors" are associated to timed constraints, meaning that their achievement is constrained by some delay. For instance, "the landing gears must be locked down within a maximum delay of 5 s". Timed constrained goals are graphically represented by rectangles with pictograms. Moreover, the fulfillment of the three goals (Push command to up, lock up the gears and close the doors) is ordered, which is graphically represented by the annotated links. Finally, the And-refinement is replaced by a milestone refinement, which consists of identifying the sub-goals as successive steps in time to satisfy the parent goal.

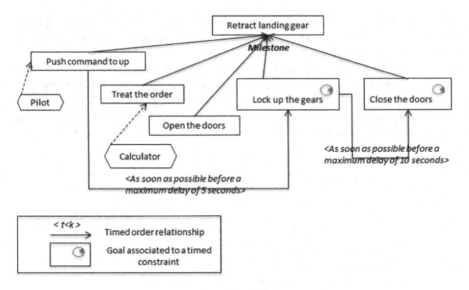

Fig. 5. An excerpt of the integrated goal model

5   Related Work

Numerous works on Cyber-physical systems have been focused on design and architectural concerns [8, 12–14]. They tried to cover many challenges of modeling aspects that arise from the intrinsic heterogeneity, concurrency and sensitivity to timing of such systems. Unfortunately, there have been few proposals that explicitly capture, from the early requirements phase, unanticipated adaptations inherent in such systems. In the following, we summarize the most popular and discuss their differences with respect to our approach.

Thanks to the concept of alternative requirements, Goal-based modeling approaches such as i* [7] and KAOS [9], have been applied to the modeling of requirements of Cyber-physical Systems. While these approaches are useful for eliciting and specifying requirements from the early requirements phase, the modeler must explicitly identify and express all possible alternative behaviors. However, it is impossible to know at the RE phase all of the possible combinations of environmental conditions that will be encountered. In addition, these approaches do not explicitly provide process models to help this modeling activity. In this paper, we go beyond by allowing unanticipated adaptations and by providing a specific process model.

AutoRELAX [10] is an approach that addresses the environmental uncertainty by identifying which goals to RELAX, which RELAX operators to apply and the shape of the fuzzy logic function that defines the goal satisfaction criteria. AutoRELAX needs a prototype of the system to be, in order to be able to generate goal models of only the FRs that the system must satisfy; it does not address NFRs. In [6], the authors propose a process model based on i* [7] to describe uncertainty in the requirements goal models. This approach considers a system as a composition of numerous target systems, each of which supports behavior for a different set of environmental conditions. At run-time, the system transitions from one target system to another, depending on the environmental conditions. Like traditional GORE approaches, this approach needs to know at requirements phase all the possible target systems. In [4], the authors use RELAX specification language to specify more flexible requirements within a goal model to handle uncertainty. This work is in some aspect close to our work as they try to integrate RELAX with goal model. The main difference is that we consider both FRs and NFRs and we explicitly analyze and describe the impact of NFRs on FRs.

6   Conclusion and Future Work

In this paper, we have investigated on how to incorporate RELAX [11] concepts into SysMLKaos [5] in order to deal with environmental uncertainty at goal level, in both FRs and NFRs. For that, we have introduced an approach that takes RELAX-ed requirements as input and then transform it into SysMLKaos goal concepts. We have illustrated the approach by applying it to the LGS of an aircraft [2].

The need to integrate RELAX with SysMLKaos arose from the fact that GORE approaches suppose that all possible alternative behaviors must explicitly be enumerated. This approach would not allow for unanticipated adaptations because possible behaviors are only those predefined by the set of enumerations. However, changing environment factors makes it difficult to anticipate all the explicit states in which the system will be during its lifetime. GORE approaches are not thus sufficient to handle the uncertainty; in particular, we must some time add flexibility to the goal in order to take into account the uncertainty. By using RELAX, the environmental uncertainty associated with RELAX-ed/adaptable requirements are captured and thus represented in the SysMLKaos models. The SysMLKaos models present different alternative solutions (thanks to the contribution goal concept) to satisfy NFGs and the impact (thanks to the impact concept) of these solutions on FGs. The use of RELAX helped us in eliciting the uncertainty factors associated with requirements and eventually the contribution goals of SysMLKaos which were not possible by using the traditional process of requirements engineering.

This is an ongoing work as till now, we treat only requirements modeling. We plan to formally verify some of these properties in the early phase of software development, using for example Event-B, as we did for SysMLKaos [19]; in this way, we can bridge the gap between the requirements phase and the initial formal specification phase. We are also interested in integrating MAPE [12] feedback loop in our proposed approach that operationalizes the system's adaptability mechanisms. We also plan to look for the requirements dependencies; once we decide to RELAX some requirements; what impact it induces on invariant requirements as for the time being, we only treat the dependency/impact between RELAX-ed requirements.

References

1. Ahmad, M., Belloir, N., Bruel, J.-M.: Modeling and verification of functional and non-functional requirements of ambient self-adaptive systems. J. Syst. Softw. **107**, 50–70 (2015). https://doi.org/10.1016/j.jss.2015.05.028
2. Boniol, F., Wiels, V.: The landing gear system case study. In: Boniol, F., Wiels, V., Ait Ameur, Y., Schewe, K.D. (eds.) ABZ 2014. CCIS, vol. 433, pp. 1–18. Springer, Cham (2014). https://doi.org/10.1007/978-3-319-07512-9_1
3. Chung, L., Nixon, B.A., Yu, E., Mylopoulos, J.: Non-Functional Requirements in Software Engineering. Kluwer Academic Publishers, Dordrecht (2000)
4. Cheng, B.H.C., Sawyer, P., Bencomo, N., Whittle, J.: A goal-based modeling approach to develop requirements of an adaptive system with environmental uncertainty. In: Schürr, A., Selic, B. (eds.) MODELS 2009. LNCS, vol. 5795, pp. 468–483. Springer, Heidelberg (2009). https://doi.org/10.1007/978-3-642-04425-0_36
5. Gnaho, C., Semmak, F., Laleau, R.: Modeling the impact of non-functional requirements on functional requirements. In: Parsons, J., Chiu, D. (eds.) ER 2013. LNCS, vol. 8697, pp. 59–67. Springer, Cham (2014). https://doi.org/10.1007/978-3-319-14139-8_8
6. Goldsby, H.-J., Sawyer, P., Bencomo, N., Cheng, B.-H.-C., Hughes, D.: Goal-based modeling of dynamically adaptive system requirements. In: Proceedings of the 15th IEEE International Conference on Engineering of Computer-Based Systems, Belfast, Northern Ireland, March 2008
7. i* Homepage. http://www.cs.toronto.edu/km/istar/
8. Kramer, J., Magee, J.: Self-managed systems: an architectural challenge. In: Briand, L.C., Wolf, A.L. (eds.) FOSE, pp. 259–268 (2007)
9. Lamsweerde, A.-V.: Requirements Engineering: From System Goals to UML Models to Software Specifications, 1st edn. Wiley, Hoboken (2009). ISBN 978EUDTE00270
10. Ramirez, A.J., Fredericks, E.M., Jensen, A.C., Cheng, B.H.C.: Automatically RELAXing a goal model to cope with uncertainty. In: Fraser, G., Teixeira de Souza, J. (eds.) SSBSE 2012. LNCS, vol. 7515, pp. 198–212. Springer, Heidelberg (2012). https://doi.org/10.1007/978-3-642-33119-0_15
11. Whittle, J., Sawyer, P., Bencomo, N., Cheng, B.-H.-C., Bruel, J.-M.: RELAX: incorporating uncertainty into the specification of self-adaptive systems. In: Proceedings of the 2009 17th IEEE International Requirements Engineering Conference, RE, RE 2009, Washington, DC, USA, pp. 79–88. IEEE Computer Society (2009)
12. Derler, P., Lee, E.A., Sangiovanni, A.: Modeling cyber-physical systems. Proc. IEEE **100** (1), 13–28 (2012)
13. Lee, E.A., et al.: Classes and inheritance in actor oriented design. ACM Trans. Embed. Comput. Syst. **8**(4), 29:1–29:26 (2009)
14. Mosterman, P.J., Vangheluwe, H.: Computer automated multi-paradigm modeling: an introduction. Simul. Trans. Soc. Model. Simul./Int. J. High Perform. Comput. Appl. **80**(9), 433–450 (2004)
15. Seong-ick, M., Lee, K.H., Lee, D.: Fuzzy branching temporal logic. IEEE Trans. Syst. Man Cybern. Part B Cybern. **34**, 1045–1055 (2004)
16. Blair, G.-S., Bencomo, N., France, R.-B.: Models@run.time. Computer **42**(10), 22–27 (2009). Run.Time@
17. Chipman, W., Grimm, C., Radojicic, C.: Coverage of uncertainties in cyber-physical systems. In: GMM/ITG/GI-Symposium Reliability by Design, ZuE 2015; 8, Siegen, Germany, pp. 1–8 (2015)

18. Zhang, M., Selic, B., Ali, S., Yue, T., Okariz, O., Norgren, R.: Understanding uncertainty in cyber-physical systems: a conceptual model. In: Wąsowski, A., Lönn, H. (eds.) ECMFA 2016. LNCS, vol. 9764, pp. 247–264. Springer, Cham (2016). https://doi.org/10.1007/978-3-319-42061-5_16

19. Tueno Fotso, S.J., Mammar, A., Laleau, R., Frappier, M.: Event-B expression and verification of translation rules between SysML/KAOS domain models and B system specifications. In: Butler, M., Raschke, A., Hoang, T.S., Reichl, K. (eds.) ABZ 2018. LNCS, vol. 10817, pp. 55–70. Springer, Cham (2018). https://doi.org/10.1007/978-3-319-91271-4_5

Assessment of Emerging Standards for Safety and Security Co-Design on a Railway Case Study

Christophe Ponsard[1]([✉]), Jeremy Grandclaudon[1], Philippe Massonet[1,2], and Mounir Touzani[2]

[1] CETIC Research Centre, Gosselies, Belgium
{christophe.ponsard,jeremy.grandclaudon,philippe.massonet}@cetic.be
[2] PhD Researcher, Toulouse, France
mtouzani64@gmail.com

Abstract. Design for safety-critical software intended for domains like transportation or medical systems is known to be difficult but is required to give a sufficient level of assurance that the system will not harm or kill people. To add to the difficulty, systems have now become highly connected and are turning into cyber-physical systems. This results in the need to address intentional cyber security threats on top of risks related to unintentional software defects. Different approaches are being defined to co-engineer both software security and safety in a consistent way. This paper aims at providing a deeper understanding of those approaches and the evolution of related standards by analysing them using a sound goal-oriented framework that can model both kind of properties and also reason on them in a risk-oriented way. In the process interesting co-design patterns are also identified and discussed. The approach is driven by a real world open specification from the railways.

Keywords: Cyber security · Safety · Goals · Threats · Co-design Standards

1 Introduction

The engineering of critical system for safety and the protection of computer systems against cyber security threats have for long been two disconnected disciplines taking place in different contexts. Both disciplines are actually risk management disciplines including quite similar identification, evaluation and reduction phases [14]. However, they are considering different kinds impacts also with different mode of occurrence of events leading to the materialisation of risks (i.e. random risks impacting human health/live or environment state vs deliberate attack resulting in loss of integrity, confidentiality or availability in the information system). More globally safety is part of dependability which shares a number of attributes with security such as integrity and availability [1].

© Springer Nature Switzerland AG 2018
E. H. Abdelwahed et al. (Eds.): MEDI 2018 Workshops, CCIS 929, pp. 130–145, 2018.
https://doi.org/10.1007/978-3-030-02852-7_12

As systems are becoming increasingly software-based and connected, there is a current evolution trend towards cyber-physical systems (CPS) tightly combining physical monitoring/control actions with an elaborated digital model inside a computation and a communication core [24]. Safety critical systems especially concerned with this evolution into CPS. CPS require to rethink about the way to design for safety and security [2]. Both dimensions have to be considered together as they can impact each other: a security vulnerability in a connected car could be used to disable braking while on a highway resulting in potential loss of control and crash [7]. Reinforcing security also impacts system usage resources that could threaten the ability to delivery safety functions. Conversely, the increased complexity required by a safety architecture can also increase the attack surface from the security point of view. The fact that many CPS and critical systems are designed to have a long service life also increases the problem of exposure, this is especially the case in aeronautics and railways [30].

Although the field is not new [22], trying to combine safety and security has gained a lot of attention over the past few years given the current evolution towards CPS. A number of methods have been proposed, some more generic [20, 23,29] while others target specific domains like automotive [19,26,27], nuclear industry [6,21], railways [5,9,10]. Most approaches use some form of analysis based on improved and/or combined version tree-based analysis that have been defined in each field (e.g. fault tree, attack tree, HAZOP, FMEA, etc).

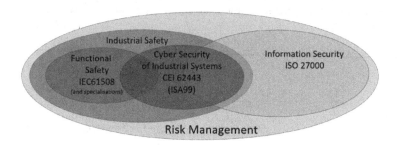

Fig. 1. Overview of risk management frameworks down to safety and security levels.

Standardisation has also started to tackle this specific area based on existing standards in both areas. Figure 1 shows the emergence of specific area for the cyber security of industrial system (with standards like CEI62443 [13]). Those are in strong intersections with the IT security domain (typically based ISO27K standards) and functional safety (typically based on IEC61508 [12] and domain-specific derivatives). The whole field is also following a standard risk assessment approach as described by the ISO31000 series [14].

The purpose of this paper and our related contribution is twofold. First, we want to *explore the currently emerging approaches, especially from a standardisation point of view* because safety and security critical systems are quite systematically subject to compliance with standards of those fields and the evolution towards combined standards has to be integrated and also provides interesting opportunities of improving processes while keeping the overhead under control.

Second, after having identified emerging approaches, *we perform a case-based assessment based on a subset of the real-world case study from the railway domain*: the automated train operation (ATO) over the European Train Control System (ETCS) which is openly available [28]. To drive this assessment, we rely on a goal-based requirements engineering framework [16]. Our aim is not to propose yet another notation to solve the problem but just use it as reference because of its proven ability to capture and reason about requirements especially for safety through the concept of obstacle [17] and for security through the concept of anti-goal [18]. We have also already proposed a combined approach [23].

This paper is structured as follows. Section 2 will give some background about specific approaches in safety and security only standards. It will also highlight our goal-oriented framework. Section 3 will describe possible emerging approaches and how standards are evolving to deal with them. Section 4 will present our case study and Sect. 5 will discuss some lessons learned. Finally Sect. 6 will draw some conclusions and identify further areas of research.

2   Background

2.1   Safety Standards

Safety standards have been defined in many different industrial sectors as depicted in Fig. 2.

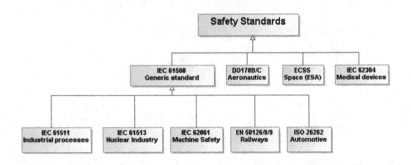

Fig. 2. Overview of safety standards across domains

A number of sectors rely on the same generic standard: the IEC 61508 [12] which is intended to be a basic functional safety standard applicable to all kinds of industry. It defines functional safety as: "part of the overall safety relating to the EUC (Equipment Under Control) and the EUC control system which depends on the correct functioning of the E/E/PE safety-related systems, other technology safety-related systems and external risk reduction facilities". It covers the complete safety life cycle and may need interpretation to develop sector specific standards. For railways, EN50126/8/9 provide such domain specific interpretations respectively for the system, software and hardware levels [4].

Standards are actually quite similar in principles and structure. This is of course quite understandable for those deriving from IEC61508. However, even other non IEC 61508 related standards have strong commonalities summarised here and fully discussed in [3].

- all domains share the same fundamental basis where the categories represent the risks associated to the end effects of the potential failures of the considered system. Risks are classically measured by a combination of their severity and occurrence probability or likelihood with different codification (SIL, ASIL, DAL, ...). These notions can be considered as equivalent provided an acceptability frontier is well defined.
- Railway systems take the same approach than aeronautics, nuclear and space: it starts from a system (top level) function, which inherits its category from the category of the risk induced by its potential failures. Then categories are derived following the functional decomposition and finally allocated to the elements implementing the functions. The situation is different for automotive where safety goals are defined for the identified risks, then further refined into safety requirements, and finally into architectural components. Categories are allocated first to the safety goals and derived to safety requirements and finally components. This provides a different perspective and an interesting way of reasoning. However, in practice the result is similar given it also relies on the propagation and end effects of failures.
- About guidance: for railways and space, there is no provided guidance: One must follow the generic allocation rule. In contrast, aeronautics and automotive standards provide detailed guidance and specific rules.

2.2 Cyber Security Standards

The landscape of security standards is very large and less structured than for safety standards. An inventory based on 25 existing overview studies identified more than 180 standards. Some of them have however emerged and are being largely adopted. Table 1 shows a widely acknowledged top ten [11].

The above standards will be described in more details with other less popular yet relevant standards for the transportation domain. The following dimensions can be used to understand the respective position of all those standards:

- Identifying attributes like: generic vs domain specific, national vs international, draft/released/revision, implicit or explicit link with another standard
- Coverage level of the workflow for the management of security including identification of threats, protecting against them, detecting an attack, responding to it and recovering from potential damage. Those 5 steps are actually the main functions defined by the NIST SP-800 in its Cyber Security Framework

Table 1. Top 10 cyber security frameworks.

Title	Source	Origin	Language	Type	Vital sector
ISO/IEC 27002	ISO/IEC	International	English	Standard	General
ISO/IEC 27001	ISO/IEC	International	English	Standard	General
NERC CIP 002 - 009	NERC	USA	English	Standard	Energy
NIST SP-800 series	NIST	USA	English	Guideline	General
ISA/IEC 62443	ISA	USA	English	Framework	Industry
AGA No. 12	AGA	USA	English	Best practices	Telecommunications
COBIT 5	ISACA	International	Multiple	Method	General
ISO/IEC 15408	ISO/IEC	International	English	Standard	General
API 1164	API	USA	English	Standard	Energy
PCI-DSS	PCI	International	Multiple	Standard	Finance

(CSF) but this kind of classification is present in the vast majority of standards. As one of the most popular, the CSF tends also to become a reference comparison point. As a further refinement step a whole hierarchy of security controls is usually associated to those high-level functions and the CSF helps in identifying adequate controls provided by various standards, each having a specific focus and coverage.

- The organisation depth of the standards which can be strategic (governance level), tactical or operational (about people, processes and technology).

2.3 The KAOS Goal-Oriented Framework

In KAOS, different abstraction levels to express goals can range from high-level strategic goals like "Maintain [SafeTrainOperation]" down to operational goals such as "Achieve [Train Stopped if ATO automatic disengagement not acknowledged]". High-level goals can be progressively refined into more concrete and operational ones through relationships, linking a parent goal to several subgoals, with different fulfilment conditions using either "AND-refinement" (all sub-goals need to be satisfied) or "OR-refinement" (a single sub-goal is enough, i.e. possible alternatives). The "WHY" and "HOW" questions can be used to conveniently navigate to parent and sub-goals, respectively. This results in a goal tree structure. The goal decomposition stops when reaching a goal controllable by an agent, i.e. answering the "WHO" question about responsibility assignment. These goals are either requirements on the software or expectations on the behaviour of agents in the environment. Domain properties can also be considered to justify a refinement. Such properties are intrinsically valid like the law of physics relating car deceleration with its mass.

A KAOS model is structured in four sub-models: the goal, agent, operation and object models which are depicted in Fig. 3. This paper will only focus on a subset of concepts represented in grey and located in the goal and agent models:

- The goal model structures functional and non-functional goals of the considered system. It also helps identify potential conflicts and obstacles related to goals and reason about their resolution. It is graphically represented as a goal tree. Obstacles can be used to reason about safety and the method supports a number of techniques to identify hazards and help in addressing them through avoidance, mitigation, repair or tolerance techniques [17]. On the security side, a more specialised concept of anti-goal is also available as well as dedicated techniques for dealing with attacks on system goals [18].

– The agent model is used to identify the agents of both the system and the environment as well as their interface and responsibilities. Attacker agents trying to intentionally disturb or disrupt the system will also be captured along with the corresponding anti-goal.

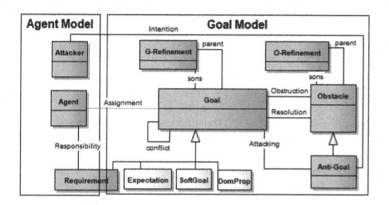

Fig. 3. Extended KAOS meta-model with obstacles and anti-goals

In order to support the above approach, we have extended the Objectiver GORE tool [25] mainly with the ability to tag goals and obstacles with their safety or security nature. This nature is modelled as an extra meta-model attribute and is graphically displayed as decorator on goal diagrams. It can be used as filter in reports and diagrams. The notion of attacker which was not yet supported was also added. Our extension takes the form of a tool plug-in [23]. It is illustrated in Fig. 4. Similar extensions can also be developed for other requirements or system engineering tools (e.g. CAPELLA).

3   Standards Addressing Safety and Security Co-Design

3.1   Overview of Possible Approaches

Considering how to cope with safety and/or security when designing system, a whole spectrum of combination can be considered, ranging from pure security to pure safety approaches as depicted in Fig. 5. A quite exhaustive literature review has been consolidated by the MERGE project [20] and more precisely identifies four possible approaches:

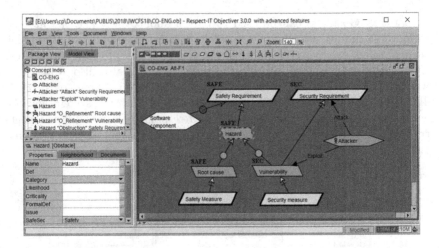

Fig. 4. Goal-based modelling notations for safety and security co-engineering

- Security and safety (especially the processes) are considered totally separately. In this case, only interactions between processes are needed.
- Security is considered at the service of safety. In this case the Safety engineering processes, methods and tools are updated with concepts and considerations from the security field. Conventional techniques for analysing Safety risks (HAZOP, FMEA, fault tree, ...) are modified to consider security giving rise to specialized versions of these methods (e.g. FMVEA, CHASSIS).
- Safety is considered to improve security practices benefiting from the maturity of safety practices. This leads security to provide a system view.
- Security and safety are addressed together by co-engineering. This approach also leads to a unification of processes, methods and tools.

Fig. 5. Spectrum of methods to address security and safety [15]

The above approaches are not all equally suitable:

- The separate approach to security and safety leads to important costs for companies due to the duplication of processes, methods, tools and the need to iterate between approaches. While temporary acceptable, it cannot remain appropriate for interconnected systems with increasing complexity.

- Dealing with security before safety does not make a lot of sense given that vulnerability connected with safety threats cannot be addressed.
- Considering security at the service of safety might also result in wrong priorities to shield the system. Some components may also have security needs disconnected from safety that are not correctly addressed.

The rest of this section will report four emerging trends with the following characteristics:

- a safety first approach based on existing standards that are combined through a combined risk assessment approach
- a safety first approach through the IEC TR 63074 "gapping" standard
- a parallel approach through the IEC TR 63069 "gapping" standard where evolving safety requirements can be managed from a security point of view
- another mixed approach proposed by International Society of Automation where a safety lifecycle is increased with security threats.

3.2 Combining Existing Safety and Security Standards

Without considering any new standards, many safety and security standards are actually risk based with many potential synergies. It is thus quite natural to consider how to combine ISO27K derivatives such as IEC62443 with standard process safety management systems (e.g. IEC 61508) in order to reach more robust safety and security outcomes but also to lower cost compared with running both management processes independently.

Starting from the risks, information security and functional safety have quite different risks and impact different kind of assets. Information security is concerned with the protection of information (computerised or paper based), the generic risks to which are confidentiality, integrity and availability (CIA). On the other hand, process and functional safety exist to protect a system by addressing its associated generic risks – people (safety), environment, asset and reputation (PEAR). A combined PEARS ('S' denoting security) approach puts safety in the forefront of security decisions while accurately identifying all relevant control system components, and addressing the impact of security on SIL (Safety Integrity Level) determination.

Experiences report several benefits to build a cyber security case on the foundations laid by a PEAR risk assessment when compared to purely security oriented approach considering its impact on PEAR later:

- it triggers early dialogue between safety engineers and security analysts
- security decisions are based on real risk opposed to just cyber risk
- the risk assessment process is simplified by chaining safety and security matrixes as shown in Fig. 6
- implementation and administration costs are reduced
- if provides a better evaluation of the impact of security on SIL.

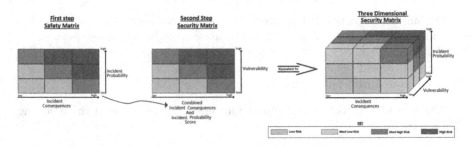

Fig. 6. Simplified risk assessment through a two-stage process [8]

3.3 IEC TR 63074 - Security Aspects Related to Functional Safety of Safety-Related Control Systems

This standard is also in elaboration phase by group TC44/WG15 of the ISO (International Standard Organisation) addressing security aspects related to functional safety of safety-related control systems. It takes the other approach advocating for performing safety analysis first to have a complete list of safety functions and assets which are passed to the security analysis. Measures produced for safety and security are also cross-checked in a realization phase. An example is the protection of a program or parameter in a PLC. The security team must know the architecture produced by the safety team (e.g. corruption against memory failure) to protect against deliberate corruption by attacker.

3.4 IEC TR 63069 - Framework to Bridge the Requirements for Safety and Security

TR 63069 is not an independent standard but aims to identify and clarify several gaps between both standards regarding concepts, terms, lifecycles, etc. It also proposes some recommendations to be able to manage the processes of each standard together. It is elaborated by group TC65/WG20 which advocate for a strong (parallel) co-engineering approach. Safety and security teams can carry work independently starting from the same design and performing risk assessment and producing counter-measures. However, if in this process additional safety functions are introduced, they need to be input to the security team for analysis. Counter-measures can be conflicting (e.g. security impacting safety) and this is detected and resolved at the common realisation phase.

3.5 ISA-TR 84.00.09-2017 - Cyber Security Related to the Functional Safety Lifecycle

This standard is intended to address and provide guidance on integrating the cyber security lifecycle with the safety lifecycle as they relate to Safety Controls, Alarms, and Interlocks (SCAI), inclusive of Safety Instrumented Systems (SIS). Its scope includes the work processes and countermeasures used to reduce the risk involved due to cyber security threats to the Industrial Automation and Control System (IACS) network. It provides recommendations to ensure SCAI are adequately secured due to the potential for cyber-attacks that can act like common mode failures that initiate a hazardous demand and prevent instrumented protection functions from performing their intended purpose. The intent is to address cyber security from both external and internal threats but not the physical plant protection. It issues a number of recommendations about secondary requirements on counter-measures, such as impact on performance, response time, interoperability, reliability and communication speed.

4   Assessment on a Railway Case Study

4.1   Case Study Presentation

Although quite a conservative industry, railways are now quickly going digital both on the trackside and the rolling stock. For example, railways signalling systems have reached such a level of interconnection and automation that they cannot be considered in isolation any more and thus require to consider a whole set of new threats. At the same time, the increasing level of automation in train operation is also introducing challenging new safety requirements.

The context is the European Rail Traffic Management System (ERTMS) composed of ETCS and GSM-R wireless communication systems for railways. It is further decomposed into a number of subsystems on the trackside (like Interlocking, Separation) and onboard (like European Vital Computer, Radio Transmission Unit, Driver Machine Interface), connected through GSM-R.

Our case study is based on the openly available specification of Automated Train Operation (ATO) over the European Train Control System (ETCS) [28]. The main goal of the ATO over ETCS is to efficiently manage varied service patterns including mixed-traffic, increase transport capacity, save energy, reduce mechanical wear and increase passenger comfort. As its name suggest, ATO provides automated train operation but it can only drive the train automatically in areas where ETCS is guaranteeing the safe train movement. Actually ETCS is providing the safety critical train protection while ATO itself is non-critical. While reasoning on the ATO system, safety requirements must eventually be assigned to safety system like the ETCS. It is composed of more than 200 requirements divided into 10 main categories (or principles) including safe movement, operation, supervision and emergency situations. Each requirement can be supported by one or several of the four Grade of Automation (GoA) modes, ie. non-automated, semi-automated, driverless and unattended train operation. Note the specification does not explicit any security requirements: those need to be discovered using the process described below.

4.2   Process Followed

In order to assess the approaches described in the previous section, we will build a goal-oriented model using a more generic approach based on obstacle and anti-goals identification and resolution techniques using the following process:

1. initial structuring of goals from the specification
2. safety-related sub-process (decorated using "SAFE") [17]
   - generate and refine obstacles using techniques such as domain regression, obstacle completion, patterns.
   - address obstacles using anticipation/resolution goals, by deidealising obstructed goals, introducing agent with extra monitor/control capabilities.
3. security-related sub-processs (decorated using "SEC")[18].
   - generate anti-goals by negating CIA goals and identify potential attackers benefiting from them
   - refine anti-goals until realizable by an attacker in terms of information that can be captured/altered, considering known vulnerabilities
   - address leaf anti-goals by reducing attacker monitor/control capabilities, using defence patterns for stronger CIA goals, detecting attackers, ...
4. perform risk/cost analysis and iterate using 2 and/or 3 over the whole goal model until residual risk acceptable.

4.3 High Level Goals

Figure 7 shows the key high level goals for implementing ATO over ETCS system. It is composed of goals covering functional safety, efficiency, interoperability and evolution. This diagram does however not claim to fully cover the source document [28]. Among the identified goals, for space reasons, only two will be detailed to show how security and safety potentially impact each other: point to point operation and management of GoA transition.

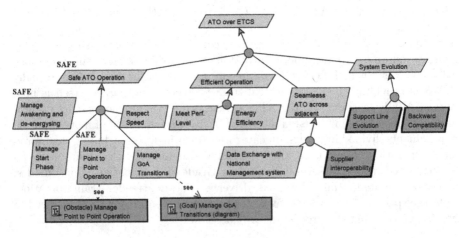

Fig. 7. High level goals of the ATO over ETCS

4.4   Analysis of Point to Point Operation

Figure 8 shows the point to point operation which follows a milestone pattern, i.e. going through successive states of departure, transportation and arrival [16]. Only the two later are detailed using the notations introduced in Sect. 2.3.

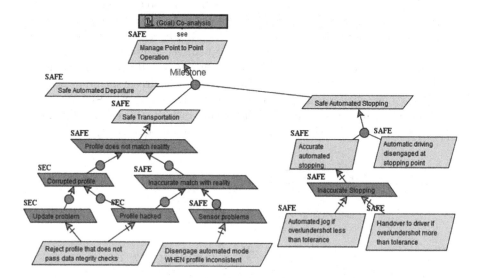

Fig. 8. Partial analysis of point to point operation

- Safe transportation can be compromised due to profile that does not match reality, the analysis can reveal it could result from corrupted profile (possibly due to communication failure or an attacker). As those are loaded prior to departure, an integrity check should avoid this. The other reason is that the train is "lost" in the profile: i.e. the experienced reality does not match the profile with enough accuracy. This could be caused by different reasons: sensor problem, change in the line or error (intentional or not) introduced in the profile. This case should be monitored and when detected, the automated system should disengage as lack of reliability can result in safety issues.
- Safe automated stopping can be inaccurate. Inaccuracy can to some extent be detected and corrected automatically but if the overshot or undershot is too high then the trains will stop safely (doors closed) until the human driver corrects the problem.

Next to each requirement, a mixed view of the result of the hazard/threat analysis is shown (those are usually presented in separate diagrams). Specific obstacles are tagged as SAFE or SEC depending on the process that identified them. Specific attacker profiles can also be captured (unique here). Some resolution techniques proposed in [18] can then be applied, e.g. to make the attack unfeasible or to reduce its impact. Some resolutions can also address mixed threats and reduce the global cost to make the whole system dependable.

4.5   Managing GoA Transitions

Another critical aspect is the management of transitions between different GoA modes. Different scenarios can result in the disengagement of the automated mode and their impact is explored in Fig. 9. In this case the driver should be warned and asked to acknowledge. The trackside can also decide to increase the GoA level which can conflict with the driver's wish to take back control, so the priority should be carefully analysed. The driver needs priority as (s)he is closer to the reality. However, on the other side if a driver is not able to ensure its duty, the system must be able to take over. On the security side, this could be exploited to take control of a train. So the link with the driver should be secured as the movement authority in charge. Of course, more sophisticated attack can be considered and can be refined at the second or even third level of residual risks if necessary (i.e. considering impact vs cost to cover the risk).

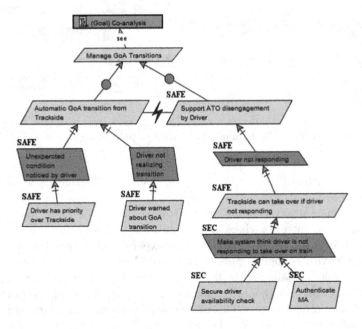

Fig. 9. Partial analysis of transitions among GoA levels

5   A Few Lessons Learned

In our partial case study, safety goal were challenged first while refining the hazard security related issues popped at some level. In some case attacks tree where introduced while improving some safety design meaning it is important to be able to have a communication channel with the security team as stressed in the 63069 standard. There was no real evidence of impact of security back to safety although competing for computation resource can result in conflicts (as stressed by ISA-TR 84.00.09). However, those can be solved using adequate architecture, typically by ensuring separation of safety and security processing.

From an engineering point of view, our work highlights scenarios involving different roles working together on the design model: the system engineer for the global system behaviour and architecture, the safety engineer to identify failure modes and their propagation, and security engineers to analyse possible attacks. Regular reviews can also take place to perform a global validation gathering all analysts. Actually rather than having a rather static view as proposed by the standards, more dynamic and tightly integrated engineering practices are also possible when considering a model-based approach because many modelling tool (including ours) are now web-based and collaborative.

Based on our current practice in railways but also on an automotive case and our review of similar work, we also believe that an interesting body of knowledge can be gathered to provide a guide into the challenging process of achieving safety and security co-design. Even if separate specialists would be required for large systems, it would give a common culture consisting of integrated analysis notation, check-lists and techniques to trigger the discovery of hazards and threats and a library of patterns capturing the interplay between security and safety (e.g. securing critical commands/sensor data, managing communication channels, performing configuration/software updates).

6   Conclusion and Future Work

In this paper, we surveyed the landscape of standards addressing the need to co-design safety and security. We identified different ways to manage both dimensions, highlighting a few realistic approaches and how standards are evolving. We used the KAOS framework to drive our decision process about a good way to perform co-engineering of safety and security in the spectrum of proposed methods and standards. We illustrated our assessment on a public railway case. Although limited in scope, our model highlights interesting knowledge we gained about how different kind of requirements and roles can interact. We also believe this can apply to other CPS where safety is crucial and challenged by security threats in constant evolution.

We plan to further refine our approach in an industrial context. We are currently recording the process on a 3 year railway development project in order to report in more details about the complexity and effort required in different phases. We will also consider runtime updates and emergent properties. We could also use formal modelling and reasoning in a targeted way.

Acknowledgements. This work was partly funded by the DIGITRANS project of the Walloon Region (grant nr. 7618). We also thanks the reviewer for their detailed comments.

References

1. Avizienis, A.: Basic concepts and taxonomy of dependable and secure computing. IEEE Trans. Dependable Secure Comput. **1**(1), 11–33 (2004)
2. Biro, M., Mashkoor, A., Sametinger, J., Seker, R.: Software safety and security risk mitigation in cyber-physical systems. IEEE Softw. **35**(1), 24–29 (2018)
3. Blanquart, J.P., et al.: Criticality categories across safety standards in different domains. In: ERTS-2012, Toulouse (2012)
4. CENELEC: EN 50128 - Railway applications - Communications, signalling and processing systems - Software for railway control and protection systems (2011)
5. Chen, B., et al.: Security analysis of urban railway systems: the need for a cyber-physical perspective. In: Koornneef, F., van Gulijk, C. (eds.) SAFECOMP 2015. LNCS, vol. 9338, pp. 277–290. Springer, Cham (2015). https://doi.org/10.1007/978-3-319-24249-1_24
6. Chen, Y.R., et al.: Unified security and safety risk assessment - a case study on nuclear power plant. In: 2014 International Conference on Trustworthy Systems and Their Applications, June 2014
7. Greenberg, A.: Hackers remotely kill a jeep on the highway-with me in it (2015). https://www.wired.com/2015/07/hackers-remotely-kill-jeep-highway
8. Hazell, P.M.: Integrating iec 62443 cyber security with existing industrial process and functional safety management systems (2017). http://bit.do/cyber-combined
9. Hessami, A.: A systems view of railway safety and security. In: Zboinski, K. (ed.) Railway Research, chap. 2. InTech, Rijeka (2015)
10. Howe, N.: Cybersecurity in railway signalling systems. Institution of Railways Signal Engineers News (2017)
11. Hulsebosch, B., van Velzen, A.: Inventory and Classification of Cybersecurity Standards. Ministry of Security and Justice of the Kingdom of the Netherlands (2015)
12. IEC: Iec 61508 - functional safety of electrical/electronic/programmable electronic safety-related systems (2010). http://www.iec.ch/functionalsafety
13. IEC: Iec 62443-4-1 security for industrial automation and control systems - part 4–1: Secure product development lifecycle requirements (2018)
14. ISO: Iso 31000:2018, risk management - guidelines, provides principles, framework (2018). https://www.iso.org/iso-31000-risk-management.html
15. Kanamaru, H.: Bridging functional safety and cyber security of SIS/SCS. In: 56th Annual Conference of the Society of Instrument and Control Engineers of Japan (2017)
16. van Lamsweerde, A.: Requirements Engineering - From System Goals to UML Models to Software Specifications. Wiley, Hoboken (2009)
17. van Lamsweerde, A., Letier, E.: Handling obstacles in goal-oriented requirements engineering. IEEE Trans. Softw. Eng. **26**(10), 978–1005 (2000)
18. Lamsweerde, A.V., Brohez, S., Landtsheer, R.D., Janssens, D.: From system goals to intruder anti-goals: attack generation and resolution for security requirements engineering. In: In Proceedings of RHAS 2003, pp. 49–56 (2003)
19. Macher, G., Höller, A., Sporer, H., Armengaud, E., Kreiner, C.: A combined safety-hazards and security-threat analysis method for automotive systems. In: Koornneef, F., van Gulijk, C. (eds.) SAFECOMP 2015. LNCS, vol. 9338, pp. 237–250. Springer, Cham (2015). https://doi.org/10.1007/978-3-319-24249-1_21
20. MERGE Project: Recommandations for Security and Safety Co-engineering. Deliverable (2016)

21. Park, J., Suh, Y., Park, C.: Implementation of cyber security for safety systems of nuclear facilities. Prog. Nuclear Energy **88**, 88–94 (2016). http://www.sciencedirect.com/science/article/pii/S014919701530127X

22. Paul, S., Rioux, L.: Over 20 years of research in cybersecurity and safety engineering: a short bibliography. In: Conference: 6th International Conference on Safety and Security Engineering (SAFE), May 2015

23. Ponsard, C., Dallons, G., Massonet, P.: Goal-oriented co-engineering of security and safety requirements in cyber-physical systems. In: Skavhaug, A., Guiochet, J., Schoitsch, E., Bitsch, F. (eds.) SAFECOMP 2016. LNCS, vol. 9923, pp. 334–345. Springer, Cham (2016). https://doi.org/10.1007/978-3-319-45480-1_27

24. Rajkumar, R., Lee, I., Sha, L., Stankovic, J.: Cyber-physical systems: the next computing revolution. In: 2010 47th ACM/IEEE Design Automation Conference (DAC), pp. 731–736, June 2010

25. Respect-IT: Objectiver. http://www.objectiver.com

26. Schmittner, C., Ma, Z.: Towards a framework for alignment between automotive safety and security standards. In: Koornneef, F., van Gulijk, C. (eds.) SAFECOMP 2015. LNCS, vol. 9338, pp. 133–143. Springer, Cham (2015). https://doi.org/10.1007/978-3-319-24249-1_12

27. Schoitsch, E., Schmittner, C., Ma, Z., Gruber, T.: The need for safety and cybersecurity co-engineering and standardization for highly automated automotive vehicles. In: Schulze, T., Müller, B., Meyer, G. (eds.) Advanced Microsystems for Automotive Applications 2015. LNM, pp. 251–261. Springer, Cham (2016). https://doi.org/10.1007/978-3-319-20855-8_20

28. Scott, G., et al.: ATO Over ETCS Operational Requirements - Version 1.7. ERTMS User Group (2016)

29. Steiner, M., Liggesmeyer, P.: Combination of safety and security analysis - finding security problems that threaten the safety of a system. In: Dependable Embedded and Cyber-physical Systems (SAFECOMP Workshop), France (2013)

30. Wolf, M., Serpanos, D.: Safety and security of cyber-physical and internet of things systems [point of view]. Proc. IEEE **105**(6), 983–984 (2017)

Generation of Behavior-Driven Development C++ Tests from Abstract State Machine Scenarios

Silvia Bonfanti[1], Angelo Gargantini[1(✉)], and Atif Mashkoor[2,3]

[1] Università degli Studi di Bergamo, Bergamo, Italy
{silvia.bonfanti,angelo.gargantini}@unibg.it
[2] Software Competence Center Hagenberg GmbH, Hagenberg, Austria
atif.mashkoor@scch.at
[3] Johannes Kepler University, Linz, Austria
atif.mashkoor@jku.at

Abstract. In this paper, we present the AsmetaVBDD tool that automatically translates the scenarios written in the AVaLLa language (used by the Asmeta validator (AsmetaV)) into Behavior-Driven Development scenarios for C++.

1 Introduction

The Behavior-Driven Development (BDD) is considered as the evolution and extension of the Test-Driven Development (TDD) [12]. It is increasingly being used to improve the code quality and reducing error rates in software. It aims at writing automated acceptance tests that represent complex system stories or *scenarios*. BDD builds upon TDD by requiring testers to write acceptance tests describing the behavior of the system from customers' point of view. While classical unit tests focus more on checking internal functionalities of classes, BDD testers take care to write tests as examples that anyone from the development team can read and understand [13]. BDD is currently supported at the level of code by several tools like Cucumber [13] for Java, PHP and C#, or Catch2 for C++[1].

The use of scenarios is common not only at the code level but also at the level of (abstract) models. The scenario-based techniques have been applied in different research areas and a variety of definitions, modes of use, and interaction mechanisms with users are given. In particular, scenarios have been used in the area of software engineering [1,10], business process reengineering [2], and user interface design [9]. The author in [8] classifies scenarios according to their use in the systems development ranging from requirements analysis, user-designer

---

The writing of this article is supported by the Austrian Ministry for Transport, Innovation and Technology, the Federal Ministry of Science, Research and Economy, and the Province of Upper Austria in the frame of the COMET center SCCH.

[1] https://github.com/catchorg/Catch2.

E. H. Abdelwahed et al. (Eds.): MEDI 2018 Workshops, CCIS 929, pp. 146–152, 2018.
https://doi.org/10.1007/978-3-030-02852-7_13

communication, examples to motivate design rationale, envisioning (imagined use of a future design), software design (examples of behavior thereof), to implementation, training, and documentation.

In the past, we have introduced the idea of using scenarios for validating Abstract State Machines [6] and developed a language AVALLA (and a corresponding tool) [7] for writing scenarios, which is integrated into the ASMETA framework [3]. With AVALLA, the designer can describe a scenario, which is briefly a sequence of external actor actions and expected reactions of the system. Scenarios can be executed in order to check whether the actual behavior of the system conforms to the requirements.

Although most ASMETA tools work at the abstract specification level, ASMETA also supports the automatic generation of C++ code [4] and of unit tests [5]. In a classical model-driven engineering approach [11], the designer writes the abstract specification and then through a process of systematic transformation, s/he can obtain the source code together with unit tests. In this way, the generated code comes with a set of unit tests that can also be used later for regression testing.

In this paper, we extend the ASMETA framework with a translator, called ASMETAVBDD, which translates an abstract scenario written in the AVALLA language to the BDD code. The paper is organized as follows. Section 2 presents some background about BDD, AVALLA, and the translation process form ASM specifications to C++. The translation from AVALLA to BDD code is presented in Sect. 3. The paper is concluded in Sect. 4 with the proposed future work.

2   Background

In this section, we present the framework we use for BDD at the level of code along with the AVALLA language and its use. However, we first introduce a simple example to show the output obtained by translating the AVALLA scenario to BDD.

The Lift Example. As a case study, we take part of a simple example of lift from [7]. The lift has for each floor one button, which, if pressed, causes the lift to visit (i.e., move to and stop at) that floor. A lift without requests should remain at its final destination and await further requests. The call of the lift is modeled in the ASM specification as a monitored function calledAtFloor: Integer -> Boolean, while the state of the lift is modeled by three controlled functions: floor that contains the floor number where the lift cabin is, state that represent whether the cabin is moving, and direction that shows the direction of a moving cabin.

2.1   BDD for C++

The are several frameworks for BDD in C++. One of the most powerful is Catch2. Catch2 is a testing framework for C++ that supports unit testing by

```#include "catch.hpp"```
 	
 ```SCENARIO("lift is called") {```
 ``` GIVEN("A lift at ground level") {```
 ```   Lift lift;```
 ```   REQUIRE(lift.floor == 0);```
 ```   REQUIRE(lift.state == STOP);```
 	
 ```   WHEN("the lift is called at floor 4") {```
 ```   lift.calledAtFloor(4);```
 ```   THEN("the lift start moving") {```
 ```   REQUIRE(v.state == MOVING);```
 ```   REQUIRE(v.direction == UP);}}```
 ```   ....```
 ```}}```
	scenario liftstarts
	 // load ASMETA specification
	 load Lift.asm
	 // check initial state
	 check floor = 0;
	 check state = STOP;
	 // lift is called at floor 4
	 set calledAtFloor(4) := true;
	 // perfrom a step
	 step
	 // lift is moving upward
	 check state = MOVING;
	 check direction = UP;
	 check floor = 1;
	 // ...

Fig. 1. A simple Catch2 BDD test   **Fig. 2.** A simple AVALLA scenario

means of macros. Moreover, it allows to write tests as a nested series of Given-When-Then statements in the style of BDD. In addition to the classic style for writing test cases, Catch2 supports an alternative syntax that allows to write tests as *executable specifications* in a classical BDD style. This set of macros include:

```
SCENARIO(scenario name)
```

that signals the start of a scenario/test case. Other macros include:

```
GIVEN(something)
WHEN(something)
THEN(something)
```

Figure 1 shows an example of a scenario written in Catch: when the lift is called to the fourth floor from the ground floor, then it starts moving upwards.

2.2   AVALLA

In [7], we have introduced a domain specific language, called AVALLA, to be used by the designer to manually describe scenarios (see Table 1). A Scenario represents a scenario of a provided ASM specification. Basically, a scenario has a name, a *spec* denoting the ASM specification to validate, and a list of target commands of type Command. A Command and its concrete sub-classes provide a classification of scenario commands. The Set command updates monitored or shared function values that are supplied by the user actor as input signals to the system. Command Step represents the reaction of the system, which executes one single ASM step. The Check class represents commands supplied by the user actor to inspect external property values and/or by the observer actor to

Table 1. The AVALLA concepts and their textual notation

Abstract syntax	Concrete syntax
Scenario	**scenario** name
	load spec_name
	$[C_1 \dots C_m]$
where C_j are commands: Set, Exec, Step, or Check	
Set	**set** loc := value;
where loc is a location term for a monitored function, and value is a term denoting	
a possible value for the underlying location	
Step	**step**
perform a machine step (compute update set and apply it to the current state)	
Check	**check** expr;
where expr is a boolean-valued term made of function and domain symbols of the ASM	
Exec	**exec** rule;
where rule is a rule of the underlying ASM	

further inspect internal property values in the current state of the underlying ASM. Finally, an Exec command executes an ASM transition rule when required by the observer actor. AVALLA supports also invariants of scenarios and the semantics of the language is given in terms of an ASM itself, so to execute a scenario ASMETA uses the ASM simulator. An example of an AVALLA scenario representing the same behavior of the C++ code is reported in Fig. 2.

2.3   ASMETA to C++

The translation from ASMs to C++, performed by the tool `Asm2C++`, has been presented in [4]. We recollect here some notions that will be used in the next section. Every ASM X is translated to a class C_X in which the monitored and controlled functions are translated to C++ fields of C_X. A step in the ASM is translated to C++ as a call of two functions: one representing the main rule, and the other one, called `updateState()`, applies the update set to the controlled part of the state.

3   Generation of BDD Tests from AVALLA

The Catch2 testing framework and AVALLA share several concepts that can be found in every BDD approach, so the translation from AVALLA to Catch2 is rather straightforward. Such translation complements the generation of C++ code [4] and the generation of C++ tests [5] already supported by ASMETA. Our translator is defined as a Model-To-Text transformation (we use Xtend[2] to define it). It takes an AVALLA scenario and produces the C++ code. Table 2 summarizes the transformation rules we have defined, which are briefly described here:

---

[2] https://www.eclipse.org/Xtext/.

Table 2. Translation of AVALLA constructs to Catch2 macros

AVALLA	Catch2

scenario name
load spec.asm
	```SCENARIO(name){```
	``` spec X; // create an instance of spec```
	``` ...```
	```}```

set block
set $l_1 = v_1$
...
set $l_n = v_n$
	```WHEN("set monitored variables"){```
	``` X.l1=v1;```
	``` ...```
	``` X.ln=vn;```
	```}```

check expr	```REQUIRE(X.C++expr);```

step	```THEN("n-th step occurs"){ .....```
	``` X.r_main();```
	``` X.updateState();```
	```}```

exec rule	add method definition **rule()** and call it

scenario is simply translated to a SCENARIO macro. The name is taken from the AVALLA scenario.

load is translated to a declaration of an instance of the class that is obtained by translating the ASM to C++. Let's call that instance X.

set all the set commands before a **step** command are grouped together and translated to a WHEN macro. Inside WHEN, every set is translated to a simple assignment to the field representing the monitored function.

check is translated to a REQUIRE macro. The argument of the check is translated to a C++ term, by reusing the translation already defined in Asm2C++.

step represents an abstract step of ASM. In C++, it is translated to a call of the function r_main() that computes the update set, and a call of the function updateState() that applies the update set to the current state in order to apply the new values of controlled location computed by the main rule.

exec allows the user to execute an arbitrary ASMETA rule. The tool translates the rule to a C++ function that is called whenever **exec** rule is invoked.

By following the rules above, the ASMETAVBDD tool generates a C++ file that can be compiled and executed. If the scenario is validated for the ASM, and translations to C++ of the ASM and of the AVALLA scenario are correct, then the BDD scenario in C++ will be correct and, when executed, no REQUIRE check will fail. However, there are two possible uses of the obtained BDD code. First, the user can manually inspect the BDD test and check whether the C++ code actually has the intended behavior. In this way, we can produce the C++ code with its tests also given in the BDD style. The use of the BDD style should increase the comprehension of the test by nontechnical stakeholders like customers or business experts. Second, the scenarios can be used for regression testing. Indeed, sometimes the C++ code is modified in order to add further details after its automatic generation. If one wants to check that the expected behaviors are still preserved after the modification, one can run the BDD tests again for confirmation.

4   Conclusions and Future Work

In this paper, we have presented an approach in which BDD tests are automatically built from AVALLA scenarios. The approach is also augmented by a prototype tool ASMETAVBDD. However, not all of the AVALLA constructs are currently supported by the tool. For instance, we do not currently take into account blocks. In the future, we plan to extend our tool in order to be able to translate any AVALLA scenario. Moreover, most of the textual information in the BDD scenario is generated automatically from the corresponding AVALLA scenario but it may not be very informative. To add specific information, we plan to extend the translator such that it can also read the comments in the AVALLA scenario, understand the commands they refer to, and translate them into BDD scenario. Currently, the comments are simply skipped since the AVALLA parser just ignores them. In this way, we loose some valuable information we already have in the abstract scenario. Furthermore, we plan to develop a feature that automatically translates a BDD scenario to an AVALLA scenario. This is useful for stakeholders involved in the validation process who do not know the AVALLA language. They can write scenarios using their preferred BDD tool and ASMETAVBDD automatically translates them into AVALLA scenarios.

Acknowledgments. We would like to thank Andrea Spalluzzi who has developed the first version of the translator during his master thesis.

References

1. Anderson, J.S., Durney, B.: Using scenarios in deficiency-driven requirements engineering. In: Proceedings of the International Symposium on Requirements Engineering, pp. 134–141. IEEE (1993)
2. Antón, A.I., McCracken, W.M., Potts, C.: Goal decomposition and scenario analysis in business process reengineering. In: Wijers, G., Brinkkemper, S., Wasserman, T. (eds.) CAiSE 1994. LNCS, vol. 811, pp. 94–104. Springer, Heidelberg (1994). https://doi.org/10.1007/3-540-58113-8_164
3. Arcaini, P., Gargantini, A., Riccobene, E., Scandurra, P.: A model-driven process for engineering a toolset for a formal method. Softw. Pract. Exp. **41**, 155–166 (2011)
4. Bonfanti, S., Carissoni, M., Gargantini, A., Mashkoor, A.: `Asm2C++`: a tool for code generation from abstract state machines to Arduino. In: Barrett, C., Davies, M., Kahsai, T. (eds.) NFM 2017. LNCS, vol. 10227, pp. 295–301. Springer, Cham (2017). https://doi.org/10.1007/978-3-319-57288-8_21
5. Bonfanti, S., Gargantini, A., Mashkoor, A.: Generation of C++ unit tests from abstract state machines specifications. In: 14th Workshop on Advances in Model Based Testing (A-MOST) @ICST 2018, Västerås, Sweden (2018)

6. Börger, E., Stark, R.F.: Abstract State Machines: A Method for High-Level System Design and Analysis. Springer, New York (2003). https://doi.org/10.1007/978-3-642-18216-7

7. Carioni, A., Gargantini, A., Riccobene, E., Scandurra, P.: A scenario-based validation language for ASMs. In: Börger, E., Butler, M., Bowen, J.P., Boca, P. (eds.) ABZ 2008. LNCS, vol. 5238, pp. 71–84. Springer, Heidelberg (2008). https://doi.org/10.1007/978-3-540-87603-8_7

8. Carroll, J.M.: Five reasons for scenario-based design. Interact. Comput. **13**(1), 43–60 (2000)

9. Carroll, J.M., Rosson, M.B.: Getting around the task-artifact cycle: how to make claims and design by scenario. ACM Trans. Inf. Syst. **10**(2), 181–212 (1992)

10. Potts, C., Takahashi, K., Antón, A.I.: Inquiry-based requirements analysis. IEEE Softw. **11**(2), 21–32 (1994)

11. Schmidt, D.C.: Model-driven engineering. Computer **39**(2), 25–31 (2006). https://doi.org/10.1109/MC.2006.58

12. Solis, C., Wang, X.: A study of the characteristics of behaviour driven development. In: 2011 37th EUROMICRO Conference on Software Engineering and Advanced Applications, pp. 383–387. IEEE, August 2011

13. Wynne, M., Hellesøy, A.: The Cucumber Book Behaviour-Driven Development for Testers and Developers. The Pragmatic Programmers, LLC, Raleigh (2012)

Hybrid Systems and Event-B: A Formal Approach to Signalised Left-Turn Assist

Guillaume Dupont[(✉)], Yamine Aït-Ameur, Marc Pantel, and Neeraj K. Singh

INPT-ENSEEIHT/IRIT, University of Toulouse, Toulouse, France
{guillaume.dupont,yamine,nsingh}@enseeiht.fr

1 Introduction

Hybrid systems represent a major part of nowadays's technology. They are present under many forms and in many safety-critical applications. Hence, the question of guaranteeing such systems' behaviour is a key issue that must be addressed.

Several approaches to this question have been proposed. Among them, we can cite hybrid automata [2], hybrid model checking [8,9], proof-based approaches [5,10], and refinement-based approaches [4,6,11].

In the context of refinement and proof based approaches, the work presented in this paper pursues the one initiated in [7]. It sets up our approach on a new[1] validation case using a case study borrowed from [3].

2 Case Study

A permissive left turn at an intersection is when a car can turn left without a dedicated traffic light phase; the car crosses the lane of opposite direction, which can result in a collision.

We target the design of a device capable of assisting the car driver in initiating her turn (thus avoiding the set up of a whole traffic light system on the road). Such a device is called a Signalised Left-Turn Assist (or SLTA for short).

2.1 System's Physics

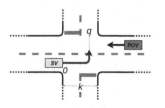

Fig. 1. Typical SLTA scenario

The situation is depicted on Fig. 1.

Let us consider k as the intersection's width. Initially, the subject vehicle (SV) is stopped at coordinate $p_{SV} = 0$ with speed and acceleration (resp.) $v_{SV} = 0$ and $a_{SV} = 0$. The primary object vehicle (POV), on the lane of opposite direction, is at position $p_{POV} > k$ with velocity $v_{POV} \in [-V_{max}, 0]$, where V_{max} is the maximum velocity reachable by the car.

---

[1] Already orally presented during the ABZ 2018 conference for [7].

© Springer Nature Switzerland AG 2018
E. H. Abdelwahed et al. (Eds.): MEDI 2018 Workshops, CCIS 929, pp. 153–158, 2018.
https://doi.org/10.1007/978-3-030-02852-7_14

When attempting its left turn, the subject vehicle is given an acceleration $a_{SV} \in [A_{min}, A_{max}]$, where A_{min} is a minimum positive acceleration (to ensure it actually reaches the end of its turn) and A_{max} is the car's maximum acceleration. The turn is complete when the SV's position exceeds q.

The system behaviour is modelled by the following differential equation:

$$\begin{cases} \dot{v}_{SV} = a_{SV} \\ \dot{p}_{SV} = v_{SV} \\ \dot{p}_{POV} = v_{POV} \end{cases} \tag{1}$$

where $\dot{x}$ is the x's first time derivative, v_{POV} is a variable that changes discretely, and a_{SV} is a given step function that ensures correct physical behaviour for the SV.

Equation 1 can be rewritten under the form of an ODE (Ordinary Differential Equation), $\dot{\eta}(t) = f(t, \eta(t))$ with $\eta = \left(v_{SV}\ p_{SV}\ p_{POV} \right)^T$ and $f\left(t, \left(x_1\ x_2\ x_3 \right)^T\right) = \left(a_{SV}\ x_1\ v_{POV} \right)^T$.

2.2 Safety

The whole goal of an SLTA is to avoid collision (and in particular collision with the POV). This safety property can be expressed as follows:

$$safe \equiv p_{POV} < k \Rightarrow (p_{SV} \geq q \vee p_{SV} \leq 0) \tag{2}$$

This assertion states that when the POV is crossing the intersection ($p_{POV} < k$), the SV either finished its turn ($p_{SV} \geq q$) or dit not began it ($p_{SV} \leq 0$).

Observe that it is possible to derive, from Eq. 1, T_{SV}, the time needed for the SV to complete its turn as well as T_{POV}, the time needed for the POV to reach the intersection (generally considering the POV is at maximum speed). The safety property is thus equivalently expressed as $T_{POV} > T_{SV}$.

2.3 System's Control

The controller acts on the SV only. It will however simulate the POV, from which it can retrieve (thanks to sensing) the position, used to determine when it is safe for SV to turn.

As shown by the automaton of Fig. 2, three states are associated with the SV's behaviour.

Initially, the SV is waiting on the lane (waiting). Then, when conditions hold ($T_{POV} > T_{SV}$) it may decide to turn (:turn) or to remain still. If the :turn transition is triggered, the SV enters the state turning. Once the turn is completed ($p_{SV} > q$), the SV leaves this state to reach the final one, passed.

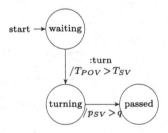

Fig. 2. System mode automaton

3   Formal Modelling with Event-B

Event-B [1] is a correct-by-construction method based on proof and refinement to design and certify systems.

The method relies on the definition of *contexts* to describe the system's static part (constants, sets, axioms, theorems) and *machines* to model the system's dynamic parts through a set of state variables modified by a set of events. Invariants defining safety properties on state variables can be defined as well.

It is possible to enrich a machine using *refinement*, by refining existing events and/or by introducing new state variables and new events.

3.1   Generic Approach

The global approach to address this case study relies on a generic machine sketched in [7]. In this machine, we define an abstract hybrid system that integrates both discrete and continuous behaviour (closed-loop modelling). This effectively factorises the core of any hybrid system. It describes:

- the state of the controller (modes of the automaton): $x_s \in$ STATES
- the set of possible values for modelling the concrete system (speed, position, temperature, etc.): $x_p \in \mathbb{R}^+ \to S$ (usually $S = \mathbb{R}^n$)
- modelling of time t together with a `Progress` event to represent the passing of time
- a set of events categorised as:
    - *sensing* events to model changes in the controller induced by the sensing of a value
    - *transition* events to record changes in the controller induced by the controller itself (including its user)
    - *actuation* events to trigger changes in the plant caused by the controller
    - *behaviour* events to model changes in the plant caused by the external environment of the system (close loop modelling).

The actuation and behaviour events, as well as the initialisation event (present in any Event-B machine) change the plant's behaviour by enforcing its values, which are functions of time, to bind to a differential equation. A before-after predicate is used for this purpose. It guarantees preservation of the past behaviour. Equation 3 defines such a binding:

$$
\begin{aligned}
x_p :\mid\ & x_p' \in \mathbb{R}^+ \to S \wedge \\
& [0, t[\lhd x_p' = [0, t[\lhd x_p' \wedge \\
& [t, +\infty[\lhd x_p' \text{ solution of the equation on } [t, +\infty[
\end{aligned}
\tag{3}
$$

where $\lhd$ denotes the *domain restriction operator* ($A \lhd f$ is defined on A and has the same value as f on this set).

3.2   Application to the Case Study

First of all, let us define the sets in which the system evolves as well as the needed constants (with associated constraints). In particular, we transcribe the mode automaton as three states (axm2) and set up the set for values to $\mathbb{R}^3$ as we will be using SV's position and speed and POV's position in the system model.

```
CONTEXT  LeftTurnAssistCtx  EXTENDS
       SystemCtx
CONSTANTS
  S, STATES, waiting, turning, passed,
  Amax, Amin, ...
  fd, fa, fam, fs
AXIOMS
  axm1:  S = ℝ × ℝ × ℝ
  axm2:  partition(STATES,{waiting},
         {turning},{passed})
  axm3-6:  Amax, Amin, ... ∈ ℝ+* ∧
          Amax > Amin
  axm7:  fd = ...
  ...
  axm11:
  [0, -v0/A [ × S ◁ fd ∈ C0 ([0, -v0/A [ × S, S) ∧
  [-v0/A, +∞[ × S ◁ fd ∈ C0 ([-v0/A, +∞[ × S, S)]
  ...
END
```

We also define the ordinary differential equations (ODEs) describing the system's behaviour. These ODEs describe how the plant behaves. We have identified four functions: stable behaviour ($a_{SV} = 0$), deceleration ($a_{SV} \in [-B, 0[$), acceleration ($a_{SV} \in]0, A_{max}]$) and acceleration with a minimum when turning ($a_{SV} \in [A_{min}, A_{max}]$).

Additionally, we also assert that these functions are piecewise continuous as per the first variable (time). This assertion is required to address later on the problem of solution existence.

At this stage, we are able to define the Event-B machine modelling the SLTA. This machine refines our generic machine. It first sets up the definition of the required state variables together with their respective constraints (note

```
MACHINE  LeftTurnAssist  REFINES  System
SEES  LeftTurnAssistCtx
VARIABLES  t, xs, pPOV, vPOV, pSV, vSV, aSV
INVARIANTS
  inv1-3:  pPOV ∈ ℝ+ → ℝ, ...
  inv4-5:  vPOV ∈ [-Vmax, 0], ...
  inv6:  ∀t · t ∈ ℝ+ ∧ pPOV(t) < k ⇒
         (pSV(t) ≤ 0 ∨ pSV(t) ≥ q)
```

that constraints on t and x_s are already handled in the abstract machine System). The safety invariant is also stated in inv6.

```
INITIALISATION  REFINES  INITIALISATION
WITH x'p: x'p = (v'SV p'SV p'POV)T
THEN
  act1-4:  t := 0, xs := waiting, vPOV := ...
  act5:  vSV, pSV, pPOV :|
         v'SV ∈ ℝ+ → ℝ ∧ p'SV ∈ ℝ+ → ℝ ∧ ...
         solutionOf(
         ℝ+, [v'SV p'SV p'POV]T,
         ODE(fs, [0 0 p0POV]T, 0)
         )
END
```

The system initialisation is quite straightforward. It starts by assigning an initial value to every discrete variable (x_s, v_{POV}, etc.) and then it binds the (continuous) system's values to an ODE, similarly to the substitution of Eq. 3 except that it does not require to preserve past values as there is no past yet ($t = 0$ at initialisation).

We consider the first type of events which models arrows in the mode automaton like :turn. This is typically a guarded transition event in our approach. When waiting, the controller/user decides to turn provided the conditions to do so are safe (modelled by guard grd2).

```
ctrl_transition_attempt_turn  REFINES
       Transition
WHERE
  grd1:  xs = waiting
  grd2:  TSV < TPOV
WITH s:  s = {turning}
THEN
  act1:  xs := turning
END
```

```
ctrl_sense_turn_end REFINES Sense
WHERE
    grd1 :  p_SV(t) ≥ q
WITH
    s :  s = {passed}
    p :  p = STATES × ℝ × {v_S, p_S, p_P | p_SV ≥ q}
THEN
    act1 :  x_s := passed
END
```

The second type of events represent arrows on the mode automaton of Fig. 2 (e.g., transition between states **turning** and **passed**). This is a case of *sensing* event that shall occur whenever its guard, referring to the plant's state, is enabled. In this case, the event models the sensing of the turn's end ($p_{SV} \geq q$) and changes the controller's mode accordingly.

The third type of event to be considered relates to the continuous transitions that happens *within* a state in a hybrid automaton. Such events model the plant's continuous evolution through functions representing its state. In this case, those functions bind to a differential equation, using the before-after predicate given in Eq. 3.

```
ctrl_actuate_turning REFINES Actuate
ANY a
WHERE
    grd1 :  x_s = turning
    grd2 :  a ∈ [A_min, A_max]
WITH
    e :  e = ODE(f_am, (v_SV(t) p_SV(t) p_POV(t))^T, t)
    s :  s = {turning}
    x'_p :  x'_p = ( v'_SV  p'_SV  p'_POV )^T
THEN
    act1 :  a_SV := a
    act2 :
        v_SV, p_SV, p_POV :|
        v_SV ∈ ℝ^+ → S ∧ ...
        [0, t[◁v'_SV = [0, t[◁v_SV ∧ ...
        solutionOf(
            ℝ^+, [t, +∞[◁ ( v'_SV  p'_SV  p'_POV )^T ,
            ODE(f_am, (v_SV(t) p_SV(t) p_POV(t))^T, t
        )
END
```

4   Assessment

The resulting model consists of 10 events (1 for transition, 1 for sense, 5 for actuation, the initialisation, **Progress** and **Behave**). Rodin generated 87 proof obligations (POs) for the machine and 20 for the context. Well-definedness (on both machine and context) accounts for 38% of them. Such obligations are generally easy to prove, although they can be cumbersome and repetitive.

Feasibility and simulation proofs account for 15% of POs in total. Those proofs are a bit more technical and often rely on high-level properties and theorems (solution existence with the Cauchy-Lipschitz theorem, smoothness, derivative, etc.).

Last, invariant proofs represent 26% of PO. Typing invariants are trivial; but other invariants like *safety* (i.e.: inv6) can be a lot more difficult and their proofs require an extensive use of theorems.

Most proofs are achieved after 10 steps; but some of them require up to 60 steps and more. The actual problem with the method right now is that the extensive use of the theory plug-in hinders proof automation, meaning that a substantial part of most proofs is fully manual.

5   Conclusion and Future Work

The work presented in this paper consolidates the relevance of our approach to formally model hybrid systems. It shows that the same method can be applied to systems with different states, values and invariants. Indeed, compared to the other developed case study, this one describes the plant using a different number of variables (three instead of two in the other one). Moreover, this case study considers two dynamic objects (vehicles) instead of one.

However, a lot of work remains. The method still needs to be extended to other types of differential equations (and not only linear autonomous ODEs). Besides, the current framework (i.e.: theories) for handling multi-valued variables is not really ergonomic; a way to properly express vectors shall thus be addressed as well.

References

1. Abrial, J.R.: Modeling in Event-B: System and Software Engineering. Cambridge University Press, Cambridge (2010)
2. Alur, R., Courcoubetis, C., Henzinger, T.A., Ho, P.-H.: Hybrid automata: an algorithmic approach to the specification and verification of hybrid systems. In: Grossman, R.L., Nerode, A., Ravn, A.P., Rischel, H. (eds.) HS 1991-1992. LNCS, vol. 736, pp. 209–229. Springer, Heidelberg (1993). https://doi.org/10.1007/3-540-57318-6_30
3. Aréchiga, N., Loos, S.M., Platzer, A., Krogh, B.H.: Using theorem provers to guarantee closed-loop system properties. In: 2012 American Control Conference (ACC), pp. 3573–3580, June 2012
4. Banach, R., Zhu, H., Su, W., Wu, X.: ASM, controller synthesis, and complete refinement. Sci. Comput. Program. **94**, 109–129 (2014)
5. Boldo, S., Clément, F., Filliâtre, J.C., Mayero, M., Melquiond, G., Weis, P.: Trusting computations: a mechanized proof from partial differential equations to actual program. Comput. Math. Appl. **68**(3), 325–352 (2014)
6. Butler, M., Abrial, J.R., Banach, R.: Modelling and refining hybrid systems in Event-B and Rodin. In: From Action Systems to Distributed Systems: The Refinement Approach. Computer and Information Science Series, pp. 29–42. Chapman and Hall/CRC (2016)
7. Dupont, G., Aït-Ameur, Y., Pantel, M., Singh, N.K.: Proof-Based approach to hybrid systems development: dynamic logic and Event-B. In: Butler, M., Raschke, A., Hoang, T.S., Reichl, K. (eds.) ABZ 2018. LNCS, vol. 10817, pp. 155–170. Springer, Cham (2018). https://doi.org/10.1007/978-3-319-91271-4_11
8. Henzinger, T.A., Ho, P.-H., Wong-Toi, H.: HyTech: a model checker for hybrid systems. In: Grumberg, O. (ed.) CAV 1997. LNCS, vol. 1254, pp. 460–463. Springer, Heidelberg (1997). https://doi.org/10.1007/3-540-63166-6_48
9. Kong, S., Gao, S., Chen, W., Clarke, E.: dReach: δ-reachability analysis for hybrid systems. In: Baier, C., Tinelli, C. (eds.) TACAS 2015. LNCS, vol. 9035, pp. 200–205. Springer, Heidelberg (2015). https://doi.org/10.1007/978-3-662-46681-0_15
10. Platzer, A., Quesel, J.-D.: KeYmaera: a hybrid theorem prover for hybrid systems (system description). In: Armando, A., Baumgartner, P., Dowek, G. (eds.) IJCAR 2008. LNCS (LNAI), vol. 5195, pp. 171–178. Springer, Heidelberg (2008). https://doi.org/10.1007/978-3-540-71070-7_15
11. Su, W., Abrial, J.R., Zhu, H.: Formalizing hybrid systems with event-b and the Rodin platform. Sci. Comput. Programm. **94**(Part 2), 164–202 (2014). Abstract State Machines, Alloy, B, VDM, and Z

Handling Reparation in Incremental Construction of Realizable Conversation Protocols

Sarah Benyagoub[1,2], Yamine Aït-Ameur[2(✉)], Meriem Ouederni[2(✉)],
and Atif Mashkoor[3,4(✉)]

[1] University of Mostaganem, Mostaganem, Algeria
[2] IRIT-INP of Toulouse, Toulouse, France
{sarah.benyagoub,yamine,meriem.ouederni}@enseeiht.fr
[3] Software Competence Center Hagenberg GmbH, Hagenberg, Austria
atif.mashkoor@scch.at
[4] Johannes Kepler University Linz, Linz, Austria
atif.mashkoor@jku.at

A main concern, already addressed by the research community, relates to the verification of Conversation Protocol (CP) realizability, which means the existence of a set of peers whose communication behavior is equivalent to a given conversation protocol. In this paper, we consider the incremental repairability of CPs identified as un-realizable using the set of composition operators, defined in [2] that satisfy sufficient conditions for realizability preservation. Reparation consists in identifying a set of changes completing intermediate un-realizable CPs so that the resulting CP becomes realizable. Our proposal is validated through a successful application of the presented approach on un-realizable CPs borrowed from the literature.

1 Introduction

In a previous work [2], we presented a correct-by-construction approach of distributed systems. There, the interaction between systems is described as a conversation protocol (CP). A set of operators allow a developer to incrementally build the distributed systems while preserving (by construction) their realizability at each application of these operators.

1.1 Basic Definitions

In the following, we summarize our correct-by-construction approach for realizable choreographies. We recall the main definitions for CP realizability as well as the set of composition operators together with their corresponding sufficient conditions.

The research reported in this paper has been partly supported by the Austrian Ministry for Transport, Innovation and Technology, the Federal Ministry of Science, Research and Economy, and the Province of Upper Austria in the frame of the COMET center SCCH.

© Springer Nature Switzerland AG 2018
E. H. Abdelwahed et al. (Eds.): MEDI 2018 Workshops, CCIS 929, pp. 159–166, 2018.
https://doi.org/10.1007/978-3-030-02852-7_15

Definition 1 (CP). *A conversation protocol CP (Fig. 1) associated with a set of peers $\{\mathcal{P}_1,\ldots,\mathcal{P}_n\}$ (Fig. 2) is a LTS CP $= (S_{CP}, s^0_{CP}, L_{CP}, T_{CP})$ where S_{CP} is a finite set of states and $s^0_{CP} \in S_{CP}$ is the initial state; L_{CP} is a set of labels and T_{CP} is the finite set of transitions.*

Definition 2 (CP_b). *A basic CP_b is a CP with a single transition defined as $CP_b = <S_{CP_b}, s^0_{CP_b}, L_{CP_b}, T_{CP_b}>$ and $T_{CP_b} = \{s^0_{CP_b} \xrightarrow{m^{\mathcal{P}_i \to \mathcal{P}_j}} s'_{CP_b}\}$ with $s^0_{CP_b} \neq s'_{CP_b}$.*

Definition 3 (Peer). *A peer is a LTS $\mathcal{P} = (S, s^0, \Sigma, T)$ where S is a finite set of states, $s^0 \in S$ is the initial state, $\Sigma = \Sigma^! \cup \Sigma^? \cup \{\tau\}$ is a finite alphabet partitioned into a set of send messages, receive messages, and the internal action, and $T \subseteq S \times \Sigma \times S$ is a transition relation.*

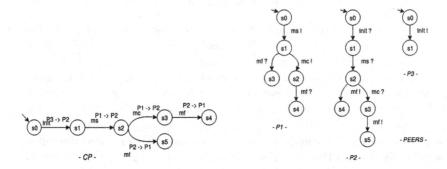

Fig. 1. Un-realizable CP.   **Fig. 2.** Projected peers.

Definition 4 (Projection). *Let the projection function $\downarrow CP$ which returns the set of peers LTSs $\mathcal{P}_i = <S_i, s^0_i, \Sigma_i, T_i>$. The set is obtained by replacing in $CP = <S_{CP}, s^0_{CP}, L_{CP}, T_{CP}>$ each label $(\mathcal{P}_j, m, \mathcal{P}_k) \in L_{CP}$ with m! if $j = i$ with m? if $k = i$ and with τ (internal action). And finally removing the τ-transitions by applying standard minimization algorithms [6].*

Figures 1 and 2 show an example of a CP and its projection respectively.

Definition 5 (Realizability). *The definition of Realizability we use in this paper is borrowed from [1]. It is decomposed as the conjunction of three properties as Realizability = Equivalence $\wedge$ Synchronizability $\wedge$ Well-formedness.*

- **Equivalence ($\equiv$).** *CP $\equiv Sys_{sync}(\downarrow CP)$ iff CP and $Sys_{sync}(\downarrow CP)$ have equal message exchanges sequences, i.e., trace equivalence.*
- **Synchronizability.** *The synchronous system $Sys_{sync}(\downarrow CP)$ and the asynchronous system $Sys_{async}(\downarrow CP)$ are synchronizable iff the system behavior is still the same in both synchronous and asynchronous communications.*

- **Well-Formedness (WF)**. $Sys_{async}(\downarrow CP)$ *is well formed, i.e.,* $Sys_{async}(\downarrow CP) \in WF$ *iff all the queues of the asynchronous system become empty at the end of system composition.*

A correctness proof of global system realizability using Event-B is available in [4]. This approach is a posteriori, it is based on the whole CP and is not incremental.

1.2   Correct-by-Construction Realizable CP's Operators

To avoid a posteriori global verification of realizablity, we have set up an incremental verification of realizability using a correct-by-construction approach to build CPs. This approach is based on the application of composition operators on basic realizable CPs. All these operators satisfy sufficient conditions which guarantee realizability. These operators are briefly described below.

Definition 6 (Sequential Composition $\otimes_{(\gg, s_{CP}^f)}$**).** *Given a CP, a state* $s_{CP} \in S_{CP}^f$, *and a* CP_b *where* $T_{CP_b} = \{s_{CP_b} \xrightarrow{l_{CP_b}} s'_{CP_b}\}$, *the sequential composition* $CP_{\gg} = \otimes_{(\gg, s_{CP})}(CP, CP_b)$ *means that* CP_b *must be executed after CP starting from* s_{CP}, *and:*

- $S_{CP_{\gg}} = S_{CP} \cup \{s'_{CP_b} |$
  $s_{CP_b} \xrightarrow{l_{CP_b}} s'_{CP_b} \in T_{CP_b}\}$
- $L_{CP_{\gg}} = L_{CP} \cup \{l_{CP_b}\}$

- $T_{CP_{\gg}} = T_{CP} \cup \{s_{CP} \xrightarrow{l_{CP_b}} s'_{CP_b}\}$
- $S_{CP_{\gg}}^f = (S_{CP}^f \setminus \{s_{CP}\}) \cup \{s'_{CP_b}\}$

Definition 7 (Choice Composition $\otimes_{(+, s_{CP}^f)}$**).** *Given a CP, a state* $s_{CP} \in S_{CP}^f$, *a set* $\{CP_{bi} \mid i = [1..n], n \in \mathbb{N}\}$ *such that* $\forall T_{CP_{bi}}, T_{CP_{bi}} = \{s_{CP_{bi}} \xrightarrow{l_{CP_{bi}}} s'_{CP_{bi}}\}$, *the branching composition* $CP_+ = \otimes_{(+, s_{CP})}(CP, \{CP_{bi}\})$ *means that CP must be executed before* $\{CP_{bi}\}$ *and there is a choice between all* $\{CP_{bi}\}$ *at* s_{CP}, *and*

- $S_{CP_+} = S_{CP} \cup \{s'_{CP_b 1}, \ldots, s_{CP'_{bn}} |$
  $s_{CP_{bi}} \xrightarrow{l_{CP_{bi}}} s'_{CP_{bi}} \in T_{CP_{bi}}\}$

- $L_{CP_+} = L_{CP} \cup \{l_{CP_{bi}}, \ldots, l_{CP_{bn}}\}$

- $T_{CP_+} = T_{CP} \cup \{s_{CP} \xrightarrow{l_{CP_{b1}}} s'_{CP_{b1}}, \ldots, s_{CP} \xrightarrow{l_{CP_{bn}}} s'_{CP_{bn}}\}$
- $S_{CP_+}^f = (S_{CP}^f \setminus \{s_{CP}\}) \cup \{s'_{CP_{b1}}, \ldots, s'_{CP_{bn}}\}$

Definition 8 (Loop Composition $\otimes_{(\circlearrowleft, s_{CP}^f)}$**).** *Given a CP, a state* $s_{CP} \in S_{CP}^f$ *and a basic CP noted* CP_b, *with* $T_{CP_b} = \{s_{CP_b} \xrightarrow{l_{CP_b}} s'_{CP_b}\}$ *and* $s'_{CP_b} \in S_{CP}$, *then the loop composition* $CP_{\circlearrowleft} = \otimes_{(\circlearrowleft, s_{CP})}(CP, CP_b)$ *is defined as follows.*

- $S_{CP_{\circlearrowleft}} = S_{CP}$
- $L_{CP_{\circlearrowleft}} = L_{CP} \cup \{l_{CP_b}\}$

- $T_{CP_{\circlearrowleft}} = T_{CP} \cup \{s_{CP} \xrightarrow{l_{CP_b}} s'_{CP_b}\}$
- $S_{CP_{\circlearrowleft}}^f = S_{CP}^f$

The condition $s'_{CP_b} \in S_{CP}$ means that the target state of CP_b is a state of CP. It defines a cycle in the built $CP_\circlearrowleft$, thus a loop and an iteration. The final states remain unchanged.

According to [2], we have identified a set of sufficient conditions which entail realizability when the CPs are built using the previously defined operators. Let us first formally define these conditions.

Condition 1 (Deterministic Choice (DC)). *Given a CP, deterministic choice property, denoted $DC(CP)$, holds iff $\forall s_{CP} \in S_{CP}$, $\nexists\{s_{CP} \xrightarrow{m^{P_i,P_j}} s'_{CP}, s_{CP} \xrightarrow{m^{P_i,P_j}} s''_{CP}\} \subseteq T_{CP}$, such that $s'_{CP} \neq s''_{CP}$.*

Condition 2 (Parallel-Choice Freeness (PCF)). *Let PCF be the set of CPs. The parallel choice freeness property (PCF), denoted as $CP \in PCF$, holds iff $\forall s_{CP} \in S_{CP}, \nexists\{s_{CP} \xrightarrow{m^{P_i,P_j}} s'_{CP}, s_{CP} \xrightarrow{m'^{P_k,P_q}} s''_{CP}\} \subseteq T_{CP}$ such that $P_i \neq P_k$ and $s'_{CP} \neq s''_{CP}$.*

Condition 3 (Independent Sequences Freeness (ISeqF)). *Let ISeqF be the set of CPs free of independent sequences. The independent sequence freeness property, denoted as $CP \in ISeqF$ holds iff $\forall s_{CP} \in S_{CP}$, $\nexists\{s_{CP} \xrightarrow{m^{P_i,P_j}} s'_{CP}, s'_{CP} \xrightarrow{m'^{P_k,P_q}} s''_{CP}\} \subseteq T_{CP}$ such that $P_i \neq P_k$ and $P_j \neq P_k$.*

The sufficient conditions associated with each composition operators can be defined. Table 1 recalls all the theorems that ensure the realizability of a CP built incrementally using each composition operator. Each theorem relies on the previously introduced sufficient conditions. More details on the definitions and proofs of these theorems are available in [2].

Table 1. Theorems for realizable by construction CPs

Theorem 1	$CP_b \in R$
Theorem 2	$CP \in R \wedge CP_b \in R \wedge CP_{\gg} = \otimes_{(\gg, s^f_{CP})}(CP, CP_b) \in ISeqF \Rightarrow CP_{\gg} \in R$
Theorem 3	$CP \in R \wedge \{CP_{bi}\} \subseteq R \wedge CP_+ = \otimes_{(+, s^f_{CP})}(CP, \{CP_{bi}\}) \in DC$
	$\wedge\ CP_+ \in ISeqF \wedge\ CP_+ \in PCF \Rightarrow CP_+ \in R$
Theorem 4	$CP \in R \wedge CP_b \in R \wedge CP_\circlearrowleft = \otimes_{(\circlearrowleft, s^f_{CP})}(CP, CP_b) \in ISeqF \Rightarrow CP_\circlearrowleft \in R$

1.3   Related work

The choreography repair technique presented in [3] depends on examining and analyzing the cause of violation of the realizablity condition [1]. In other words, the approach propose a realizability verification and reparation on the whole CP, to check the equivalence, the synchronizability and the well-formedness properties. Both verification and reparation techniques require building of synchronous and asynchronous traces that increase the complexity of verification and reparation.

The verification and reparation approach of [5] proposes an automated and non-intrusive solution for enforcing realizability when a choreography is not realizable. Their idea is to generate distributed controllers that are in charge of correcting ordering issues to make the corresponding distributed peers respect the choreography requirements. To do this, both synchronous and asynchronous communications are needed to check the realizability condition given in [1]. Notice that, the reparation proposed in [5] is not a generic repair method. Such that, a choreography is not repairable when at some point in its behavior there is a choice between interactions involving different sending peers. In that case, realizability cannot be enforced.

To avoid the aforementioned situations, the idea is, instead of checking and repairing the realizability on the whole system, we propose to check and repair the CP incrementally starting from an empty CP. To achieve this objective, our reparation strategy is based on the sufficient conditions satisfied by the set of composition operators [2]. Each operator can build a realizable CP from another realizable CP and a basic one without needing the projected peers or the synchronous and asynchronous traces. Notice that, there is no general repair method for un-realizable CP. Each violated sufficient condition gives rules for reparation, by adding a synchronization transition which reestablishes the sufficient conditions that restore the CP realizability.

1.4   Case study

In order to illustrate our approach, we use a case study borrowed from [3]. The choreography describes a simple file transfer protocol where P_1 is a client asking for the file transfer, P_2 is a file server and P_3 initializes the communication between a client and a server. This CP is depicted in Fig. 1. First, the client sends a message ($init$) to the server to request the server to start the transfer (ms). When the transfer is finished, the server sends the "Transfer Finished" (mf) message and the protocol terminates. However, the client may decide to cancel the transfer before hearing back from the server by sending a "Cancel Finished" message (mc) in which case the server responds with "Transfer Finished" (mf) message, which, again, terminates the protocol.

In order to check the realizability condition given in Definition 5, we rely on a stepwise correct-by-construction approach to build incrementally a realizable CP. The approach consists in applying the different operators on a set of basic CPs by checking the sufficient conditions associated with each composition operator. A sequence of steps is set up to build the conversation protocol of Fig. 1 as follows.

1. Identification of the set of basic CPs involved in the CP of Fig. 1.

- $CP = \varnothing$
- $CP_{b0} = s_0 \xrightarrow{Init^{P3 \to P2}} s_1$
- $CP_{b1} = s_1 \xrightarrow{ms^{P1 \to P2}} s_2$

- $CP_{b2} = s_2 \xrightarrow{mc^{P1 \to P2}} s_3$
- $CP_{b3} = s_3 \xrightarrow{mf^{P2 \to P1}} s_4$
- $CP_{b4} = s_2 \xrightarrow{mf^{P2 \to P1}} s_5$

2. Application of the composition operators.
   (a) $CP_1 = \otimes_{(\gg, s_{CP}^1)}(CP, cp_{b0})$, ✓ $CP_1 \in$ ISeqF
   (b) $CP_2 = \otimes_{(\gg, s_{CP}^1)}(CP_1, cp_{b1})$, × $CP_2 \notin$ ISeqF.

The sequence of composition starts from an empty CP. The sufficient condition ISeqF holds for the first composition CP_1. So, by Theorem 1 of Table 1, CP_1 (a) is realizable. However, realizability does not hold for CP_2 (b) where the ISeqF property is violated.

In the following section, we show how such un-realizable CPs can be repaired.

2 Incremental Reparation

2.1 General Idea

The sufficient conditions are not satisfied by the CP in Fig. 1. In this example, both sequences and branches violate the associated sufficient conditions.

Therefore, the CP must be transformed in order to restore ISeqF and PCF properties while preserving the initial communication purpose. To address this issue, we propose to introduce synchronization transitions with synchronization messages. These messages are not relevant for the communication purpose, but they are added for synchronization and realizability purposes.

Two reparation cases can be distinguished for both sequence and branch operators as follows.

- *Sequence property repair.* Following the ISeqF definition, the reparation of the sequence transitions (ISeqF violation) requires the introduction of a novel transition with message $Sync0$ (bold-dotted in Figs. 3 and 4) between the two independent sequences. This transition exchanges a synchronization message between the sender or the receiver peers of the first transition and the sender of the second transition.
- *Branch properties repair.* Following the PCF definition, the reparation of the branch transitions, (PCF violation) requires the introduction of a novel transition with message $Sync1$ (bold-dotted in Figs. 5 and 6) before one of the branches transitions. This transition exchanges a synchronization message between the same sender peer as the other branches and the receiver one.

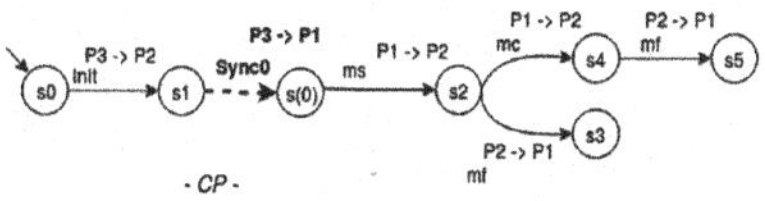

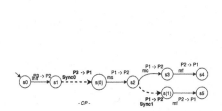

Fig. 3. ISeqF repair proposition 1. 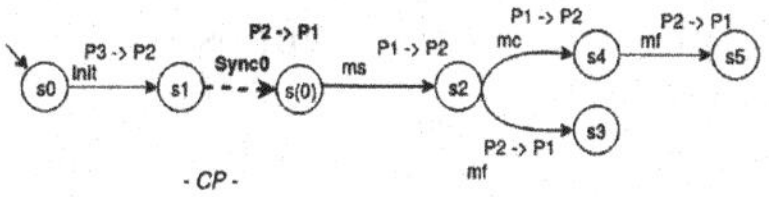   **Fig. 4.** ISeqF repair proposition 2.

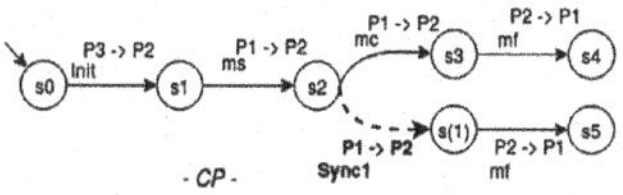

Fig. 5. PCF repair proposition 1. 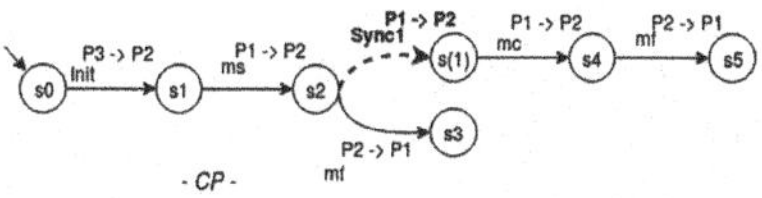   **Fig. 6.** PCF repair proposition 2.

2.2 Application to the Case Study

According to the previous reparation possibilities, four reparation scenarios are possible. One of the possible CP reparation is obtained by combination one reparation from the two sequence reparations and one from the two branches reparations. The CP of Fig. 1 is depicted in Fig. 7. The realizable projection is presented in Fig. 8.

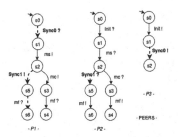

Fig. 7. Un-realizable CP repair.   **Fig. 8.** Projected peers repair.

In the sequel, we show that there exists a sequence of compositions of operators that lead the CP depicted in Fig. 7. This sequence is defined as follows.

– Identification of the set of basic CPs and initialization of CP

- $CP = \varnothing$
- $CP_{b0} = s_0 \xrightarrow{Init^{P3 \rightarrow P2}} s_1$
- $CP_{b1} = s_1 \xrightarrow{Sync0^{P3 \rightarrow P1}} s(0)$
- $CP_{b2} = s(0) \xrightarrow{ms^{P1 \rightarrow P2}} s_2$

- $CP_{b3} = s_2 \xrightarrow{mc^{P1 \rightarrow P2}} s_3$
- $CP_{b4} = s_3 \xrightarrow{mf^{P2 \rightarrow P1}} s_4$
- $CP_{b5} = s_2 \xrightarrow{Sync1^{P1 \rightarrow P2}} s(1)$
- $CP_{b6} = s(1) \xrightarrow{mf^{P2 \rightarrow P1}} s_5$

- Application of the composition operators.
  1. $CP_1 = \otimes_{(\gg, s^1_{CP})}(CP, CP_{b0})$, ✓ $\qquad\qquad CP_1 \in \text{ISeqF}$
  2. $CP_2 = \otimes_{(\gg, s(0)_{CP})}(CP_1, CP_{b1})$, ✓ $\qquad\qquad CP_2 \in \text{ISeqF}$
  3. $CP_3 = \otimes_{(+, s^2_{CP})}(CP_1, \{CP_{b3}, CP_{b5}\})$, ✓ $CP_3 \in \text{ISeqF} \wedge CP_3 \in$ DC $\wedge CP_3 \in$ PCF
  4. $CP_4 = \otimes_{(\gg, s^3_{CP})}(CP_3, CP_{b4})$, ✓ $\qquad\qquad CP_2 \in \text{ISeqF}$
  5. $CP_5 = \otimes_{(\gg, s(1)_{CP})}(CP_4, CP_{b6})$, ✓ $\qquad\qquad CP_5 \in \text{ISeqF}.$

The previous composition operators are successfully applied. So, the obtained CP is realizable.

3   Conclusion

In this paper, we present a top down approach to repair an un-realizable distributed systems. The proposal is based on the application of composition operators to check the realizability of systems. In case where the sufficient conditions associated with each operator are not satisfied, intermediate CPs, behaving as synchronization transitions, are introduced for adaptation purposes. In the future, we aim at implementing the reparation strategy we have introduced in this paper using the correct-by-construction Event-B method. The idea consists in introducing reparation events corresponding to the different situations of sufficient conditions violations.

References

1. Basu, S., Bultan, T., Ouederni, M.: Deciding choreography realizability. In: Proceedings of POPL 2012, pp. 191–202. ACM (2012)
2. Basu, S., Bultan, T.: Automatic choreography repair (2015)
3. Basu, S., Bultan, T.: Automatic choreography repair. Theor. Comput. Sci. (2015)
4. Farah, Z., Ait-Ameur, Y., Ouederni, M., Tari, K.: A correct-by-construction model for asynchronously communicating systems. Int. J. STTT 1–21 (2016)
5. Güdemann, M., Poizat, P., Salaün, G., Ye, L.: Verchor: a framework for the design and verification of choreographies. IEEE Trans. Serv. Comput. 9(4), 647–660 (2016)
6. Hopcroft, J.E., Ullman, J.D.: Introduction to Automata Theory, Languages and Computation. Addison Wesley, Boston (1979)

Analyzing a ROS Based Architecture for Its Cross Reuse in ISO26262 Settings

Xabier Larrucea[1(✉)], Pablo González-Nalda[2],
Ismael Etxeberria-Agiriano[2], Mari Carmen Otero[2], and Isidro Calvo[2]

[1] Tecnalia. Parque Tecnológico de Bizkaia, Calle Geldo, Edificio 700, 48160
Derio, Spain
xabier.larrucea@tecnalia.com
[2] University of the Basque Country (UPV/EHU), Nieves Cano, 12, 01006
Vitoria-Gasteiz, Spain
{pablo.gonzalez,ismael.etxeberria,mariacarmen.otero,
isidro.calvo}@ehu.eus

Abstract. The automotive industry is applying the latest technological advances in order to provide safety and security to drivers and pedestrians. In this sense, Robot Operating System (ROS) is used as a middleware to be adapted and deployed in cars. However, ROS has not been tested enough to be used in safety environments. Therefore, this paper reports an analysis of a ROS based architecture running in a prototype. We define a safety case based on the ISO 26262 Safety Element out of Context (SEooC) for its cross reuse, and we generate the required evidences related to the identified characteristics and thresholds. Goal Structuring Notation (GSN) is the notation used for the safety case definition and to argue conformance with respect to ISO 26262.

Keywords: ROS · ISO 26262 · SEooC · Safety case

1 Introduction

Recently, Robot Operating System (ROS) is used as a middleware to be adapted and deployed in cars [1]. Car manufacturers, such as BMW[1] [2], are using ROS[2] as a standard collection of open source software libraries to implement a middleware for message passing communications among modules within robot applications. Several experiences such as [3, 4], are applying ROS in automotive scenarios. ROS allows simplifying the construction of architectures, and this aspect can be extrapolated to the automotive domain. In our prototype, we embed ROS to build a modular component to be reused in several systems. In the automotive domain, this component is called a Safety Element out of Context (SEooC) as defined by the ISO 26262 [5]. This standard is becoming the reference certification model for the automotive industry covering the whole development life cycle.

---

[1] http://www.bmw-carit.com/.
[2] http://www.ros.org.

© Springer Nature Switzerland AG 2018
E. H. Abdelwahed et al. (Eds.): MEDI 2018 Workshops, CCIS 929, pp. 167–180, 2018.
https://doi.org/10.1007/978-3-030-02852-7_16

However, ROS has not been sufficiently tested to be used in safety environments [6]. In this sense, this paper reports an industrial experience where we analyze a running ROS based prototype, and we identify the ROS characteristics and threshold values in order to reuse this ROS component in several cars/prototypes. Some experiences analyzing the ISO26262 SEooC [6] have been carried out by some of the authors [7, 8] including safety cases [9]. Therefore, we identify requirements and design assumptions to be conformant to ISO26262 SEooC [6]. These assumptions, such as timing constraints [10], impact on the SEooC requirements and design, and they must be reflected in the safety cases/assurance cases [9].

In addition, it is not clear enough how these aspects are included during the safety certification [11] especially in safety critical software systems [12]. Certification of electronic components in cars, and in particular their embedded software, is a major goal for the automotive industry [13]. Some tools have been developed for supporting this life cycle such as OASIS [14] where authors present a part of a tool chain supporting properties checking, model correction, fault tree generation and FMEA (Failure Modes and Effects Analysis) table generation. In this sense, OpenCert [15] provides a complimentary approach for defining assurance cases. Safety certification relies on the demonstration that a software system is acceptably safe when it satisfies a set of objectives that the safety standards require for compliance [9]. Some European projects, such as CESAR [16], SafeCer [17], OPENCOSS [18] and CertWare [19], have been dealing with this topic. It is also aligned with the certification of safety critical domains, and it proposes the use of safety cases [10].

This paper deals with the following research questions (RQ):

- **RQ1**: *What are the required characteristics and thresholds for a ROS based architecture?* Our running architecture includes sensor, controller and actuator. The relationships among them are essential to understand how these elements interact. At the end we identify what thresholds are acceptable.
- **RQ2**: *What safety assumptions are defined during the safety case definition?* This industrial experience assumes that this ROS based component is going to be reused in several prototypes (cars), and it must be conformant to the ISO26262 SEooC definition. At the end, we need to provide a set evidences supporting our assumptions and arguments in order to declare that the component is acceptably safe.
- **RQ3**: *What ROS aspects are relevant for cross reuse and for its certification?* We need to understand and clarify the expected behaviour of a ROS based component.
- The remainder of the paper is structured as follows. A background analysis in ISO 26262 certification and SEooC, Software Reliability Certification, ROS and Safety Cases is first provided. Afterwards we define our ROS based architecture, including what aspects are measured, and the main results are provided. Finally, a discussion section argues the research questions and a conclusions section ends this paper.

2 Background

In this section we analyse the background of various important topics in this context: SEooC within an ISO 26262 certification, Robot Operating System and Safety Cases.

2.1 ISO 26262 Certification and SEooC

The ISO 26262 international standard [20] was released in 2011 and modified[3] in 2012. This standard includes a specific part entitled "Guideline on ISO 26262" for dealing with the Safety Element out of Context (SEooC) [5]. The automotive industry does not require to certify all their components based on ISO 26262. However, it is becoming a reference model for the automotive industry [16, 17]. In addition, the emergence of autonomous vehicles will increase the relevance of this certification. For the sake of simplicity, we are considering the certification process as a compliance process or as an assessment process such as [21], and as a process where product characteristics are assessed [22]. Concerning the software aspect, ISO 26262 states on its Part 6: Product development at the software level, Clause 6.4.2:

> "The specification of the software safety requirements shall be derived from the technical safety concept and the system design in accordance with ISO 26262-4:2011, 7.4.1 and 7.4.5, and shall consider:[..]
> e) the timing constraints;
> '....'[4].

Our work is, therefore, aligned with the evaluation of timing constrains of the proposed architecture. All these requirements impact on a wide set of ISO 26262 clauses such as specification of software safety requirements, software unit design and implementation, and software unit testing.

Voas defined a certification process for off-the-shelf components [23] which is based on the analysis of quality characteristics, considering components as black boxes. A component is considered to be certifiable if its quality characteristics are met. Voas' approach does not define what high quality [23] means, and our approach extends his approach with our ROS based architecture. He also considers wrappers to limit its component's behaviour, and the analysis of its operational system which can also affect the component behaviour. Other certification approaches based on standards [37] define basic steps for carrying out a certification process.

2.2 Software Reliability Certification

The Software Reliability [24] basic steps are: list related systems, implement operational profiles, define necessary reliability, prepare for test, execute test and guide test. A similar approach is the Software Reliability Engineering Process [25], where once the reliability objective is determined and the operational profile is developed, we proceed with the software testing, collection of failure data, and so on. Concerning

---

[3] https://www.iso.org/obp/ui/#iso:std:iso:26262:-10:ed-1:v1:en.

[4] The bold typeface is ours.

certification, certifying the reliability of software [26] is not an easy task, and all these approaches agree on the fact that we need to set up the operational profiles. In fact, a certification process will take into account these operational profiles as a basis. In this context safety evidences [27] are used to support certification processes, and they are also a cornerstone in software component certification [22]. There are techniques used in the certification process such as Software Fault Injection (SFI) which can be used for software certification in order to analyse a component behaviour and response in faulty conditions. Wholin and Regnell defined a reliability certification of software components for different usage profiles [28]. In our context we identify and characterize a usage profile for a SEooC component as well as its reliability. This is needed because during the certification process the auditor/evaluator checks these characteristics in the resulting product by means of measurable attributes.

2.3   Robotic Operating System (ROS)

According to Bruyninckx [56] robotics software has several chronic problems in several industrial domains due to the lack of standardization, interoperability and reuse of software libraries, both proprietary and open source. In order to produce a healthy software ecosystem the following relevant problems must be prevented: (1) lack of code reuse; (2) higher needs of integration of components and (3) finding the appropriate trade-off between efficiency and robustness. As a solution, Free and Open Source Software (FOSS) initiatives such as the Robot Operating System (ROS) were promoted.

ROS [29] is a message-passing middleware providing operating system-like and package tools. It defines different entities including nodes, message topics and services. Nodes are processes or software modules that can communicate with other nodes through simple messages (or data structures) by means of publisher/subscriber mechanisms on top of TCP or UDP standard network protocols. In ROS a service is modelled as a pair of messages, one for request and another for reply. ROS has several client libraries implemented in different languages such as C++, Python, Octave or Java in order to create ROS applications. Its major advantage is code reuse and sharing [30]. ROS has been successfully used in different kinds of robots such as autonomous guided vehicles [31–33].

2.4   Safety Cases

There is an existing debate on whether safety cases are enough to provide confidence in order to consider a system safe [34]. However, we consider safety cases as a useful way to provide enough confidence using structured arguments and evidences [8] in safety critical applications [6]. Our approach uses Safety Cases for gathering primary assets during certification process, and we are using Goal Structuring Notation[5] (GSN) [35] as a notation for representing arguments and evidences. Another representation for the

---

[5] http://www.goalstructuringnotation.info/.

same purpose is Claims, Arguments and Evidence[6] (CAE) from Adelard. Both initiatives are focused on providing confidence to safety critical scenarios.

The OMG is devoting efforts with a special task force[7] and a dependability assurance framework[8]. They have released a metamodel for representing assurance cases, the so-called Structured Assurance Case Metamodel[9] (SACM). In this paper we use safety cases and GSN notation for arguing conformance with respect to ISO 26262.

3   The ROS Based Architecture

In this section we briefly introduce the ROS architecture used and describe the experimentation carried out.

3.1   ROS Description: Operational Profile

We define our SEooC as a generic architecture containing two processing devices which communicate between them using a ROS wrapper. The two processing devices are specialized as follows:

1. Advanced Level Processing (ALP), implemented on a higher processing device with higher computation and connectivity capabilities
2. Low Level Processing (LLP), implemented on a device with limited processing and memory capabilities, directly connected with sensors and actuators.

So, while ALP nodes typically communicate to similar nodes by means of standard interfaces, such as AUTomotive Open System ARchitecture (AUTOSAR) interfaces, communication between APL and LLP nodes can use proprietary mechanisms. ROS is adopted in order to avoid low level communication programming details. For the sake of testing this architecture it has been implemented with two different and easily available devices: A Raspberry Pi board as ALP node, which processes the data acquired from an Arduino Board as LLP node, both linked via an USB serial connection. Figure 1(a) provides a detailed representation of the proposed implementation of this architecture, which is deployed in a vehicle as shown in Fig. 1(b). The use of the SEooC within this vehicle is out of the scope of this paper.

3.2   Architecture Used in the Experiments

Since this architecture is aimed at building components that could be connected into a broader system, typically for measuring or actuation purposes, they must be represented externally by a limited set of chosen parameters. In order to ease the integration of the component it is of key importance that these parameters represent only the most

---

[6] http://www.adelard.com/asce/choosing-asce/cae.html.

[7] http://sysa.omg.org/.

[8] http://www.omg.org/hot-topics/cdss.htm.

[9] http://www.omg.org/spec/SACM/1.1/.

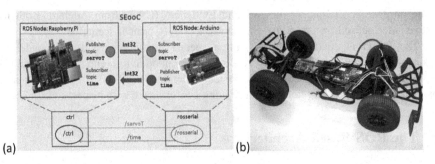

Fig. 1. (a) Implementation of our SEooC with Raspberry Pi (ALP) & Arduino (LLP); (b) Raspberry Pi & Arduino SEooC integrated in our car prototype

relevant aspects of the component behaviour, while wrapping to a maximum the characteristics of the internal off-the-shelf components involved, i.e. ROS framework and devices at ALP and LLP layers. For this set of experiments, we have fixed the size of the exchanged messages to a 32 bits word. This will be the typical message size associated with the limited processing and memory storage capacity of the ALP (e.g. our Arduino UNO has 2 KB of RAM). More specifically, the message payload used in the experiments is a message number generated consecutively by the ALP (Raspberry Pi). Messages are sent with a fixed frequency, the period. This information is asynchronously echoed by the LLP (Arduino) and then used to calculate the time required for the communication by the LLP upon reception, if received.

The selected parameters are:

1. **Period**: It describes the time interval, in milliseconds, of messages published by the ALP (Raspberry Pi) to be received by the LLP (Arduino) nodes.
2. **Granularity**: Parameter related to the ROS message-passing mechanism representing the message delivery frequency. While some invocations will result in no information exchange other may result in one or more messages delivered. It is expressed in kHz.
3. **Queue size**: ROS stores messages in fixed length queues following the Publisher/Subscriber paradigm. This parameter is the internal size of these queues.

3.3   Safety Case and Evidence

We have identified which assumptions and arguments are required for defining an ISO26262 SEooC component. As result we have defined a safety case (Fig. 2) which require some evidences: "ROS characteristics are under control". These characteristics are the parameters defined in previous section: period, granularity and queue size.

According to [28] we need to identify different profiles for the usage of our SEooC component. At least we need to identify the reliability communications behaviour for the ROS based architecture. A quantitative technique for profiling the runtime behaviour is based on testing workloads [37]. We test our ROS based architecture by sending messages. In this sense stress testing [38] has been used in the past, and it is an essential activity in safety-critical software [39]. Therefore, we define fault as an

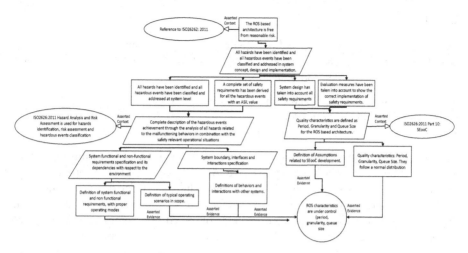

Fig. 2. A fragment of our safety case (GSN notation)

abnormal condition that can cause an element (clause 1.32) or an item (clause 1.69) to fail [20]. An error is a discrepancy between a computed, observed or measured value or condition, and the true, specified or theoretically correct value or condition. Finally, a failure is a termination of the ability of an element (clause 1.32) to perform a function as required.

In our definition, we are just considering lost messages as faults. Underlying protocols provided by ROS guarantee message integrity. A lost message means, for example, that the information sent to an actuator is not received, and therefore not processed. These faults can also be considered as relative errors in this context. In this sense, we are going to measure the following aspects for each experiment:

- Faults: number of undelivered messages or messages arrived after a certain latency threshold.
- Mean: mean latency of all arrived messages.
- Median: central latency of all arrived messages.
- Standard Deviation: variation of arrived messages.
- Minimum: minimum latency value of all arrived messages.
- Maximum: maximum latency value of all arrived messages.
- Confidence Interval (CI) 95% (lower and upper): thresholds delimiting outliers. We only consider outliers latencies higher than Upper CI 95%.
- Undelivered Density: number of undelivered messages per total number of messages sent.
- Outlier Density: number of outliers per total number of arrived messages.
- Reference Interval (RI) 99% (lower and upper): thresholds delimiting 99% of the arrived messages.

3.4   Results

We need to assess software operational quality based on stressing our SEooC. So, we identified 40 different configurations ($5 \times 2 \times 4 = 40$) for our SEooC component, being their input variables and values:

- **Period** values: 2, 3, 4, 5 and 8 ms.
- **Granularity** values: 5 and 10 kHz.
- **Queue size** values: 1, 2, 10 and 100.

Each experiment combination was executed 24 times during 10 min, therefore resulting altogether in 960 executions (see Annexes-URL). These empirical cases provided an overview of the SEooC component behaviour under stress conditions.

In a preliminary data analysis we determine which experiments were meaningful. Figure 3 depicts the latency of two executions of out SEooC component. X axis represents the execution time in seconds (10 min altogether). Y axis represents the latency of each message over time in milliseconds. Undelivered messages are shown as having null latency. Figure 3 (a) shows a high density of messages delivered within the range from 6 to 12 ms latency. Four spots close to the X axis (zero latency value) correspond to undelivered messages. On the upper zone of the thick stripe, loose dots represent messages with a high-out of common latency. Figure 3(b) depicts a completely different scenario. At the beginning, some messages are delivered with an extremely high latency (more than 150 s). Further to a given point (around 300 s execution time) messages no longer arrive, so that they all remain null (representing undelivered messages). Clearly, in this case the component cannot be considered reliable as messages mostly remain undelivered. The whole experiment set with a period of 2 ms behaves similarly. Furthermore, they are not comparable and we shall exclude them from the remaining of our study. This reduces our data set to 768 (24 executions of $4 \times 2 \times 4 = 32$ experiments). Similar figures to those provided in Fig. 3 are obtained for the whole set of 768 valid executions and in general terms they all look like Fig. 3 (a). We have visually compared the figures of the 24 executions under the same experimental conditions and they are consistent. All summarised information has been collected and compared in spread sheets with two different sorting views: (1) blocks of the 24 executions under each experimental condition and (2) blocks of all experiments under the same execution number. All this information can be consulted in the Annexes.

Figure 4 provides a different representation of the execution illustrated in Fig. 3(a) 3 ms, 5 kHz, queue size 2. A similar representation of Fig. 3(b) is also show in the Annexes. However, as these data sets corresponding to Period 2 ms do not follow a Gaussian distribution they do not make much sense. They have therefore been eliminated.

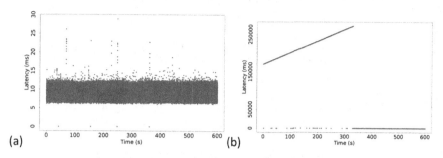

Fig. 3. Data plots of two executions of the SEooC component, (a) 3 ms, 5 kHz, queue size 2; (b) 2 ms, 5 kHz, queue size 2

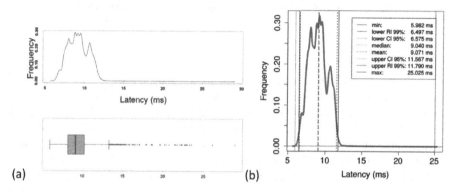

Fig. 4. (a) Density plot vs boxplot of execution in Fig. 2 (a); (b) density plot of execution 19, period 3 ms, granularity 5 kHz, queue size 1

Another visual representation utilised in our analysis has been the density plot. Figure 4(b) shows an execution instance of our SEooC. In order to formally analyse the experimental results we need to check if they follow a normal distribution to apply the Central Limit Theorem. When sample size is 8 to 29 (in our case, 24), we need to verify whether the Shapiro-Wilk and Kolmogorov-Smirnov normality test is fulfilled. Since the mean latency values do not violate the normal assumption, the Confidence Intervals (CI) 95% can be calculated as in Eq. (1).

$$\text{Confidence Interval } 95\% = \mu \pm 2\sigma \tag{1}$$

Having carried out this verification we can state that they follow the normal distribution. The R script utilised to verify this fact can be found in the provided Web site. All our executions and data are available. Figure 5 represents graphically all periods by means of boxplots.

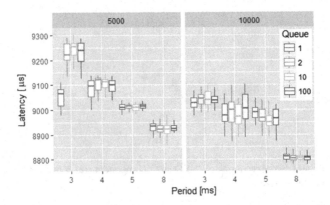

Fig. 5. Boxplots for all period (ms), granularity (Hz) and queue size

4 Discussions

Our ROS based architecture is characterised in terms of timing. We have identified which characteristics and thresholds are available for this ROS based architecture. Therefore RQ1 (RQ1: What are the required characteristics and thresholds for a ROS based architecture?) is answered. Note that a different architecture (sensor, controller and actuator configuration) can generate other values. However, this research provides an overview of the acceptable thresholds when using a ROS based architecture.

When defining our safety case, we identify a set of assumptions and arguments required for supporting ISO 26262 SEooC concept, especially for reusing this component across different domains/systems. All these assumptions, safety aspects and asserted evidences supporting goals argue that a specific instantiation of a ROS based architecture is acceptably safe and compliant to the ISO 26262 clauses related to SEooC. So, our second research question (RQ2: What safety assumptions are defined during the safety case definition?) is accomplished.

Our approach for certification is straightforward. We have used existing approaches for assessing that we are fulfilling with the requirements. In fact, we are just focused on providing the evidences that are summarizing the behaviour of a ROS based component. All these parameters (Characterisitics) are the main elements to be used for reusing this component in a different system/domain. Therefore, RQ3 (RQ3: What ROS aspects are relevant for cross reuse and for its certification?) is reached. However, these arguments and evidences can vary depending on each situation. If this ROS component is going to be integrated in a more complex scenario, additional arguments and evidence should be defined and analysed.

Our ROS based architecture is tested on a basic platform which is not a complex system where several components (some of them ROS based) are interacting among them. Deeper studies are required on complex infrastructures and mechanisms. For example, the current bus communicator is a Universal Serial Bus (USB), and traditionally communications in automotive domain use the so called CAN bus [40]. However it can be used with USB for connecting other automotive components. In addition, further research should be devoted to security/safety? issues which are not covered in CAN bus systems representing a main weakness.

The presented approach helps to identify what use of a ROS component can be defined by the designer. In fact, it is under the designer's responsibility to accept or to decline a specific configuration according to one specific application requirements. Our ROS characterization provides an overview of the acceptable values considering Confidence Intervals (95%) and Reference Intervals (99%). During a certification process these values are taken as reference values. These aspects are used during ISO 26262 SEooC component definition.

So, according to our study we can identify the ideal set of parameters for an application, which would be a period of 8 ms, granularity of 5 kHz, and queue size of 100 in order to minimise the number of undelivered messages. In our example the percentage of undelivered messages is 0.01%. We consider that each message can be an instruction (order) for our autonomous car, and it cannot be lost. For example, if an autonomous car identifies an obstacle in the way it should be avoided immediately, otherwise the car might crash against it. A message redirecting its path is sent, it cannot be lost and it should be processed as soon as possible.

5   Conclusions and Future Work

The automotive industry is applying the latest technological advances such as Robot Operating System (ROS) for providing safety and security to drivers and pedestrians. Despite some initial ROS based experiences, it has not been tested enough to be used in safe environments. Therefore, this paper reports an assessment of a running ROS based prototype in order to identify the main characteristics to be used as a ISO 26262 Safety Element out of Context (SEooC). In fact, we have identified a safety case to argue conformance to the ISO 26262. We have used Goal Structuring Notation (GSN) as the notation language. As the timing is a relevant factor in our context, we analyse the following ROS messaging parameters: period, granularity and queue size. Based on a specific configuration we have generated the evidences related to the identified characteristics and thresholds. All these parameters can be used as reference values when a ROS component is reused in another system.

As future work, we have identified behavioural improvements modifying the Linux kernel. In this sense there are some interesting initiatives such as Linux for automotive[10], and how ROS can be smoothly integrated with this operating system. Another set of experiments could be carried out using as a parameter the message size since much variability is not possible due to the limited capabilities of the LLP (Arduino).

Acknowledgments. This work has been partially supported by the Basque Government Project CPS4PSS Etortek14/10.

---

[10] https://www.automotivelinux.org/.

Annexes

A more detailed description of the experimental environment and the individual execution results are available in data and graphical modes at the following annexes web address:

  http://lsi.vc.ehu.eus/CPS-annexes.

References

1. Kato, S., Takeuchi, E., Ishiguro, Y., Ninomiya, Y., Takeda, K., Hamada, T.: An open approach to autonomous vehicles. IEEE Micro 35(6), 60–68 (2015). https://doi.org/10.1109/MM.2015.133
2. Aeberhard, M.: Automated Driving with ROS at BMW, Open Source Robotics Foundation (2016). https://www.osrfoundation.org/michael-aeberhard-bmw-automated-driving-with-ros-at-bmw/. Accessed 13 Sep 2017
3. Ainhauser, C., et al.: Autonomous driving needs ROS. ROS as a platform for autonomous driving functions, BMW Group, BMW Car IT GmbH (2013)
4. Noh, S., Park, B., An, K., Koo, Y., Han, W.: Co-pilot agent for vehicle/driver cooperative and autonomous driving. ETRI J. 37, 1032–1043 (2015). https://doi.org/10.4218/etrij.15.0114.0095
5. International Standard Organisation. Road vehicles – Functional safety; ISO 26262- part 10 (2012)
6. Larrucea, X., Combelles, A., Favaro, J.: Safety-critical software [Guest editors' introduction]. IEEE Softw. 30, 25–27 (2013). https://doi.org/10.1109/MS.2013.55
7. Larrucea, X., Mergen, S., Walker, A.: A GSN approach to SEooC for an automotive hall sensor. In: Kreiner, C., O'Connor, R.V., Poth, A., Messnarz, R. (eds.) EuroSPI 2016. CCIS, vol. 633, pp. 269–280. Springer, Cham (2016). https://doi.org/10.1007/978-3-319-44817-6_23
8. Larrucea, X., Walker, A., Colomo-Palacios, R.: Supporting the management of reusable automotive software. IEEE Softw. 34(3), 40–47 (2017). https://doi.org/10.1109/MS.2017.68
9. Hawkins, R., Habli, I., Kelly, T., McDermid, J.: Assurance cases and prescriptive software safety certification: a comparative study. Saf. Sci. 59, 55–71 (2013). https://doi.org/10.1016/j.ssci.2013.04.007
10. Hernandez, C., Abella, J.: Timely error detection for effective recovery in light-lockstep automotive systems. IEEE Trans. Comput.-Aided Integr. Circuits Syst. 34, 1718–1729 (2015). https://doi.org/10.1109/TCAD.2015.2434958
11. Gallina, B.: A model-driven safety certification method for process compliance. In: IEEE International Symposium Soft Reliability Engineering Workshops, pp. 204–209 (2014). https://doi.org/10.1109/ISSREW.2014.30
12. Areias, C., Cunha, J.C., Iacono, D., Rossi, F.: Towards certification of automotive software. In: IEEE International Symposium Software Reliability Engineering, pp. 491–496 (2014). https://doi.org/10.1109/ISSREW.2014.54
13. Adedjouma, M., Hu, H.: Process model tailoring and assessment for automotive certification objectives, pp. 503–508. IEEE (2014). https://doi.org/10.1109/ISSREW.2014.23
14. Mader, R., Armengaud, E., Grießnig, G., Kreiner, C., Steger, C., Weiß, R.: OASIS: an automotive analysis and safety engineering instrument. Reliab. Eng. Syst. Saf. 120, 150–162 (2013). https://doi.org/10.1016/j.ress.2013.06.045

15. OpenCert: Evolutionary Assurance and Certification for Safety-Critical Systems n.d. https://
www.polarsys.org/introducing-opencert-evolutionary-assurance-and-certification-safety-
critical-systems. Accessed 13 Mar 2018

16. Rajan, A., Wahl, T. (eds.): EU Project CESAR - Cost-Efficient Methods and Processes for
Safety-Relevant Embedded Systems. Springer, Heidelberg (2013). https://doi.org/10.1007/
978-3-7091-1387-5_1

17. EU project SafeCer - Safety Certification of Software-Intensive Systems with Reusable
Components. http://safecer.eu/. Accessed 20 Apr 2017

18. EU project OPENCOSS - Open Platform for EvolutioNary Certification of Safety-critical
Systems. http://opencoss-project.eu. Accessed 20 Apr 2017

19. Barry, M.R.: CertWare: a workbench for safety case production and analysis, pp. 1–10.
IEEE (2011). https://doi.org/10.1109/AERO.2011.5747648

20. International Standard Organisation. Road vehicles – Functional safety; ISO 26262 (2011)

21. Taylor, W., Krithivasan, G., Nelson, J.J.: System safety and ISO 26262 compliance for
automotive lithium-ion batteries, pp. 1–6. IEEE (2012). https://doi.org/10.1109/ISPCE.2012.
6398297

22. Morris, J., Lee, G., Parker, K., Bundell, G.A., Lam, C.P.: Software component certification.
Computer **34**, 30–36 (2001). https://doi.org/10.1109/2.947086

23. Voas, J.M.: Certifying off-the-shelf software components. Computer **31**, 53–59 (1998).
https://doi.org/10.1109/2.683008

24. Verma, A.K., Ajit, S., Karanki, D.R. (eds.): Software Reliability. Reliability Safety
Engineering, pp. 193–228. Springer, London (2010). https://doi.org/10.1007/978-1-84996-
232-2

25. Lyu, M.R.: Software reliability engineering: a roadmap, pp. 153–170. IEEE (2007). https://
doi.org/10.1109/FOSE.2007.24

26. Currit, P.A., Dyer, M., Mills, H.D.: Certifying the reliability of software. IEEE Trans. Softw.
Eng. **SE-12**, 3–11 (1986). https://doi.org/10.1109/TSE.1986.6312914

27. Panesar-Walawege, R.K., Sabetzadeh, M., Briand, L.: Using model-driven engineering for
managing safety evidence: challenges, vision and experience, pp. 7–12. IEEE (2011). https://
doi.org/10.1109/WoSoCER.2011.8

28. Wohlin, C., Regnell, B.: Reliability certification of software components. IEEE Comput.
Soc. 56–65 (1998). https://doi.org/10.1109/ICSR.1998.685730

29. Quigley, M., Conley, K., Gerkey, B., Faust, J., Foote, T., Leibs, J., et al.: ROS: an open-
source robot operating system. In: ICRA Workshop Open Source Software, vol. 3, p. 5
(2009)

30. Staranowicz, A., Mariottini, G.L.: A survey and comparison of commercial and open-source
robotic simulator software, p. 1. ACM Press (2011). https://doi.org/10.1145/2141622.
2141689

31. Noh, S., Han, W.-Y.: Collision avoidance in on-road environment for autonomous driving,
pp. 884–889. IEEE (2014). https://doi.org/10.1109/ICCAS.2014.6987906

32. Silva, M., Garrote, L., Moita, F., Martins, M., Nunes, U.: Autonomous electric vehicle:
steering and path-following control systems. In: IEEE Mediterranean Electrotechnical
Conference, pp. 442–445. (2012). https://doi.org/10.1109/MELCON.2012.6196468

33. Pérez, J., et al.: Robotic manipulation within the underwater mission planning context. In:
Carbone, G., Gomez-Bravo, F. (eds.) Motion and Operation Planning of Robotic Systems.
MMS, vol. 29, pp. 495–522. Springer, Cham (2015). https://doi.org/10.1007/978-3-319-
14705-5_17

34. Wassyng, A., Maibaum, T., Lawford, M., Bherer, H.: Software certification: is there a case against safety cases? In: Calinescu, R., Jackson, E. (eds.) Monterey Workshop 2010. LNCS, vol. 6662, pp. 206–227. Springer, Heidelberg (2011). https://doi.org/10.1007/978-3-642-21292-5_12
35. Spriggs, J.: GSN - The Goal Structuring Notation. A Structured Approach to Presenting Arguments. Springer, London (2012). https://doi.org/10.1007/978-1-4471-2312-5
36. Fachet, R.: Re-use of software components in the IEC-61508 certification process, vol. 2004, p. 8. IEEE (2004). https://doi.org/10.1049/ic:20040532
37. Sârbu, C., Johansson, A., Suri, N., Nagappan, N.: Profiling the operational behavior of OS device drivers. Empir. Softw. Eng. **15**, 380–422 (2010). https://doi.org/10.1007/s10664-009-9122-z
38. Jiang, B., Chen, P., Chan, W.K., Zhang, X.: To what extent is stress testing of android TV applications automated in industrial environments? IEEE Trans. Reliab. 1–17 (2015). https://doi.org/10.1109/TR.2015.2481601
39. Baker, R., Habli, I.: An empirical evaluation of mutation testing for improving the test quality of safety-critical software. IEEE Trans. Softw. Eng. **39**, 787–805 (2013). https://doi.org/10.1109/TSE.2012.56
40. Davis, R.I., Burns, A., Bril, R.J., Lukkien, J.J.: Controller area network (CAN) schedulability analysis: refuted, revisited and revised. R.-Time Syst. **35**, 239–272 (2007). https://doi.org/10.1007/s11241-007-9012-7

REMEDY 2018 Workshop

Introduction to the International Workshop on Formal Models for Mastering Multifaceted Systems (REMEDY 2018)

Welcome to the Workshop on 'Formal Models for Mastering Multifaceted Systems' which was held in Marrakech on October 24, 2018.

My colleague and friend Yamine Ait Ameur suggested to organize this satellite event at the MEDI conference. Patricia Derler (National Instruments, Berkeley, USA) and Martin Törngren (KTH Royal Institute of Technology, Stockholm, Sweden) accepted despite their numerous engagements to contribute to organizing and managing the scientific aspects of the workshop as co-chairs. Their encouragement and dedication contributed to the success of this workshop.

We focused the topics of the workshop on "Formal Models for Mastering Multi-faceted Systems." The emphasis was on not only the main topics in models and engineering of MEDI, but also our daily concerns in teaching and research activities.

Indeed, numerous software-based systems are distinguished by their needs to handle simultaneously multiple facets: complex behaviors, intensive data, continuous reactions with their environment, evolving physical environments, time properties, robustness to failure, etc.

Modeling, analyzing, and building such multifaceted systems are still challenging research concerns. The purpose of the workshop is to connect researchers and praction working on various aspects of such systems that involve heterogeneous components, distributed and embedded systems, reactive systems, etc.

We thank the colleagues and students who contributed, despite the short submission deadlines, by proposing their work to the workshop and also the authors who actively participated at the conference.

We believe that the meeting in Marrakech gave attendees the opportunity to initiate relationships and stimulate fruitful discussions and collaborations for the future.

We want to express our deep gratitude to the Program Committee members who reviewed and evaluated within a tight schedule all the submitted papers.

We also thank all the MEDI Conference organizers and the satellite workshop organizers for their hard works.

October 2018

Patricia Derler
Christian Attiogbé
Martin Törngren

REMEDY 2018 Workshop Chairs

Patricia Derler	National Instruments, USA
Christian Attiogbé	University of Nantes, France
Martin Törngren	KTH, Sweden

REMEDY 2018 Program Committee

Christian Attiogbé	University of Nantes, France
Yamine Ait Ameur	ENSEEIHT, France
Luis Barbosa	University of Minho, Portugal
Mohamed Tahar Bhiri	University of Sfax, Tunisia
Maurice ter Beek	ISTI-CNR Pisa, Italie
Imen Ben Hafaiedh	University of Tunis El Manar, Tunisia
DeJiu Chen	KTH, Sweden
Patricia Derler	National Instruments, USA
Mamoun Filali	IRIT, France
Stephan Hallerstade	Aarhus University, Denmark
Eric Madelaine	Inria Sophia Antipolis, France
Dominique Mery	University of Nancy, France
Mohamed Messabihi	University of Tlemcen, Algeria
Hassan Mountassir	University of Besançon, France
Manuel Núñez	Universidad Complutense of Madrid, Spain
Jérôme Rocheteau	ICAM/LS2N, France
Martin Torngren	KTH, Sweden
Stavros Tripakis	University of Aalto, Finland
Marina Walden	Abo Akademi University, Finland
Virginie Wiels	ONERA, France

Reliability in Fully Probabilistic Event-B: How to Bound the Enabling of Events

Syrine Aouadi and Arnaud Lanoix[⊠]

University of Nantes/LS2N UMR CNRS 6004, Nantes, France
syrine.aouadi@eleves.ec-nantes.fr
arnaud.lanoix@univ-nantes.fr

Abstract. In previous work, we have proposed a fully probabilistic version of Event-B where all the non-deterministic choices are replaced by probabilistic ones and, particularly, the events are equipped with weights that allow us to consider their enabling probability. In this work, we focus on the reliability of the system by proposing to constraint the probability of enabling an event (or a set of events) to control its importance with regard to the intended system behaviour. We add a specific upper bound which must limit the enabling probabilities of the chosen events and we consider the necessary proof obligations to check that the considered events respect the bound. At the end, we illustrate our work by presenting a case study specified in probabilistic Event-B and where bounding the enabling of some events is mandatory.

Keywords: Event-B · Probabilistic Event-B
Probabilistic properties · Reliability · Weight · Proof obligations

1 Introduction

Systems using randomized algorithms [1], probabilistic protocols [2] or failing components become more and more complex. It is then necessary to add new modeling features in order to take into account the inherent complexity of the system properties such as reliability [3], responsiveness [4,5], continuous evolution, energy consumption etc. One of these features is probabilistic reasoning, which can be used in order to introduce uncertainty in a model or to mimic randomized behavior. Probabilistic modeling formalisms have therefore been developed in the past, mainly extending automata-based formalisms [6,7]. Abstraction [8,9], refinement [10] and model-checking algorithms [11,12] have been successfully studied in this context. However, the introduction of probabilistic reasoning in proof-based modeling formalisms has been, to the best of our knowledge, quite limited [13–20]. Although translations from proof-based models to automata-based models are always possible, the use of automata-based verification techniques in the context of proof-based models is most of the time inconvenient because of possible state-space explosion introduced in the translation.

Event-B [21] is a proof-based formal method used for modeling discrete systems. It is equipped with *Rodin* [22], an open toolset for modeling and proving

© Springer Nature Switzerland AG 2018
E. H. Abdelwahed et al. (Eds.): MEDI 2018 Workshops, CCIS 929, pp. 185–199, 2018.
https://doi.org/10.1007/978-3-030-02852-7_17

systems. This toolset can easily be extended, which makes Event-B a good candidate for introducing probabilistic reasoning in a proof-based modeling formalism.

So far, several research works have focused on the extension of Event-B to allow the expression of probabilistic information in Event-B models. In [23], Abrial *et al.* have summarized the difficulties of embedding probabilities into Event-B. This paper suggests that probabilities need to be introduced as a refinement of *non-determinism*. In Event-B, non-determinism occurs in several places such as the choice between enabled events in a given state, the choice of the parameter values in a given event, and the choice of the value given to a variable through some non-deterministic assignments. To the best of our knowledge, the existing works on extending Event-B with probabilities have mostly focused on refining non-deterministic assignments into probabilistic assignments. Other sources of non-determinism have been left untouched. In [24], Hallerstede *et al.* propose to focus on a qualitative aspect of probability. They refine non-deterministic assignments into *qualitative* probabilistic assignments where the actual probability values are not specified, and adapt the Event-B semantics and proof obligations to this new setting. In [25], the same authors study the refinement of qualitative probabilistic Event-B models and propose tool support inside Rodin. Other works [26–28] have extended this approach by refining non-deterministic assignments into *quantitative* probabilistic assignments where, unlike in [24], the actual probability values are specified. This new proposition is then exploited in order to assess several system properties such as reliability and responsiveness.

Unfortunately, sources of non-determinism other than assignments have been left untouched, although the authors argue that probabilistic choice between events or parameter values can be achieved by transformations of the models that embed these choices inside probabilistic assignments. While this is unarguably true, such transformations are not trivial and greatly impede the understanding of Event-B models. Moreover, these transformations would need to be included in the refinement chain when designers need it, which would certainly be counter-intuitive to engineers.

In previous works [29, 30] we pursued these works by proposing a probabilistic extension of Event-B and presenting some ways of introducing probabilistic reasoning within Event-B. We have proposed some new syntactic elements for writing fully probabilistic Event-B models in the Event-B framework. The consistency of such models has been expressed, as in standard Event-B, in terms of proof obligations. In the standard Event-B setting, *convergence* is a required property for proving a refinement step as soon as new events are introduced in the model. The counterpart property in the probabilistic setting is *almost-certain convergence*, which has already been studied in [24], in the context of non-deterministic models with only probabilistic assignments. We therefore have exhibited new sufficient conditions, expressed in terms of proof obligations, for the almost-certain convergence of a set of fully probabilistic events. While the conditions we exhibit are more constrained than those from [24] concerning events and parameters, they are also less restrictive concerning probabilistic assignments. Finally, some of the previously mentioned results have been implemented in a prototype plugin for Rodin.

In the probabilistic Event-B context, the probabilistic events are equipped with weights, in order to easily consider the enabling probability of each event in any configuration. In this paper, we extend the previous work by considering a kind of probabilistic invariant that allows us to model and verify properties concerning reliability: we add a specific upper bound to constraint the enabled probability of an event (or a set of events) in order to limit their importance with regards to the system behavior. As in the previous work, we check that the considered events respect the bound by means of new proof obligations. These new proof obligations ensure that in any configurations where the considered event can be enabled, this enabled probability is lower than the considered bound. Finally, we illustrate our work on an industrial simplified case study: the PCB manufacturing and control system [31,32]. Particularly, we show the requirements for applying the enabled bound property on a realistic used system.

Outline. The paper is structured as follows. Section 2 presents the scientific background of this paper in terms of Probabilistic Event-B. In Sect. 3, we focus on how to constraint the enabling of events, and the necessary proof obligations on such models. Section 4 introduces our case study: a simple PCB manufacturing and control system which illustrate the use of the previously mentioned property. Finally, Sect. 5 concludes the paper.

2   Preliminaries: Probabilistic Event-B

Event-B [21] is a formal method used for the development of complex discrete systems. Systems are described in Event-B by means of models. We have previously extended standard Event-B models to introduce probabilistic reasoning. In Event-B, non-determinism can appear in three places: the choice of the enabled event to be executed, the choice of the parameter value to be taken and the choice of the value to be assigned to a given variable in a non-deterministic assignment. To obtain a *fully probabilistic Event-B model*, we have proposed to replace all these non-deterministic choices with probabilistic ones.

```
MODEL
   M
VARIABLES
   v̄
INVARIANTS
   I(v̄)
VARIANT
   V(v̄)
EVENTS
   Init ≙ ...
   e₁ ≙ ...
   ...
   eₙ ≙ ...
END
```

For the sake of simplicity, we assume in the rest of the paper that a fully probabilistic Event-B model is expressed by a tuple $M = (\bar{v},\ I(\bar{v}),\ V(\bar{v}),\ \mathsf{PEvts},\ \mathsf{Init})$ where $\bar{v} = \{v_1 \ldots v_n\}$ is a set of variables, $I(\bar{v})$ is an invariant, $V(\bar{v})$ is an (optional) variant used for proving the (almost-certain) convergence of the model, PEvts is a set of probabilistic events and $\mathsf{Init} \in \mathsf{PEvts}$ is the initialization event. The invariant $I(\bar{v})$ is a conjunction of predicates over the variables of the system specifying properties that must always hold.

Probabilistic Events. A probabilistic event has the following structure where e_i is the name of the event, $W_i(\bar{v})$ is the weight of the event, $\bar{t} = \{t_1 \ldots t_n\}$ represents the (optional) set of parameters of the event, $G_i(\bar{t}, \bar{v})$ is the (optional) guard of the event and $S_i(\bar{t}, \bar{v})$ is the action of the event. A probabilistic event is *enabled* in a given valuation of the variables (also called a configuration) if and only if *(i)* there exists a parameter valuation such that its guard $G_i(\bar{t}, \bar{v})$ is fulfilled in this context and *(ii)* its weight $W_i(\bar{v})$ is strictly positive.

In standard Event-B, when several events are enabled, the event to be executed is chosen non-deterministically. The weight $W_i(\bar{v})$ of the event resolves this non-deterministic choice: in configurations where several probabilistic events are enabled, the probability of enabling one of them will therefore be computed as the ratio of its weight against the total value of the weights of all enabled events in this state. Moreover, for the sake of expressibility, we propose to express the weight $W_i(\bar{v})$ of a probabilistic event e_i as an expression over the vari-

```
event e_i ≙
weight
  W_i(v̄)
any t̄ where
  G_i(t̄,v̄)
then
  SP_i(t̄,v̄)
end
```

ables $\bar{v}$ of the fully probabilistic Event-B model. The probability of enabling a given event can therefore evolve as the system progresses.

For the events equipped with parameters $\bar{t}$, a valuation of the parameters is chosen such that the guard $G_i(\bar{t}, \bar{v})$ of the event is satisfied. In standard Event-B, when there are several such parameter valuations, one of them is selected non-deterministically. We therefore have proposed to replace this non-deterministic choice by a uniform choice over all parameter valuations ensuring that the guard of the event is satisfied.

Probabilistic Assignments. The action $SP_i(\bar{t}, \bar{v})$ of a probabilistic event may contain several assignments that are executed in parallel. An assignment can be expressed in one of the following forms:

- **Deterministic assignment:** $x := E(\bar{t}, \bar{v})$ means that the expression $E(\bar{t}, \bar{v})$ is assigned to the variable x.
- **Predicate probabilistic assignment:** $x :\oplus Q(\bar{t}, \bar{v}, x, x')$ means that the variable x is assigned a new value x' such that the predicate $Q(\bar{t}, \bar{v}, x, x')$ is satisfied. Instead of choosing non-deterministically among the values of x' such that the predicate $Q(\bar{t}, \bar{v}, x, x')$ is true as in standard predicate non-deterministic assignments, we propose to choose this new value using an uniform distribution.
- **Enumerated probabilistic assignment:** $x := E_1(\bar{t}, \bar{v}) @ p_1 \oplus \ldots \oplus E_n(\bar{t}, \bar{v}) @ p_n$ means that the variable x is assigned the expression E_i with probability p_i. In order to define a correct probability distribution, each p_i must be strictly positive and smaller or equal to 1, and they must sum up to 1. Although rational numbers are not natively handled in Event-B, we assume that an adequate context is present. That can be done by defining a "Rational" theory in Rodin using the theory plug-in providing capabilities to define and use mathematical extensions to the Event-B language and the proving infrastructure [33].

Before-After Predicate and Semantics. The formal semantics of an assignment is described by means of a before-after predicate (BA) $Q(\bar{t}, \bar{v}, x, x')$, which describes the relationship between the values of the variable before (x) and after (x') the execution of an assignment.

- The BA of a deterministic assignment is $x' = E(\bar{t},\bar{v})$.
- The BA of a predicate probabilistic assignment is $Q(\bar{t}, \bar{v}, x, x')$.
- The BA of an enumerated probabilistic assignment is $x' \in \{E_1(\bar{t}, \bar{v}) \ldots E_n(\bar{t}, \bar{v})\}$.

Recall that the action $S_i(\bar{t}, \bar{v})$ of a given event e_i may contain several assignments that are executed in parallel. Assume that $v_1 \ldots v_i$ are the variables assigned in $S_i(\bar{t}, \bar{v})$ – variables $v_{i+1} \ldots v_n$ are thus not modified – and let $Q(\bar{t}, \bar{v}, v_1, v'_1) \ldots Q(\bar{t},\bar{v},v_i,v'_i)$ be their corresponding BA. Then the BA $S_i(\bar{t}, \bar{v}, \bar{v}')$ of the event action $S_i(\bar{t}, \bar{v})$ is:

$$S_i(\bar{t},\bar{v},\bar{v}') \;\hat{=}\; Q(\bar{t},\bar{v},v_1,v'_1) \;\wedge\; \ldots \;\wedge\; Q(\bar{t},\bar{v},v_i,v'_i) \;\wedge\; (v'_{i+1}{=}v_{i+1}) \;\wedge\; \ldots (v'_n{=}v_n)$$

Proof Obligations. The consistency of a standard Event-B model is characterized by means of *proof obligations* (POs) formally defined in [21] which must be discharged. Discharging all the necessary POs allows to prove that the model is sound with respect to some underlaying behavioral semantics. The consistency of a fully probabilistic Event-B model is also characterized by means of POs to be discharged. Among all of them, the first ones are adaptation of the standard POs and the second ones are POs specific to fully probabilistic Event-B.

In the following, we recall the adaptation of the most important of the standard POs: (event/pINV) for *invariant preservation*, which states that the invariant still holds after the execution of each probabilistic event in the Event-B model M. Given an event e_i with a guard $G_i(\bar{t}, \bar{v})$ and an action $S_i(\bar{t}, \bar{v})$, this PO is expressed as follows:

$$I(\bar{v}) \;\wedge\; G_i(\bar{t},\bar{v}) \;\wedge\; W_i(\bar{v}) > 0 \;\wedge\; SP_i(\bar{t},\bar{v},\bar{v}') \;\vdash\; I(\bar{v}') \qquad \text{(event/INV)}$$

Then, we give some of the new POs specific to fully probabilistic Event-B:

- we impose that the expression $W_i(\bar{v})$ representing the weight of a given probabilistic event must evaluate to natural numbers.

$$I(\bar{v}) \;\wedge\; G_i(\bar{t},\bar{v}) \;\vdash\; W_i(\bar{v}) \in NAT \qquad \text{(event/WGHT/NAT)}$$

- In order to be able to use a discrete uniform distribution over the set of parameter valuations ensuring that the guard of a probabilistic event is satisfied, we impose that this set must be finite.

$$I(\bar{v}) \;\vdash\; \text{finite}\,(\{\bar{t} \mid G_i(\bar{t},\bar{v})\}) \qquad \text{(event/param/pWD)}$$

- Probability values p_i in enumerated probabilistic assignments are strictly positive and smaller or equal to 1.

$$\vdash \; 0 < p_i \leq 1 \qquad\qquad\qquad\qquad \text{(event/assign/pWD1)}$$

- The sum of the probability values $p_1 \ldots p_n$ in enumerated probabilistic assignments must be equal to 1.

$$\vdash \; p_1 + \ldots + p_n = 1 \qquad\qquad\qquad \text{(event/assign/pWD2)}$$

Feasibility of enumerated probabilistic assignments is trivial: as soon as at least one expression $E_i(\bar{t}, \bar{v})$ is present and well-defined, it always returns a value.

- In order to define a discrete uniform distribution over the set of values of a variable x making the predicate $Q_x(\bar{t}, \bar{v}, x')$ of the corresponding assignment satisfied, we impose that this set must be finite.

$$I(\bar{v}) \wedge G_i(\bar{t},\bar{v}) \wedge W_i(\bar{v}) > 0 \;\vdash\; \text{finite } (\{x' \mid Q_x(\bar{t},\bar{v},x')\})$$
$$\text{(event/assign/pWD3)}$$

Feasibility of predicate probabilistic assignments is ensured by the standard feasibility PO [21] inherited from Event-B. It ensures that the set $\{x' \mid Q_x(\bar{t}, \bar{v}, x')\}$ is not empty.

3   Contribution: Limiting the Enabling of Probabilistic Events

We recall that, in standard Event-B, when several events are enabled in a given configuration, the event to be executed is chosen non-deterministically. In order to resolve this non-deterministic choice, we have proposed to equip each event with a *weight* $W_i(\bar{v})$ that is an expression over the variables $\bar{v}$ of the fully probabilistic Event-B model. Note that using weights instead of actual probability values is convenient as the set of enabled events evolves with the configurations of the system. Using probability values instead would require to normalize them in all configurations.

Enabling Probability. A probabilistic event is enabled in a given configuration if and only if there exists a parameter valuation such that its guard $G_i(\bar{t}, \bar{v})$ is fulfilled and its weight $W_i(\bar{v})$ is strictly positive. In configurations where several probabilistic events are enabled, the probability of choosing one of them will therefore be computed as the ratio of its weight against the total value of the weights of all enabled events in this configuration. Formally, this *enabling probability* is defined as follows.

Let $M = (\bar{v}, I(\bar{v}), V(\bar{v}), \mathsf{PEvts}, \mathsf{Init})$ be a fully probabilistic Event-B model. Given an event e_i in PEvts and a valuation σ of the variables $\bar{v}$ of the model, the enabling probability of e_i in σ is formally defined by

$$P(e_i, \sigma) = \frac{[\sigma]W_i(\bar{v})}{\sum_{e_j \in PEvts} \left([\sigma]W_j(\bar{v} \mid [\sigma]W_j(\bar{v}) > 0 \land \exists\, \theta'.[\sigma,\theta']G_j(\bar{v},\bar{t}) = \top\right)} \quad (1)$$

$$\text{if } \exists\, \theta.[\sigma,\theta]G_i(\bar{v},\bar{t}) = \top \text{ and } [\sigma]W_i(\bar{v}) > 0 \quad (2)$$

$$= 0 \text{ otherwise} \quad (3)$$

where θ and θ' are possible valuations of the parameters $\bar{t}$.

The probability of enabling a given event can therefore evolve as the system progresses. Equation (1) represents the ratio of the weight of the considered event e_i against the total value of the weights of all the enabled events (including the weight of e_i), when Eq. (2) is verified i.e. the event e_i is enabled. Otherwise as Eq. (3) the enabling probability of e_i is equal to 0.

Enabled Bound Property. In standard and probabilistic Event-B, the events for which we want to study their termination are annotated as **convergent**. We adopt the same principle and we annotate by **bounded** the events for which we want to limit their enabling probabilities. We also introduce a specific upper bound $EB(\bar{v})$ (notice **ENABLED_BOUND** into the B model) as an expression over the variables $\bar{v}$ of the fully probabilistic Event-B model to limit the enabling probability of the **bounded** events. Note that this upper bound can evolve as the system progresses.

Considering a **bounded** event e_i, it must verify the *enabled bound property*, i.e. in all configurations in which e_i could be enabled, then its enabling probability must be lower than or equal to the value of the enabled upper bound $EB(\bar{v})$ in that configuration. Formally

$$\forall \sigma.\ \exists\, \theta.[\sigma,\theta]G_i(\bar{v},\bar{t}) = \top \land [\sigma]W_i(\bar{v}) > 0 \Rightarrow P(e_i,\sigma) \leq [\sigma]EB(\bar{v}) \quad (4)$$

Proof Obligations. Checking standard or probabilistic Event-B models consists of discharging proof obligations. We then propose necessary POs to check the above mentioned enabled bound property on a fully probabilistic Event-B model.

Let $M = (\bar{v},\ I(\bar{v}),\ V(\bar{v}),\ PEvts,\ Init)$ be a fully probabilistic Event-B model. Let e_i be a **bounded** event from $PEvts = \{e_1 \ldots e_i \ldots e_n\}$. Let $EB(\bar{v})$ be the enabled upper bound. Then, the necessary POs are defined as follows.

1. The enabled upper bound $EB(\bar{v})$ must always be a rational number i.e. a positive non-zero value strictly lower than 1:

$$\boxed{\quad I(\bar{v}) \vdash 0 < EB(\bar{v}) < 1 \qquad\qquad\qquad (\text{eBOUND/WD}) \quad}$$

2. Each **bounded** event e_i satisfies the enabled bound property (see Eq. (4)), i.e. its enabling probability is always lower than or equal to the enabled upper bound.

$$\boxed{\begin{array}{l} I(\bar{v}) \land G_i(\bar{t},\bar{v}) \land W_i(\bar{v}) > 0 \vdash \qquad\qquad (\text{event/WGHT/eBOUND}) \\[2mm] \dfrac{W_i(\bar{v})}{\sum (e_j).(W_j(\bar{v}) \mid G_j(\bar{t},\bar{v}) \land W_j(\bar{v}) > 0)} \leq EB(\bar{v}) \end{array}}$$

4 Case Study: The PCB Manufacturing and Control System

In this section, our purpose is to highlight on a concrete case study the interest of the enabled bound property. We then propose a fully probabilistic Event-B model of a simplified industrial case study: the Printed Circuit Boards (PCB) manufacturing and control system [31, 32]. This case study interests electronic cards manufacturers that face the ever increasing requirement of reducing their cost and improving products quality. That requires having a fine control strategy through which we evaluate the produced electronic cards by detecting possible errors from the tests performed.

In the considered case study, we will focus on two kinds of tests: the ICT ("In Circuit Testing") tests check the presence of all the attempted components and the FCT ("Functional Testing") tests verify the functional behavior of each PCB.

Our proposed model simply abstracts the manufacturing and control process. We only identify each manufactured card by a unique identifier and we introduce two events, one representing the fair cards manufacturing, the other modeling the deficient cards manufacturing. The PCB manufacturing and control system must provide a history about the produced PCB and the error reporting.

Informal description of this system imposes two probabilistic requirements

(i) the risk of having a deficient card must decrease with the increasing number of reported errors;

(ii) having fair cards increases with correct cards production rise.

In fact, the manufacturing and control system must be a self-corrective maneuver on the PCB production line.

Event-B Context. To model the static aspects of the system, we propose the Event-B context as depicted by Fig. 1. Precisely,

- the constant Max_Cards models the maximum number of cards that can be produced whereas the constant Max_Errors models the maximum number of errors that can be reported;
- the set Error_State represents the tree kind of errors that can be reported during the test phase:
  - the constant ICT_error designs an "In Circuit" error;
  - the constant FCT_error Designs a "Functional" error;
  - the constant ICT_FCT_error designs a double error, i.e. "In Circuit" and "Functional" errors simultaneously.

Note that Error_State is syntactically expressed as a partition between ICT_error, FCT_error and ICT_FCT_error, i.e. Error_State = {ICT_error, FCT_error, ICT_FCT_error}.

The maximum number of reported errors must be lower than or equal to the maximum number of produced cards. Only one kind of error is reported for a specific card.

```
CONTEXT
  PCBctx
SETS
  Error_State
CONSTANTS
  Max_Cards
  Max_Errors
  ICT_Error
  FCT_Error
  ICT_FCT_Error
AXIOMS
    Max_Cards ∈ ℕ₁
  ∧ Max_Errors ∈ℕ₁
  ∧ partition (Error_State,{ICT_Error},{FCT_Error},{ICT_FCT_Error})
  ∧ Max_Errors ≤ Max_Cards
END
```

Fig. 1. PCB manufacturing system context

Event-B Model. We propose to model the system's state by means of three state variables, as depicted by Fig. 2:

– the set Cards represents all the produced cards;
– the partial function Errors models the history of all the cards which have reporting errors, i.e. it associates to each necessary card, the corresponding reported error;
– the variable Next_ID identifies the nextly produced card.

We then model the dynamic of the system using three (probabilistic) events.

– the event init initializes the model: regarding Cards and Errors, they are initialized to empty sets and Next_ID is initialized to any chosen integer value (10 on the illustrated specification);
– the event Manufacturing_OK models the fair cards production. Cards could be produced when the maximum number of produced cards is not reached and the maximum number of errors is also not reached; The number of the newly produced card is added to Cards, and the Next_ID is incremented;
– the event Manufacturing_Error represents the production of deficient cards: The event's parameter error chooses a kind of errors among the Error_State, i.e. a "In Circuit" error, a "Functional" error or the both simultaneously. The newly produced card is also registered, the Next_ID is incremented and the reported error is added to Errors: Next_ID ↦ error.

```
MODEL
  PCBsystem
SEES
  PCBctx
VARIABLES
  Cards
  Errors
  Next_ID
INVARIANTS
    Cards ⊆ ℕ₁
  ∧ Errors ∈ Cards⇸Error_State
  ∧ Next_ID ∈ ℕ₁
  ∧ finite (Cards)
  ∧ finite (Errors)
  ∧ card(Cards) ≤ Max_Cards
  ∧ card(Errors) ≤ Max_Errors
ENABLED_BOUND
  (Max_Cards+card(Cards)+1) / (Max_Cards+card(Cards)+Max_Errors−card(Errors)+2)
EVENTS
  event init ≙
  begin
    Next_ID:= 10
    Cards := ∅
    Error := ∅
  end
  event Manufacturing_OK ≙
  weight
    Max_Cards + 1 + card(Cards)
  when
    card(Cards) < Max_Cards ∧ card(Errors) ≤ Max_Errors
  then
    Cards := Cards ∪ {Next_ID}
    Next_ID := Next_ID + 1
  end
  event Manufacturing_Error ≙
  bounded
  weight
    Max_Errors + 1 − card(Errors)
  any error where
    error ∈ Error_State ∧ card(Cards) < Max_Cards ∧ card(Errors) < Max_Errors
  then
    Cards := Cards ∪ {Next_ID}
    Next_ID := Next_ID + 1
    Errors := Errors ∪ {Next_ID ↦error}
  end
END
```

Fig. 2. PCB manufacturing system model

We note that the system stops running when the allowed numbers of reported errors or total cards produced are reached.

Probabilities appear in weights associated to each events and in the uniform choice between the kind of errors in the event Manufacturing_Error. We recall that informal description of this system imposes two probabilistic requirements: the risk of having a deficient card must decrease with the increasing number of reported errors and having fair cards increases with cards production rising, due to the manufacturing and control system must be a self-corrective maneuver on the PCB production line. In other words, the more errors are reported, the less errors will be reported, whereas the more cards are produced, the more fair care will be produced. As the events Manufacturing_OK and Manufacturing_Error will be enabled simultaneously, their respective probabilities computed from their weights translate the requirements:

- the weight of the event Manufacturing_OK increases with the number of produced cards, that corresponds to the requirement "the more cards are produced, the more fair care will be produced";
- the weight of the event Manufacturing_Error decreases with the number of reported errors, that correspond to the requirement "the more errors are reported, the less errors will be reported".

To illustrate the attempted behavior of the specified system, we give in Fig. 3 a sub-part of the corresponding probabilistic transition system, with Max_Errors fixed to 2 and Max_Cards fixed to 3.

Verification. We consider that the consistency of the Event-B model PCBsystem presented above is verified by discharging all the necessary consistency proof obligations. We only focus on the verification of the *enabled bound property* depicted in Sect. 3. we annotate by **bounded** the event Manufacturing_Error and we add an **ENABLED_BOUND**: the enabling probability of Manufacturing_Error must be always limited by the value of the **ENABLED_BOUND**. We have chosen as **ENABLED_BOUND** an expression which corresponds to the enabling probability of the event Manufacturing _OK to ensure that always errors are reported less than fair cards are produced; it is a specific case: in a more general case, any expression could be chosen with respect to the case study.

To prove that the enabled bound property is verified, we must discharge the POs (eBOUND/WD) and (event/WGHT/eBOUND). The PO (eBOUND/WD) is instantiated as follows on the Event-B model PCBsystem:

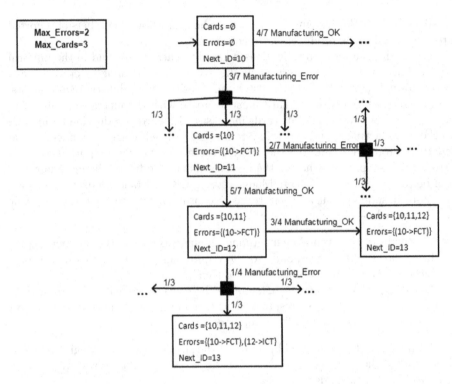

Fig. 3. Extract of the transition system of PCBsystem with Max_Errors = 2 and Max_Cards = 3

```
1   Max_Cards ∈ ℕ₁
2   Max_Errors ∈ℕ₁
3   Max_Errors ≤ Max_Cards
4   Cards ⊆ ℕ₁
5   Errors ∈ Cards↛Error_State
6   finite (Cards)
7   finite (Errors)
8   card(Cards) ≤ Max_Cards
9   card(Errors) ≤ Max_Errors
10  |− − − − − − − − − − − − − − − − − − − − −
11  0 <
12  ( Max_Cards + card(Cards) +1 )
13  / ( Max_Cards + card(Cards) + Max_Errors − card(Errors) +2 )
14  < 1
```

We have to show that the goal (lines 11–14) could be established using the hypotheses (lines 1–9). It is obvious since the sum given line 12 is strictly positive when taking account of the hypotheses lines 1 and 8. The hypotheses lines 5 and 9 imply that the difference (Max_Errors + 1 − Max_Cards) is also strictly positive. Thus, numerator given line 12 is strictly lower than denominator given line 13.

So, the considered fraction is strictly lower than 1 and the PO (eBOUND/WD) is discharged.

Secondly, we instantiate the PO (event/WGHT/eBOUND) in the context of the **bounded** event Manufacturing_Error. Note that the event Manufacturing_Ok could always be triggered with Manufacturing_Error so the PO becomes as follows:

```
1   Max_Cards ∈ ℕ₁
2   Max_Errors ∈ℕ₁
3   Max_Errors ≤ Max_Cards
4   Cards ⊆ ℕ₁
5   Errors ∈ Cards↦Error_State
6   Next_ID ∈ ℕ₁
7    finite (Cards)
8    finite ( Errors )
9   card( Cards ) < Max_Cards
10  card( Errors ) < Max_Errors
11  |— — — — — — — — — — — — — — — — — — —
12  ( Max_Errors − card(Errors) +1)
13  / ( Max_Cards + card(Cards) + Max_Errors − card(Errors) +2 )
14  <
15  ( Max_Cards + card(Cards) +1 )
16  / ( Max_Cards + card(Cards) + Max_Errors − card(Errors) +2 )
```

Clearly, when we take account the hypothesis given line 3, the goal is obviously discharged.

In this example, we showed how demonstrate the necessary POs by hand, but in an industrial context, the Rodin toolset will be used and their embedded automatic provers will be in charge of discharging the POs. Discharging the POs (eBOUND/WD) and (event/WGHT/eBOUND) ensures that the enabled bound property is proved on the PCBsystem, i.e. always errors on cards are less reported than fair cards are produced.

5 Conclusion

Some properties as invariance, deadlock-freeness or convergence are natively managed in Event-B. In our probabilistic extension of Event-B, we have studied the almost certain convergence of a set of events. Moreover, a variety of research works treated the expression and verification of other probabilistic properties such as reliability or reactivity. In this paper we pursue our investigation of probabilistic properties and how to verify them using proof-based techniques. We proposed to express and check an enabled bound property where an event's probability is bounded by a fixed limit described during the requirements specification phase. This property can be used in a wide class of industrial systems, especially those where errors execution have a limit that must not be crossed. Hence, we illustrated a simplified use case of control and manufacturing of printed circuit boards where the enabled bound property was imperative to check if the likelihood of manufacturing an erroneous card can be at most equal to that of producing a correct card.

References

1. Motwani, R., Raghavan, P.: Randomized Algorithms. Chapman & Hall/CRC, Boca Raton (2010)
2. Abrial, J.R., Cansell, D., Méry, D.: A mechanically proved and incremental development of IEEE 1394 tree identify protocol. Form. Asp. Comput. **14**(3), 215–227 (2003)
3. Villemeur, A.: Reliability, Availability, Maintainability and Safety Assessment: Assessment, Hardware, Software and Human Factors, vol. 2. Wiley, Hoboken (1992)
4. Chu, W.W., Sit, C.M.: Estimating task response time with contentions for real-time distributed systems. In: Proceedings of the Real-Time Systems Symposium, pp. 272–281. IEEE (1988)
5. Trivedi, K.S., Ramani, S., Fricks, R.: Recent advances in modeling response-time distributions in real-time systems. Proc. IEEE **91**(7), 1023–1037 (2003)
6. Stoelinga, M.: An introduction to probabilistic automata. Bull. EATCS **78**(176–198), 2 (2002)
7. Puterman, M.L.: Markov Decision Processes: Discrete Stochastic Dynamic Programming. Wiley, Hoboken (2014)
8. Katoen, J.-P.: Abstraction of probabilistic systems. In: Raskin, J.-F., Thiagarajan, P.S. (eds.) FORMATS 2007. LNCS, vol. 4763, pp. 1–3. Springer, Heidelberg (2007). https://doi.org/10.1007/978-3-540-75454-1_1
9. Dehnert, C., Gebler, D., Volpato, M., Jansen, D.N.: On abstraction of probabilistic systems. In: Remke, A., Stoelinga, M. (eds.) Stochastic Model Checking. Rigorous Dependability Analysis Using Model Checking Techniques for Stochastic Systems. LNCS, vol. 8453, pp. 87–116. Springer, Heidelberg (2014). https://doi.org/10.1007/978-3-662-45489-3_4
10. Jonsson, B., Larsen, K.G.: Specification and refinement of probabilistic processes. In: Logic in Computer Science. LICS 1991, pp. 266–277. IEEE (1991)
11. Bianco, A., de Alfaro, L.: Model checking of probabilistic and nondeterministic systems. In: Thiagarajan, P.S. (ed.) FSTTCS 1995. LNCS, vol. 1026, pp. 499–513. Springer, Heidelberg (1995). https://doi.org/10.1007/3-540-60692-0_70
12. Baier, C., Katoen, J.P., et al.: Principles of Model Checking. MIT Press, Cambridge (2008)
13. Haghighi, H., Afshar, M.: A Z-based formalism to specify Markov chains. Comput. Sci. Eng. **2**(3), 24–31 (2012)
14. Sere, K., Troubitsyna, E.: Probabilities in action systems. In: Proceedings of the 8th Nordic Workshop on Programming Theory, pp. 373–387 (1996)
15. Hoang, T.S.: The development of a probabilistic B-method and a supporting toolkit. Ph.D. thesis. The University of New South Wales (2005)
16. Goldreich, O.: Probabilistic proof systems. In: Modern Cryptography, Probabilistic Proofs and Pseudorandomness. AC, vol. 17, pp. 39–72. Springer, Heidelberg (1999). https://doi.org/10.1007/978-3-662-12521-2_2
17. Barthe, G., Fournet, C., Grégoire, B., Strub, P.Y., Swamy, N., Zanella-Béguelin, S.: Probabilistic relational verification for cryptographic implementations. In: ACM SIGPLAN Notices, vol. 49, pp. 193–205. ACM (2014)
18. Hurd, J., McIver, A., Morgan, C.: Probabilistic guarded commands mechanized in HOL. Electron. Not. Theoret. Comput. Sci. **112**, 95–111 (2005)
19. Audebaud, P., Paulin-Mohring, C.: Proofs of randomized algorithms in Coq. Sci. Comput. Program. **74**(8), 568–589 (2009)

20. Hurd, J.: Formal verification of probabilistic algorithms. Ph.D. thesis. University of Cambridge, Computer Laboratory (2003)
21. Abrial, J.R.: Modeling in Event-B: System and Software Engineering. Cambridge University Press, Cambridge (2010)
22. Abrial, J.R., Butler, M., Hallerstede, S., Hoang, T.S., Mehta, F., Voisin, L.: Rodin: an open toolset for modelling and reasoning in Event-B. Int. J. Softw. Tools Technol. Transf. **12**(6), 447–466 (2010)
23. Morgan, C., Hoang, T.S., Abrial, J.-R.: The challenge of probabilistic *Event B— extended abstract—*. In: Treharne, H., King, S., Henson, M., Schneider, S. (eds.) ZB 2005. LNCS, vol. 3455, pp. 162–171. Springer, Heidelberg (2005). https://doi.org/10.1007/11415787_10
24. Hallerstede, S., Hoang, T.S.: Qualitative probabilistic modelling in Event-B. In: Davies, J., Gibbons, J. (eds.) IFM 2007. LNCS, vol. 4591, pp. 293–312. Springer, Heidelberg (2007). https://doi.org/10.1007/978-3-540-73210-5_16
25. Yilmaz, E.: Tool support for qualitative reasoning in Event-B. Ph.D. thesis, Master thesis. ETH Zürich (2010)
26. Tarasyuk, A., Troubitsyna, E., Laibinis, L.: Reliability assessment in Event-B development. In: NODES 2009 (2009)
27. Tarasyuk, A., Troubitsyna, E., Laibinis, L.: Integrating stochastic reasoning into Event-B development. Form. Asp. Comput. **27**(1), 53–77 (2015)
28. Tarasyuk, A., Troubitsyna, E., Laibinis, L.: Towards probabilistic modelling in Event-B. In: Méry, D., Merz, S. (eds.) IFM 2010. LNCS, vol. 6396, pp. 275–289. Springer, Heidelberg (2010). https://doi.org/10.1007/978-3-642-16265-7_20
29. Aouadhi, M.A., Delahaye, B., Lanoix, A.: Moving from Event-B to probabilistic Event-B. In: Proceedings of the 32nd Annual ACM Symposium on Applied Computing. ACM (2017)
30. Aouadhi, M.A., Delahaye, B., Lanoix, A.: Introducing probabilistic reasoning within Event-B. Softw. Syst. Model. (2017)
31. Gaiero, D., Zola, U.: ICT Vs FCT Test: case studies, June 2014
32. Electronics notes: PCP Inspection Techniques and Technologies. https://www.electronics-notes.com/articles/test-methods/automatic-automated-test-ate/pcb-inspection.php
33. Butler, M., Maamria, I.: Practical theory extension in Event-B. In: Liu, Z., Woodcock, J., Zhu, H. (eds.) Theories of Programming and Formal Methods. LNCS, vol. 8051, pp. 67–81. Springer, Heidelberg (2013). https://doi.org/10.1007/978-3-642-39698-4_5

Systematic Construction of Critical Embedded Systems Using Event-B

Pascal André$^{(\boxtimes)}$, Christian Attiogbé, and Arnaud Lanoix

LS2N CNRS UMR 6004 - University of Nantes, Nantes, France
{pascal.andre,christian.attiogbe,arnaud.lanoix}@univ-nantes.fr

Abstract. We propose a method to build critical embedded control systems in a systematic way. The method covers the modelling of both the digital part and the physical environment of a considered system, and their refinement until more concrete levels. It is based on Event-B in order to benefit from its materials, stepwise refinements and tools. Two main processes are distinguished: one to capture the global model, the other to detail the global model; they are made of several refinement steps which are accompanied with guidelines. The precise description of the interface between the digital and physical parts is used to start the modelling process. The recurrent categories of variables and events in control systems are described and used as guidelines to conduct a systematic construction. We illustrate the method with the landing gear system case study.

Keywords: Embedded control systems · Specification method
Event-B patterns

1 Introduction

Modelling and analysis of complex systems without dedicated methods is painful, inefficient and time-consuming. Methods and tools are required for efficient system engineering; this is particularly true for formal software engineering.

Unlike many other types of software, embedded systems are often developed for specific target environments (processors, vehicles, medical devices, etc.) and very often they should run for long times (even years), once they have been implemented in their so called critical environments. Therefore, embedded systems and their construction have stringent robustness requirements; one have to develop them accordingly to get them reliable at runtime. The target environments for the development of each embedded system do not help the advent or the expansion of tools and methods dedicated to this type of software. But, there are numerous models for embedded real-time systems [15].

Considering that *(i)* the requirements for reliability and correct construction of the models and the derived embedded systems are of great importance, and that *(ii)* the development of these systems lacks of methods to guide the developers, we are motivated to contribute to fill the gap between these needs and the state of the art.

© Springer Nature Switzerland AG 2018
E. H. Abdelwahed et al. (Eds.): MEDI 2018 Workshops, CCIS 929, pp. 200–216, 2018.
https://doi.org/10.1007/978-3-030-02852-7_18

In this work we propose a correct-by-construction method dedicated to critical embedded control systems. This method, based on Event-B, is intended to guide step by step the specifier or the engineer to drive its development from requirements to concrete software, defining abstract models, and refining them in a systematic way.

In Sect. 2 we introduce the proposed method with the details of each step. Section 3 illustrates the application of the method on a common case study, called the landing gear system. In Sect. 4 we evaluate the application of the method and the case study and comment related studies. Section 5 concludes this work.

2   A Method to Construct Correct Embedded Systems

We present a stepwise and systematic method (named Heñcher) to construct critical embedded control systems using Event-B. We reuse the approach already established and demonstrated in several case studies [1,9,10], following which complex systems can be constructed by combining (1) horizontal refinement with *feature augmentation* where we have to build a global abstract model of a the whole system (a controller and its physical environment) (Sect. 2.1) and (2) *structural refinement* (making the abstract structures more and more concrete (Sect. 2.2). But we extend it and provide dedicated guidelines at different steps,

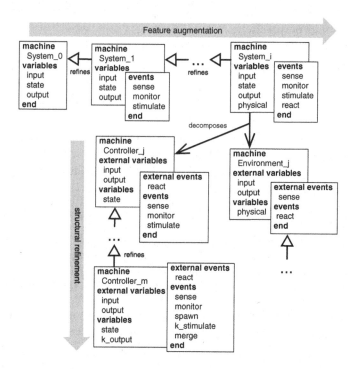

Fig. 1. Synoptic structure of the Event-B models of the construction

which help the developers to reach quickly a correct control system. Figure 1 illustrates the Event-B patterns from the most abstract model which describes only the interface of the controller, to the systematic decomposition into two parts: the Controller and the physical Environment.

2.1 Horizontal Process: Building an Abstract Global Model of the System

The high level state space of any control system can be described by the **elicitation of the interface variables** between the digital part (the controller) and the physical part (the controlled environment) of the considered system.

Step 1: Characterise the abstract model of a considered system

Figure 2 depicts a general principle that may govern the organisation of *event-based models* of control systems. The dashed ovals are representative of the parametric events families; They should be replaced by the effective events related to the logic of a specific case study. Besides, the identified physical devices to be controlled should be precisely listed. The behaviour of each one will be specified later.

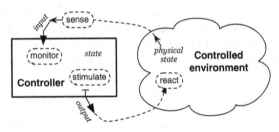

Fig. 2. A generic shape for event-based model of a control system

Step 1.1: Elicit the interface. We distinguish in our method, a first step which consists in the *description of the interface variables of the controller*. There are three categories of variables at the interface of a controller with the controlled environment.

- the *input* variables: they give the sensed state of the environment (the value given by sensors); they are read by the controller;
- the *state* variables: they are set and modified by the controller; they are used for monitoring the whole system;
- the order *output* variables: they are those used to send the orders that stimulate the physical environment; their values will be used by actuators.

These categories of variables will be used at different levels of the modelling and refinement of the system at hand: to introduce the events of the first abstract model and, for refining gradually the first model. Additionally, we have the category of *internal* variables, which are only used inside the controller.

Step 1.2: Elicit the global properties of the system. The required system properties, including safety, liveness and non-functional properties should be explicitly named and listed in their informal form. These properties will be formalised and gradually introduced with their formal form during the various construction steps of our method.

Step 1.3: Start with a first abstract model. Use the interface variables resulting from Step 1.1 to build a first Event-B abstract model. This abstract model comprises in the related B machine clauses, the interface variables together with the appropriate abstract sets and properties which characterise them. This Event-B model will be enriched to obtain a global abstract model of the system including its control part, its physical part and their related properties. Global properties of the system (among those already listed in Step 1.2) should be formalised and introduced according to the available variables. Notice that the enrichment incorporates gradually the details of the physical environment (sensors and actuators) and the corresponding properties.

Step 1.4: List the events of the abstract model. The Event-B abstract model resulting from the previous step will be enriched with a series of events built by defining a family of events related to each category of the interface variables: *sense events, monitor events* and *stimulate events.*

- **Sense events family.** This family gathers the events used to set and to modify the values of the *input* variables. For each variable of this category, define an event named after the variable, with the prefix *sense_*. The link with the physical (state variables of the) environment is done later by refining these events in Step 2.2.
- **Monitor events family.** These events modify the appropriate *state* variables. For each variable of this category, define an event named after the variable with the prefix *monitor_*, to set the variable according to the current state of the controller and the input data.
- **Stimulate events family.** The events of this family modify the order *output* variables; each variable of this category is set with an event named after the variable with the prefix *stmlt_*. These events use the internal variables, the input variables and the output variables. Associated with these events to stimulate the physical devices, we may have as many events to stop the stimulation of the devices; accordingly these events have their name prefixed with stop_.

These three families of events, together with the **reaction events family** introduced later, are compliant with the standard sense-decision-control of the control cycle.

Step 2: Extend the abstract global model

Use *feature augmentation* [1,9,10] to integrate the controlled environment. This is precisely achieved on the basis of the sense events family, which in turn need the description of the controlled environment. The global properties listed before are also gradually formalised in the model, as invariants, as soon as the appropriate variables are available. Two sub-steps are distinguished but no matter their order during the development.

Step 2.1: Introduce the physical environment and the reaction events family. It consists in adding successively to the model, events to propagate the values of interface *output* variables inside the physical environment. These events simulate or stop the behaviours of physical devices via the actuators. The feature augmentation is used to introduce the *physical state* variables, invariants and appropriate behaviours. Depending on the cases, either one simulates the behaviour of the physical devices with an abstract model, or the values of the output variables (from the interface) result in signals sent to the environment. In this last case we do not have dedicated events in the abstract model. Accordingly, the behaviours of the physical devices should be formally described. These behaviours, systematically guarded by the values of the output variables, may impact the state of the environment and finally they may impact the sensors. State automata can often be used to capture the behaviour of a physical device; describing the automata with B events is then straightforward. The description of the physical part behaviour results in the ***family of reaction events***. These events should be named using as prefix the identifier of the physical part that they describe.

Step 2.2: Detail the sense events family. Each event of the *sense family*, updates an *input* variable according to the state of the sensors; for this purpose the event needs the model and the behaviour of its related sensor. Therefore the feature augmentation consists in introducing the model of the sensors and their related behaviour, as variables, invariants and related events. The behaviour of the sensors should consider the possible failures (anomalies, malfunctioning or physical defects); specific events should be described for each such possible failure.

Practically during all the refinement steps, it is recommended to proceed incrementally with several small refinement steps dedicated to variables and events. This is necessary to master the proof complexity.

Step 3: Introduce the specific properties
According to the system one has to build, besides the global properties gradually introduced with the variables, additional specific properties should be integrated at the abstract level to constrain the functioning of the system.

1. *Reachability property with partial ordering:* specific events (not at the same granularity with the Event-B events) with timestamps may be systematically used to order and to reason on reachability properties.
2. *Non functional properties:* specific properties related to nonfunctional requirements should be gradually introduced here. No matter the way they are described, provided that the mathematical support of Event-B is very large, and that external modules may be used to analyse them.

2.2   Vertical Process: Building the Concrete Parts of the System

The aim of this second process is to build the digital part and possibly the physical part of the system. The global Event-B abstract model resulting from the horizontal process should then be decomposed into various parts leading to specific components. At least we have a decomposition into a control software and a physical part. The decomposition can be performed as soon as one want to go into the details of one of the specific part by considering that the other part will stay as it is; that means no modification of the other part cannot be considered when we are refining a given one. Typically, from a decomposition step, the digital part will be refined until code by considering the events and variables of the physical part as they was at the decomposition step.

Step 4: Refine the global abstract model

We recommend to perform structural refinements as needed by the specific model to be refined. New internal B events may be added to refine the events of each family of events (*sense, monitor,* or *stimulate*). The state space variables of the global abstract model may be refined with more details in the invariant. At the end of this step, be sure that, the events of both parts are all in place, that the global required properties of the system are all in place (they cannot be introduced later after the decomposition).

Like with other formal models, an Event-B model can be animated, *i.e.* when appropriate values are provided for the variables in the model, its behaviour can be observed step by step according to the semantics of the model. Animation capabilities are helpful during all the refinement steps where we still have all the events of the global system together; it will not be possible to animate the whole system after its decomposition.

Step 5: Decompose into software and physical parts

A decomposition paradigm is already supported by the Event-B method. It consists in splitting a given machine into several ones which will be refined independently. The decomposition splits the variables of the state space and/or the behaviour of the machine; however resulting machines cannot contradict each other by modifying the variables and their related properties once they have been separated. Two approaches exist for this purpose: the Abrial'style decomposition (called the A-style decomposition) [2] based on shared variables, and the Butler'style decomposition (called the B-style decomposition) [7,19] based on shared events. In the A-style decomposition, events are first split between Event-B sub-components and then shared variables of the sub-components are used to introduce external events in the sub-components; these external events should be refined in the same way. In the B-style decomposition, variables are first partitioned between the sub-components and then shared events (which use the variables of both sub-components) are split between the sub-components according to the used variables.

We adopt the A-style decomposition which is more relevant when considering a list of specific events to be split relatively to a control part and a physical part. The methodological guide to achieve the decomposition is as follows: the digital part is made with all the events defined in the *sense events*, the *monitor events* and the *stimulate events* families whereas the physical environment gathers all the events defined in the *reaction events* families. Moreover, each part must have an abstract view of the other through external variables and events.

Step 6: Refine the control software and the physical environment separately

Step 6.1: Refining the control software. Use *Structural refinements* based on the *stimulate* events family to refine the controller. The involved categories of variables are the *input* variables, the *state* variables and the *output* variables. Typically, the values of the *output* variables are synthesised from the other ones. This can be done through simple control functions or through sub-modules.

When there are sub-modules, the *input* variables may be spawned inside the sub-modules; in the same way *output* variables may be updated by promotion from the sub-modules if any. Therefore one have to incorporate successively in the Event-B model the events to set and modify the *output* variables; they describe the result of the behaviour of the control part. State automata help to catch these behaviours; then the events of the B models encode the automata. We give now some recurrent patterns to help in modelling control part.

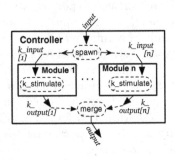

Fig. 3. Modules redundancy

(i) *Composition of several redundant sub-modules:* when a controller is made of several redundant modules, it is straightforward to describe a generic module and use an indexing function to compose several instances of such modules (see Fig. 3).

  – *Encasing variables inside modules:* the values coming from outside one or several modules can be systematically encased inside the modules with a dedicated event that spawn the events.
  – *Promoting variables outside a module:* in a symmetric way, the values going outside a module or several modules can be systematically described using a **promotion pattern** (with a dedicated event) for merging the output variables of the internal computing modules.

(ii) When the modules are not redundant, each one should be refined separately, but the treatment we have described for the inputs and outputs variables is the same.

Step 6.2: Refining the controlled (physical) environment. Many cases can be considered depending on the system to be studied; either the physical devices are already available, or one has to build the physical devices from the formal models, or one has to build a part of the physical devices. Nevertheless, the exchange of signal with actuators is the standard way to act on physical devices.

(i) In the case where the physical devices are available, with the related actuators, the refinement is straightforward; it consists for the events of the physical part to output the correct signal values (for example on/off values are encoded as voltage) as input of the actuators. But the physical devices may be emulated in preliminary studies before implementing the control part on the real devices. Mathematical models and dedicated system engineering tools are available as explained hereafter.

(ii) When the output variables of the controller cannot be immediately encoded as signal values, transformation can be achieved via appropriate mathematical functions and models. This should be done, starting from the requirements and the properties of the previous model, for example by external modules or functions written with tools like Matlab or Simulink[1] or SciLab[2]; related works can be found in [21]. These tools generate executable codes dedicated to the target devices. They are also equipped with specific functions to handle time requirements.

3   A Running Case Study

The proposed method is applied on the *Landing Gear* (LG) case study, a benchmarking example proposed at the ABZ'2014 conference to compare different formal methods in terms of expressivity, performance, and ease of use. A prerequisite for reading this section is the detailed specification of this critical embedded system given in [5]. A summary of the LG system is depicted in Fig. 4.

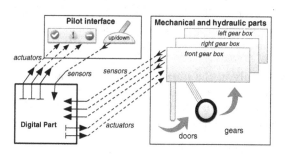

Fig. 4. Global architecture of the LG system

The LG system is in charge of manoeuvring 3 landing boxes: front, left and right. Each landing box contains a landing gear, an associated door and the corresponding hydraulic cylinders in charge to move gears and doors. The system is made of a controller (the *digital part*) and the controlled physical environment (i.e. the 3 landing gear boxes and a pilot interface) which interact via sensors and actuators; the sensors provide to the digital part the information on the state of its physical part; the actuators engage the orders of the controller on the physical part. The physical devices already exist, we will not build them; the challenge deals with the digital control part only (see p. 2 of [5]).

3.1   Horizontal Process: Building an Abstract Global Model of the System

We give the main elements resulting from the successive application of the steps proposed in the method (Sect. 2).

---

[1] http://uk.mathworks.com/products/control/.
[2] http://www.scilab.org.

Step 1.1: Elicitation and modelling of the interface variables. The requirement document listed several triplicated *input* variables: handle, analogical switch, gear states, doors, ⋯. We model (**Step 1.3**) them with a type $TRIPLE = \{1, 2, 3\}$ used as an index of the function variables:

$GEAR$	$= \{FG, LG, RG\}$	$analogical\_switch \in TRIPLE \rightarrow AnalSWSTATE$	
$DOOR$	$= \{FD, RD, LD\}$	$handle \in TRIPLE \rightarrow HSTATE$	
$HSTATE$	$= \{hDown, hUp\}$	$gear\_extended \in (TRIPLE \times GEAR) \rightarrow BOOL$	
$AnalSWSTATE = \{openSW, closedSW\}$		$door\_closed \in (TRIPLE \times DOOR) \rightarrow BOOL$	
...		...	

The function variable $handle \in TRIPLE \rightarrow HSTATE$ captures precisely the requirement $handle_i \in \{hDown, hUp\}$ with $i \in \{1, 2, 3\}$. The *state* variables are the states of the gears, doors, anomalies, etc. They are modelled as follows:

$gears\_locked\_down \in BOOL \quad \wedge \quad gears\_maneuvering \in BOOL \quad \wedge \quad anomaly \in BOOL \wedge \cdots$

The *output* variables hold the values computed for various electro-valves:

$general\_EV \in BOOL \quad \wedge \quad close\_EV \in BOOL \quad \wedge \quad open\_EV \in BOOL \wedge \cdots$

The lights which indicate the position of the gears and doors to the pilot are described as *internal* variables: $greenLight$, $orangeLight$, $redLight$. These variables are bound to the output state variable $gears\_locked\_down$ with an invariant predicate. Another *internal* variable $order$ is used to record the action of the pilot on the handle.

The LG system is controlled digitally in the *normal* mode until an anomaly is detected. A permanent failure leads to an *emergency* mode where the system is controlled analogically. Accordingly the *internal* boolean variable *anomaly* is used to denote that an anomaly has been detected or not.

Step 1.2: Elicitation of the global properties of the LG system. Most of the normal mode requirements are safety properties. Some identified ones are the following:

R_{21}	We can not observe a retraction sequence (consequence of the order hUp) if the handle is down. Using the enumerated set $HSTATE$ which permits only one value from two for the variable *order*.
R_{31}	The gears outgoing event occurs if doors are open locked.
R_{41}	Opening and closing doors electro-valve are not stimulated simultaneously.
R_{51}	It is not possible to stimulate the manoeuvring EV (opening, closure, outgoing or retraction) without stimulating the general EV.

The first Event-B abstract model resulting from **Step 1.3**, gathers all the variables of the interface, their related invariants and initialisations. Event-B contexts are used to model the static part with the various sets and definitions that we have introduced.

Step 1.4: The families of events of the abstract model. A thorough analysis of the two action sequences (*outgoing sequence* and *retraction sequence*) described in the LG system helps us to capture the behaviour of the digital part and to derive the events. We use here state automata to make it clear the interaction between the different components (actions of the pilot, the controller, the orders received by the environment).

In the *sense event* family we have listed for example the event sense_gear to modify the input variable *gear_extended* listed above. In the same way we have listed the other events sense_door, etc. Examples of events we have identified for the *control events* family are: stmlt_general_EV to stimulate the general electro valve, stmlt_door_opening, stmlt_gear_outgoing, stop_stmlt_general_EV, stop_ stmlt_gear_outgoing, etc.

Each one modifies its related variable, for instance the event stop_stmlt_gear_outgoing sets the variable *extend_EV* to $FALSE$. Examples of event we have classified in the *monitor events* family are: monitor_ anomaly, monitor_gears_locked_Down, monitor_ gears_maneuvering.

Step 2: Extension of the abstract global model with the event families. We achieve many refinement steps, by feature augmentation, to integrate gradually the variables and events related to the physical devices: the sensors, the doors and the gears.

Following **Step 2.1**, we define the behaviours of physical devices. For instance, the door behaviour is first captured with a state automata; the transitions of the automata are then described as events. For this purpose we use a transition function $doorState \in DOOR \rightarrow DSTATE$ where $DSTATE = \{ClosedLocked, ClosedUnlocked, OpenUnlocked\}$ is the enumerated set of the identified door states. The set $DOOR$ contains the three door identifiers. The function *doorState* is a total function; this captures the requirement that all the three doors are controlled via the state transition.

The starting transition of the door behaviour is enabled by the *open_EV* order given by the digital part. Therefore there is a synchronisation between the digital part and the motion of the doors. We only give below the description of the starting event Door_openDoor_cl2cu; the other necessary events are similar.

```
event Door_openDoor_cl2cu
/* Door's Behaviour (for the three doors). The first transition of the Door Automata */
where
      @g1  open_EV = TRUE // all the doors Electro Valves are on
      @g2  ran(doorState) = {notOpenLocked}
then
      @a1  doorState := DOOR × {notOpenNotLocked} // door is being opened
end
```

The following event describes an event of the *control event* family.

```
event stmlt_gear_outgoing
/* stimulate gear outgoing electro valve once the three doors are in the open position */
where
        @g0  general_EV = TRUE
        @g1  order = hDown
        @g2  ran(handle) = {hDown}
        @g3  ran(door_closed) = {FALSE} // the three doors are in the open position
```

```
        @g4  ran(door_open) = {TRUE}
        @next  nextOGseq = 3
        @gano  anomaly = FALSE // no anomaly detected
        @notretract  retract_EV = FALSE
then
        @a1  extend_EV := TRUE
        @a2  nextOGseq := nextOGseq + sequenceStep
end
```

The variable $nextOGseq$ controls the evolution of the outgoing sequence; it indicates in the event guards, the next step in the outgoing sequence. We note that the events in the *sense event* family anticipate their real future specifications, which are related to the physical part introduced later. When we have introduced the various events families and the related variables, it becomes clear for us that we have the complete control loop. Following **Step 2** the properties (listed in **Step 1.2** above) are formalised as first order predicates, integrated into the invariant of the abstract model and, proved along the horizontal refinement. As an example, the requirement R_{51} is described as follows.

```
((open_EV = TRUE ∨ close_EV = TRUE ∨ extend_EV = TRUE ∨ retract_EV = TRUE)
   ⇒ general_EV = TRUE)
```

To sum up, the global Event-B abstract model results from a series of refinement of contexts and machines.

Step 3: Dealing with specific properties. In this case study, reachability is one of the specific properties. Based on the idea of Lamport's logical clocks [16], we implement a technique that captures the reachability requirement R_1 given in page 13 of [5]. For that purpose, we introduce the notion of *control cycle*, a period of time during which one can observe several events, especially a chain of events denoting an outgoing sequence or a retraction sequence; a typical control cycle is one starting with an event ($downH$) which denotes the $hDown$ order and terminating by an event ($dcge$) which denotes the fact that *"the gears are locked down and the doors are seen closed"*; similarly, another control cycle is started when the handle triggers an order hUp. A dedicated variable $endCycle$ is used to control the start and the end of each control cycle.

Given a set $obsEvents$ of events (for instance the starting of an outgoing sequence, a door closed, a gear locked in a position, etc.) and a logical clock modelled as a natural number, the occurrences of the events can be ordered by the timestamps given by the clock. In our case two events cannot happen at the same time. We use a partial function $ldate \in obsEvents \nrightarrow \mathbb{N}$ to record the timestamps of the events. We can compare and reason on the timestamps of any events happening during a sequence and specifically within the specific event sequence called *control cycle*. An example is as follows.

$$\forall dj.(((dj \in \mathbb{N}) \land (dcge \in dom(ldate)) \land (dj = ldate(dcge))$$
$$\land (endCycle = TRUE) \land dj < llc) \Rightarrow$$
$$\exists di.((di \in \mathbb{N}) \land (downH \in dom(ldate)) \land (di = ldate(downH)) \land (di < dj) \land$$
$$\forall ii.(ii \in \mathbb{N} \land di = ii \land ii < dj \Rightarrow ldate \sim [\{ii\}] \neq \{upH\})))$$

To put into practice in Event-B with Rodin, we defined the set *obsEvents* in the context of our machines, and the above property is included in the invariants of the abstract model.

3.2   Vertical Process: Building the Concrete Parts of the LG System

The vertical process includes several refinements (in **Step 4**) described below following the proposed method. We end our process with the **Step 5**. The **Step 6** was not performed for the LG case study because only the digital part will be refined with the objective to build the software part. The variables and events which are specific to the behaviour of the physical part are not refined but we keep them in the model in order to preserve *animation capabilities*. This approach is very pragmatic.

Step 4: Structural refinements of the global abstract model. The requirement document details the inner structure of the digital part; it is made of two redundant computing modules. We achieve structural refinement steps to overcome the details of the behaviour of the digital part.

(a) Introducing the two computing modules with refinements. Both modules have the same interface (*input* and *output* variables) inherited from the abstract model of the digital part. Each interface variable of a module k (where $k \in \{1, 2\}$) is inherited from a variable (for instance *gear_extended*) of the digital part of the abstract model and it is denoted by $k\_gear\_extended(k)$ where k is an index. An enumerated set $CompModule = \{1, 2\}$ is used for the indexes. Therefore each interface variable of the computing modules is specified with the following shape:

$$k\_gear\_extended \in CompModule \rightarrow ((TRIPLE \times GEAR) \rightarrow BOOL)$$

The binding between the two modules interface variables and those of the abstract module is achieved via refinements where new variables and related events are introduced.

(b) Spawning the inputs inside the computing modules with refinements. We introduced new events (prefixed with **spawn_**) to push the value of each *input* variable (for example *handle*) at the abstract level, in the corresponding variable (for example k_handle) of each computing module. As the inputs of the modules should be the same, an invariant is defined in each case of variable spawning in order to guarantee the correctness of the binding between the *input* variable of the digital part and the same input of the computing modules. The following event pattern spawns the variables at the interfaces of the computing modules.

```
event spawn_handleDown // spawn handleDown within the k CompModules
where @g1   ran(handle) = {hDown}
then
      @a1   k_handle := {1 ↦ (TRIPLE × (ran(handle))), 2 ↦ (TRIPLE × (ran(handle)))}
end
```

We have identified a reusable **specification rule**: a new event is introduced along with each new k-indexed variable. This event should copy the variable at high level (the digital part) into the indexed variables at the low level. Furthermore, the existing events, whose guards or actions involve the spawned variables, should be refined by extending their guards and actions in order to satisfy the binding between the variables and the associated k-indexed variables. One noticeable feature in this case is that when we have a non-deterministic event of abstract level (as for the value of the sensors), then in the refinement the event should be refined (not extended). This is another reusable **specification rule** we have identified.

(c) Merging the outputs of the computing modules with refinements. As depicted in Fig. 3, the k-indexed *output* variables (for example $k\_extend\_EV(1)$ and $k\_extend\_EV(2)$) are merged using a logical OR to set the corresponding variable (for example $extend\_EV$) at the output of the digital part. Therefore the event that sets the variable should be guarded by the availability of the merged value. As explained before, a binding invariant should be provided for each variable and the related k-indexed variable. Several refinements are used to introduce the appropriate events.

(d) Specifying the behaviour of the computing modules. The two computing modules have the same behaviour. It is made of the events that monitor the system and set accordingly the state output variables and the input variables of the digital part, the events that give orders (control decision) to the physical part through the order output variables. It results in the k-indexed form of the events related to the three categories of the interface variables and the internal variables.

We stopped our construction at this stage. However following the guidelines provided in the method, it remains to perform the decomposition step in the basis of the *sense, monitor, control* events families (**Step 6**). Fortunately, the decomposition modules of Rodin provide assistance for this purpose. In our case the Abrial's style of decompostion which is based on share variables [2] is the most appropriate. Indeed, the decompostion is precisely based on the families of events: the *sense* family should be used for a (physical) machine while *monitor* and *control* families should be used for another (software) machine.

4   Assessment and Discussion

Coverage. Applying the proposed method helped us a lot in mastering the case study. The resulting Event-B model presented in this article covers the main aspects of the landing system: the digital part with modules redundancy, its physical part and their interactions. The model covers mainly the safety properties of the LG system; liveness properties are treated by adapting Lamport's logical clocks [16]; but we have not deal with time constraints. Code generation was out of the scope of the current work. Nevertheless the management of huge B models is still tedious, since modifying the models already equipped with a lot of variables an events, at more abstract level requires redoing several steps of modelling, refinements and proving.

Experimentation with Rodin and Statistics. The Rodin tool is very efficient for proving the Event-B models; a very high percentage (~90%) of proof obligations was automatically discharged. The specifications are available online[3]. The current version is partial as we focus on representative events instead of being exhaustive. Statistics on Proof Obligations are given in Table 1. From a total of 619 POs, 547 of them were automatically discharged by Rodin and 6 of them were interactively discharged. Most of the POs at the abstract levels were proved. The undischarged POs are related to the structural refinement and specifically they are related to the binding invariants.

Managing very large models requires a rigorous slicing and several small steps of refinements. This is the reason why we have introduced many refinements, but it is still not enough, the slicing should be of finer grain. Moreover a good naming discipline is necessary at each level of the mod-

Table 1. Statistics of PO generated and proved with Rodin

	Total	Auto	Manual	Review.	Undis.
LandingSys5	619	547	6	0	66
Abstract model					
Landing_DP_Ctx	0	0	0	0	0
LandingSysDP_A	115	114	1	0	0
LandingSysDP_SWITCH_A	5	3	0	0	2
LandingSysDP_DOOR_A	42	42	0	0	0
LandingSysDP_DOOR_GEAR_A	79	79	0	0	0
LandingSysDP_DOOR_GEAR_TIME_A	2	2	0	0	0
Models of the vertical refinement					
LandingSysDP_DGT_R1_In	52	50	0	0	2
LandingSysDP_DGT_R2_INOUT	56	56	0	0	0
LandingSysDP_DGT_R3_INOUTDOOR	128	81	5	0	42
LandingSysDP_DGT_R3INOUTDOORGEAR	140	120	0	0	20

elling. As far as the ProB animation tool (integrated in Rodin) is concerned, it is very helpful to tune the Event-B models.

Related Works. The state of the art lacks of assistance methods. The four-variable model of software-controlled embedded systems originally proposed by Parnas and Madey has been used successfully in the development of safety-critical applications in various industries. But as mentioned by [18], the model does not explicitly specify the software requirements, but rather bounds them by specifying the system requirements and the input and output hardware interfaces of the system. We share the same the motivations with [13]. However the authors propose a method to synthesise the controller from the environment.

---

[3] http://www.lina.sciences.univ-nantes.fr/aelos/softwares/LGS/index_en.php.

They introduced the controller and its interface as a solution to the problem of maintaining a desired behaviour of an *autonomous system*. In our approach the controller is not synthesised to maintain a specific behaviour; it is built simultaneously with the environment according to the given control requirements, but the environment behaviour is less constrained by the controller. As far as method is concerned in the treatment of the LG system benchmark, all the related B specifications of the LG System are based on refinements. They do not describe a precise methodological process. Often, the authors need about ten refinements to include properties and requirements. The distinction between them is rather the way the refinements are organised rather than on methodological assumptions.

Su and Abrial [20] mentioned that there is no definitive answer for applying some recipe since the question varies from one project to another. They propose a light methodology with three steps: informal requirements, refinement strategy and formal model. They excluded features like redundancy and simplified time constraints. The systematic refinement strategy integrates progressively the devices, which is specific to the case study. Accordingly, our method focuses on a more general refinement strategy.

Mammar and Laleau adopted the four-variable model of software-controlled embedded systems originally proposed by Parnas and Madey. They used a series of refinements [17] first according to a variable classification first (monitor, control, output) then including timing aspects, failure cases and last properties. Mammar and Laleau focused on the control part only. Since it appears to be a logical organisation, a separation of concerns, this ordering delays most of the proof work to the last refinements. It lost modularity and extensibility. R. Banach used Hybrid Event-B to lead his study [4]; this extension enables one to carry continuous varying behaviours. R. Banach proposed a proof of concept of the language extension rather than a method or a full answer to the case study. However, hybrid-B seems adequate to refine the physical part of our current specification and especially to model time requirements.

Hansen et al. focused on the validation of the case using ProB rather than on the methodology of specifying with B [12]. As a matter of fact, the temporal properties are naturally introduced using LTL expressions. Another interesting feature is the ability to visualise the system execution. The counterpart is a simplified specification (no redundancy, no physical part, no failure). The refinements start with physical devices (door, gears, electro-valves), then the output, sensor and controllers are introduced as refinements and finally the general control (switch, valves, lights).

In [8] the authors present a technique for feature interactions for telecommunication services; it is a very close approach but our method is more general than the feature interactions. We plan to investigate more the connection of our approach with works on system engineering approaches [14], and cyber-physical systems where interconnected entities are interacting with the physical world [11].

5   Conclusion

We proposed a method (named Heñcher) to guide step by step the construction of embedded control systems with Event-B. We build on the well-known structure of control systems and on the experiments of several case studies where the Event-B was used and where some methodological guidelines was provided [9,10]. We provide a systematic use of the interface of the controller to build the components of the abstract model of the control system and, also how the features of the control system should be used to guide the successive refinements of the abstract model. A non trivial case study served as illustration and assessment of the proposal.

One flaw of the Event-B top-down approach is the constraint imposed by the evolution of the global abstract model defined before its refinement to the concrete models. This constraint prevents for an incremental model evolution. Indeed, if we miss some features in the abstract state, we will have to reconsider completely the structural refinements. It would be interesting to be able to mix both horizontal and vertical refinements in an incremental view of the design method. In [3] Back, have proposed guidelines for this purpose; an adaptation of this work to Event-B is likely to be interesting.

The reuse of existing independent models, with a bottom-up approach, would be interesting for managing large Event-B models. A typical example is the composition of existing models to build a given abstract model where each part can be modified and refined separately.

We plan to develop an assistance tool to help the user with various patterns, in the form of Event-B machines derived from the interface variables which will be extracted from a sketched graphical view of its control system (as in Fig. 2).

References

1. Abrial, J.R.: Modeling in Event-B - System and Software Engineering. Cambridge University Press, Cambridge (2010)
2. Abrial, J.R., Hallerstede, S.: Refinement, decomposition, and instantiation of discrete models: application to Event-B. Fundam. Inform. **77**(1–2), 1–28 (2007)
3. Back, R.-J.: Software construction by stepwise feature introduction. In: Bert, D., Bowen, J.P., Henson, M.C., Robinson, K. (eds.) ZB 2002. LNCS, vol. 2272, pp. 162–183. Springer, Heidelberg (2002). https://doi.org/10.1007/3-540-45648-1_9
4. Banach, R.: The landing gear case study in hybrid Event-B. In: Boniol et al. [6], pp. 126–141 (2014). https://doi.org/10.1007/978-3-319-07512-9_9
5. Boniol, F., Wiels, V.: The landing gear system case study. In: Boniol et al. [6], pp. 1–18 (2014). https://doi.org/10.1007/978-3-319-07512-9_1
6. Boniol, F., Wiels, V., Ait Ameur, Y., Schewe, K.-D. (eds.): ABZ 2014. CCIS, vol. 433. Springer, Cham (2014). https://doi.org/10.1007/978-3-319-07512-9
7. Butler, M.: Decomposition structures for Event-B. In: Leuschel, M., Wehrheim, H. (eds.) IFM 2009. LNCS, vol. 5423, pp. 20–38. Springer, Heidelberg (2009). https://doi.org/10.1007/978-3-642-00255-7_2

8. Cansell, D., Méry, D.: Playing with abstraction and refinement for managing features interactions. In: Bowen, J.P., Dunne, S., Galloway, A., King, S. (eds.) ZB 2000. LNCS, vol. 1878, pp. 148–167. Springer, Heidelberg (2000). https://doi.org/10.1007/3-540-44525-0_10

9. Damchoom, K., Butler, M.: Applying event and machine decomposition to a flash-based filestore in Event-B. In: Oliveira, M.V.M., Woodcock, J. (eds.) SBMF 2009. LNCS, vol. 5902, pp. 134–152. Springer, Heidelberg (2009). https://doi.org/10.1007/978-3-642-10452-7_10

10. Damchoom, K., Butler, M., Abrial, J.-R.: Modelling and proof of a tree-structured file system in Event-B and rodin. In: Liu, S., Maibaum, T., Araki, K. (eds.) ICFEM 2008. LNCS, vol. 5256, pp. 25–44. Springer, Heidelberg (2008). https://doi.org/10.1007/978-3-540-88194-0_5

11. Lee, E.A., Seshia, S.A.: Introduction to Embedded Systems - A Cyber-Physical Systems Approach. MIT Press, Cambridge (2017)

12. Hansen, D., Ladenberger, L., Wiegard, H., Bendisposto, J., Leuschel, M.: Validation of the ABZ landing gear system using prob. In: Boniol et al. [6], pp. 66–79 (2014)

13. Hudon, S., Hoang, T.S.: Development of control systems guided by models of their environment. Electron. Notes Theor. Comput. Sci. **280**, 57–68 (2011)

14. Dragomir, I., Ober, I., Lesens, D.: A case study in formal system engineering with SysML. In: 2012 IEEE 17th International Conference on Engineering of Complex Computer Systems, pp. 189–198 (2012)

15. Jard, C., Roux, O.H. (eds.): Communicating Embedded Systems: Software and Design. Wiley-ISTE (2009)

16. Lamport, L.: Time, clocks, and the ordering of events in a distributed system. Commun. ACM **21**(7), 558–565 (1978)

17. Mammar, A., Laleau, R.: Modeling a landing gear system in Event-B. In: Boniol et al. [6], pp. 80–94 (2014). https://doi.org/10.1007/978-3-319-07512-9_6

18. Patcas, L.M., Lawford, M., Maibaum, T.: From system requirements to software requirements in the four-variable model. ECEASST **66** (2013). http://journal.ub.tu-berlin.de/eceasst/article/view/887

19. Silva, R., Butler, M.: Shared event composition/decomposition in Event-B. In: Aichernig, B.K., de Boer, F.S., Bonsangue, M.M. (eds.) FMCO 2010. LNCS, vol. 6957, pp. 122–141. Springer, Heidelberg (2011). https://doi.org/10.1007/978-3-642-25271-6_7

20. Su, W., Abrial, J.R.: Aircraft landing gear system: approaches with Event-B to the modeling of an industrial system. In: Boniol et al. [6], pp. 19–35 (2014). https://doi.org/10.1007/978-3-319-07512-9_2

21. Su, W., Abrial, J.-R., Zhu, H.: Complementary methodologies for developing hybrid systems with Event-B. In: Aoki, T., Taguchi, K. (eds.) ICFEM 2012. LNCS, vol. 7635, pp. 230–248. Springer, Heidelberg (2012). https://doi.org/10.1007/978-3-642-34281-3_18

Component Design and Adaptation Based on Behavioral Contracts

Samir Chouali[1](✉), Sebti Mouelhi[2], and Hassan Mountassir[1]

[1] Univ. Bourgogne Franche-Comté, FEMTO-ST Institute/CNRS, Besançon, France
{schouali,hmountas}@femto-st.fr
[2] ECE Paris - Graduate School of Engineering, Paris, France
sebti.mouelhi@ece.fr

Abstract. In this paper, our objective is to propose an adaptation approach to generate a component adaptor that ensures a correct interaction between mismatched components. Compared to the related works on component adaptation, the originality of our proposition relies on two main contributions. In the first, we design component behavioral contracts in order to generate component adaptor. So, we propose to specify component interfaces as behavioral contracts, to enrich the exhibited informations in component interfaces. Our behavioral contracts express all component facets: their action signatures, their actions semantics, and their protocol. We consider that these informations are important when generating component adaptors. In the second contribution, we propose to specify component behavioral contracts with the formalism based on interface automata that we enrich to specify the semantics of component actions. So, our adaptation approach is also an extension of the interface automata approach to handle the problem of component adaptation.

Keywords: Components · Behavioral contracts · Adaptation

1 Introduction

The development of component-based systems is principally based on component reusability which allows the use of components in diverse environments without affecting their codes. However, in many cases, reusability is constrained with mismatches that may occur between components and their new environments during their interaction. The mismatches are caused by components that do not match perfectly the requirements of their environment. In this case, component adaptation should be performed in order to generate software entities, called *adaptors*, capable of enabling a correct interaction between components when mismatches occur.

In this paper, we focus on adapting components whose interfaces are described with behavioral contracts, which exhibit all component facets at the levels of action signatures (signatures of component operations), component protocols (scheduling of operation calls), and action semantics (semantic of component operations). We believe that consideration of all these informations in

© Springer Nature Switzerland AG 2018
E. H. Abdelwahed et al. (Eds.): MEDI 2018 Workshops, CCIS 929, pp. 217–230, 2018.
https://doi.org/10.1007/978-3-030-02852-7_19

component interfaces lead to generate suitable and reliable adaptors. To specify formally component contracts, we propose to exploit the interface automata formalism [1] that we enrich by the semantic of component actions, because interface automata express only the scheduling of components actions without their semantics. So, we annotate the actions in interface automata by pre and post-conditions expressed on their parameters. This new formalism led us to adapt the compatibility verification approach, based on interface automata, to handle with the semantic of actions, because the adaptor generation relies on the verification of component compatibility.

Previously, we treated only adaptation at the protocol level [6]. Our purpose was to generate automatically an adaptor (interface automaton in-the-middle) for exactly two component interface automata according to a mapping that establishes a number of rules relating their mismatched input and output actions. In this paper, the main contribution relies on proposing a methodological approach to treat the problem of component adaptation at signature, semantic, and protocol levels, by exploiting component behavioral contracts. We show how to cooperate between the adaptation at the protocol level, and the semantic adaptation to generate a suitable adaptor for components specified with enriched interface automata that specify component contracts.

The paper is organized as follows. In Sect. 2, we present the formalization of component behavioral contracts with the interface automata, enriched with the semantics of component actions. In Sect. 3, we show how to verify the compatibility between components specified with behavioral contracts. When the compatibility does not hold between components, we present in Sect. 4 the specification of the mapping rules between the mismatched components that we exploit to generate adaptors. Section 5, is dedicated to present our proposition to adapt components at signature, semantic, and protocol levels. Finally, we discuss the related work to our approach in Sect. 6 and conclude the paper in Sect. 7.

2   Component Behavioral Contracts

Interface automata (IAs) have been defined by Alfaro and Henzinger [1], to model the behavior of software component. Every component is described with an interface, which is specified with one interface automaton. This latter describes the scheduling of input, output, and hidden component actions, such that, input actions are used to model methods that can be called, and the end of receiving messages from communication channels, as well as the return values from such calls. Output actions are used to model method calls, message transmissions via communication channels, and exceptions that occur during the methods executions. Local operations are called hidden actions. The alphabet of an interface automaton consists of the names of actions annotated by "?" for input actions, by "!" for output actions, and by ";" for hidden actions. In the interface automata approach, the verification of the compatibility between two component is based on the composition of their interface automata, which is achieved by synchronizing their shared input and output actions. The compatibility holds between two interface automata where there is an environment (third component) which prevents the reachability of *illegal states* (states where the synchronization between the shared actions is not achieved) in their composition. This approach is considered optimistic because the existence of illegal states in the composition is not sufficient to decide on the incompatibility between components. The composition approach of the other automata-based formalisms describing the interface protocols of components are considered pessimistic.

In this paper, we propose to specify component behavioral contracts with interface automata formalism, enriched with the explicit description of the semantics of each action. These contracts specify component behaviors by showing the scheduling of the actions calls, and the interface automata formalism is suitable to specify component behaviors. However our behavioral contracts should express also the semantics of component actions, with pre and post conditions that should be satisfied by the environment in order to call or to provide component actions. And interface automata are not enough expressive to specify the semantics of component actions, therefore we propose to enrich this formalism to cope with action semantics.

In our proposal, we consider that the signature of an input (resp. output) component action a is of the form $a(i_1, \ldots, i_n) \rightarrow (o)$. The set $P_a^i = \{i_1, \ldots, i_n\}$ represents the set of input parameters of a. The set of output parameters P_a^o is defined by the singleton $\{o\}$ (we assume that an action has at most a unique return value). The set of all parameters of an action a is denoted by P_a. The absence of input or output parameters is denoted by (). For a parameter p, we define a domain D_p which is a set of values that p can take. The semantics of actions is represented by the pre and post-conditions defined on action parameters. We express these conditions as formulas of the first-order logic. Given a set of variables V, we denote by $Preds(V)$, the set of first-order logic predicates whose free variables belong to V.

Definition 1 (Interface Automaton for a behavioral contract). *Let B be a behavioral contract associated to a component interface. An* interface automaton *to specify B is a tuple $A = \langle S_A, i_A, \Sigma_A^I, \Sigma_A^O, \Sigma_A^H, \delta_A, \Psi_A \rangle$ such that:*

- S_A *is a finite set of states. A is called* empty *iff $S_A = \emptyset$;*
- $i_A \in S_A$ *is the initial state;*
- Σ_A^I, Σ_A^O, *and Σ_A^H are respectively the sets of names of input, output, and hidden actions. Let $\Sigma_A = \Sigma_A^I \cup \Sigma_A^O \cup \Sigma_A^H$;*
- $\delta_A \subseteq S_A \times \Sigma_A \times S_A$ *is the set of transitions betweens states;*
- Ψ_A *is a function, $\Psi_A : \Sigma_A \mapsto Preds(P_a^i) \times Preds(P_a^i \cup P_a^o)$, that associates, for each action $a \in \Sigma_A$, a tuple $\langle Pre_{\Psi_A(a)}, Post_{\Psi_A(a)} \rangle$ that represents the pre and post conditions of component actions.*

We require that interface automata are deterministic, *i.e.* for all $(s, a, s_1) \in \delta_A$ and $(s, a, s_2) \in \delta_A$, we have $s_1 = s_2$.

The set Σ_A^{ext} of *external* actions of interface automaton A is defined by the union $\Sigma_A^I \cup \Sigma_A^O$. The set Σ_A^{loc} of *locally controlled* actions of A is defined by the union $\Sigma_A^O \cup \Sigma_A^H$. We define by $\Sigma_A^I(s)$, $\Sigma_A^O(s)$, $\Sigma_A^H(s)$, $\Sigma_A^{ext}(s)$, and $\Sigma_A^{loc}(s)$

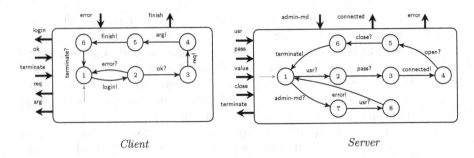

Fig. 1. A variant of a client/server system

respectively the input, output, hidden, external and locally controlled actions enabled from s. The set $\Sigma_A(s)$ includes all the enabled actions from s.

Example 1. Let us consider the two composable interface automata *Client* and *Server*, that specify component behavioral contracts, shown in Fig. 1. After authentication, *Client* sends a request *req*! to open a file in read-only or write mode. After that, it sends an action *arg*! containing the name of a file to be open. *Server* receives the two actions by executing an action *open*? that open the file in readonly or write mode. After using the file, *Client* sends a signal *finish*! indicating to *Server* that the file is ready to be closed (action *close*?). Finally, *Server* sends a signal *terminate*! to terminate the session. The action *admin-md*? is a super signal received from the administrator of the system to open a super user session. When a client username is received by the server after receiving the *admin-md*! signal from an administrator, then an error is detected. For example, the signatures and the semantics of the action *login* in *Client* and *usr* in *Server* are defined as follows.

Signatures: $login(uname, passwd, lu, lp) \rightarrow (exist)$,
$usr(username, lengthu) \rightarrow ()$.

The semantics of the action *login* is defined as:
$Pre_{\Psi_{Client}(login)} \equiv 1 < lu \leq 20 \wedge 8 \leq lp \leq 10$,
$Post_{\Psi_{Client}(login)} \equiv exist = 1 \vee exist = 0$
The semantics of the action *usr* is defined as:
$Pre_{\Psi_{Server}(usr)} \equiv 1 < lengthu \leq 30, Post_{\Psi_{Server}(usr)} \equiv true$

3   Component Compatibility Based on Behavioral Contracts

In this section we show how to verify the compatibility between two components specified with their behavioral contracts. Our proposition relies on the extension of the interface automata approach to cope with the semantics of component actions expressed with their pre and post condition on their parameters. To verify the compatibility between two components that are specified with two interface automata A_1 and A_2, we have first to verify their composability and then compute their composition by their synchronized product.

Before defining the composition between, A_1 and A_2, we present in the following the conditions that should be respected by both automata, that specify component behavioral contracts, in order to authorize their composition.

The Composability Conditions: Two interface automata A_1 and A_2 associated to two behavioral contracts are *composable* if:

– The condition on the non shared input and output actions is satisfied:

$$\Sigma^I_{A_1} \cap \Sigma^I_{A_2} = \Sigma^O_{A_1} \cap \Sigma^O_{A_2} = \Sigma^H_{A_1} \cap \Sigma_{A_2} = \Sigma^H_{A_2} \cap \Sigma_{A_1} = \emptyset.$$

– The condition on the shared actions is satisfied:
$Shared(A_1, A_2) = (\Sigma^I_{A_1} \cap \Sigma^O_{A_2}) \cup (\Sigma^I_{A_2} \cap \Sigma^O_{A_1})$ is the set of shared input and output actions of A_1 and A_2. For each action $a \in Shared(A_1, A_2)$ such that its signature is given by $a(i_1, \ldots, i_n) \rightarrow (o)$ in A_1 and by $a(i'_1, \ldots, i'_n) \rightarrow (o')$ in A_2 then, $D_{i_k} \subseteq D_{i'_k}$ for $1 \leq k \leq n$ and $D_o \subseteq D_{o'}$ in the case where $a(i_1, \ldots, i_n) \rightarrow (o) \in \Sigma^O_{A_1}$ and $a(i'_1, \ldots, i'_n) \rightarrow (o') \in \Sigma^I_{A_2}$. Otherwise, $D_{i_k} \supseteq D_{i'_k}$ for $1 \leq k \leq n$ and $D_o \supseteq D_{o'}$. This property is called the *domain inclusion* of the parameters of shared actions. The intuition behind this condition comes from the fact that the output actions specify the method calls and the input ones specify the methods that can be called.

If the above conditions are satisfied between two interface automata A_1 and A_2, then we have to perform the renaming of parameter names in their pre and post-conditions in order to realize their composition.

Definition 2 (Parameter renaming). Given an action a in Shared (A_1, A_2), the signature of a is defined by $a(i_1, \ldots, i_n) \rightarrow (o)$ in A_1 and by $a(i'_1, \ldots, i'_n) \rightarrow (o')$ in A_2. The *renaming* of parameters in the semantics $\Psi_{A_1}(a)$ and $\Psi_{A_2}(a)$ is the substitution of i'_1 by $i_1, \ldots, i'_n$ by i_n, and o' by o in $\text{Pre}_{\Psi_{A_2}(a)}$ and $\text{Post}_{\Psi_{A_2}(a)}$ or the opposite in $\text{Pre}_{\Psi_{A_1}(a)}$ and $\text{Post}_{\Psi_{A_1}(a)}$.

We denote by $\Psi_{A_1/A_2}(a)$ and $\Psi_{A_2/A_1}(a)$, the semantics of a after the parameter renaming respectively in A_1 and A_2. We can now define properly the notion of the semantic compatibility of shared external actions.

Definition 3 (Semantic compatibility). Given an action a $\in$ Shared(A_1, A_2), if one of the following conditions is true, then the action a in A_1 is *semantically compatible* with the same action a in A_2 i.e. $\text{SemComp}_a(A_1, A_2)$ is true (*otherwise* $\neg\text{SemComp}_a(A_1, A_2)$ is true):

– if a $\in \Sigma^O_{A_1} \wedge \text{Pre}_{\Psi_{A_1/A_2}(a)} \Rightarrow \text{Pre}_{\Psi_{A_2/A_1}(a)} \wedge \text{Post}_{\Psi_{A_2/A_1}(a)} \Rightarrow \text{Post}_{\Psi_{A_1/A_2}(a)}$,
– if a $\in \Sigma^I_{A_1} \wedge \text{Pre}_{\Psi_{A_2/A_1}(a)} \Rightarrow \text{Pre}_{\Psi_{A_1/A_2}(a)} \wedge \text{Post}_{\Psi_{A_1/A_2}(a)} \Rightarrow \text{Post}_{\Psi_{A_2/A_1}(a)}$.

Definition 4 (Synchronized product ⊗). Given two composable interface automata A_1 and A_2, the *synchronized product* $A_1 \otimes A_2$ of A_1 and A_2 is defined by:

- $S_{A_1 \otimes A_2} = S_{A_1} \times S_{A_2}$ and $i_{A_1 \otimes A_2} = (i_{A_1}, i_{A_2})$; $\Sigma^I_{A_1 \otimes A_2} = (\Sigma^I_{A_1} \cup \Sigma^I_{A_2}) \setminus$ Shared (A_1, A_2);
- $\Sigma^O_{A_1 \otimes A_2} = (\Sigma^O_{A_1} \cup \Sigma^O_{A_2}) \setminus$ Shared(A_1, A_2); $\Sigma^H_{A_1 \otimes A_2} = \Sigma^H_{A_1} \cup \Sigma^H_{A_2} \cup \{a \in Shared(A_1, A_2) \mid SemComp_a(A_1, A_2)\}$;
- $((s_1, s_2), a, (s'_1, s'_2)) \in \delta_{A_1 \otimes A_2}$ iff
  - $a \notin$ Shared $(A_1, A_2) \wedge (s_1, a, s'_1) \in \delta_{A_1} \wedge s_2 = s'_2$ or $a \notin$ Shared$(A_1, A_2) \wedge (s_2, a, s'_2) \in \delta_{A_2} \wedge s_1 = s'_1$ or $a \in$ Shared$(A_1, A_2) \wedge (s_1, a, s'_1) \in \delta_{A_1} \wedge (s_2, a, s'_2) \in \delta_{A_2} \wedge SemComp_a(A_1, A_2)$;
- $\Psi_{A_1 \otimes A_1}$ is defined by:
  - Ψ_{A_1} for $a \in \Sigma_{A_2} \setminus Shared(A_1, A_2)$;
  - Ψ_{A_2} for $a \in \Sigma_{A_2} \setminus Shared(A_1, A_2)$;
  - $\langle Pre_{\Psi_{A_1}(a)}, Post_{\Psi_{A_2}(a)} \rangle$ for $a \in Shared(A_1, A_2) \cap \Sigma^O_{A_1}$ such that $SemComp_a(A_1, A_2)$;
  - $\langle Pre_{\Psi_{A_2}(a)}, Post_{\Psi_{A_1}(a)} \rangle$ for $a \in Shared(A_1, A_2) \cap \Sigma^I_{A_1}$ such that $SemComp_a(A_1, A_2)$;

The incompatibility between two interface automata A_1 and A_2 could happen due to (i) the existence of states (s_1, s_2) in the product $A_1 \otimes A_2$ such that there exists at least one action a in $Shared(A_1, A_2)$ enabled from s_1 and it is not from s_2 or inversely, or (ii) the action a is enabled from s_1 and s_2 but $\neg SemComp_a(A_1, A_2)$ is valid. These states are therefore illegal in the product $A_1 \otimes A_2$.

Definition 5 (Illegal states). The set of *illegal states*, denoted by Illegal$(A_1, A_2) \subseteq S_{A_1} \times S_{A_2}$, in $A_1 \otimes A_2$ is defined by $\{(s_1, s_2) \in S_{A_1} \times S_{A_2} \mid (\exists\, a \in Shared(A_1, A_2) \mid$ the condition $C_1 \oplus C_2$ is true[1] $)\}$.

$$C_1 = \begin{pmatrix} (a \in \Sigma^O_{A_1}(s_1) \wedge a \notin \Sigma^I_{A_2}(s_2)) \vee (a \in \Sigma^O_{A_1}(s_1) \wedge a \in \Sigma^I_{A_2}(s_2)) \\ \wedge \neg SemComp_a(A_1, A_2)) \end{pmatrix}$$

$$C_2 = \begin{pmatrix} (a \in \Sigma^O_{A_2}(s_2) \wedge a \notin \Sigma^I_{A_1}(s_1)) \vee (a \in \Sigma^O_{A_2}(s_2) \wedge a \in \Sigma^I_{A_1}(s_1)) \\ \wedge \neg SemComp_a(A_1, A_2)) \end{pmatrix}$$

Reaching states in *Illegal*(A_1, A_2) is not sufficient to decide that A_1 and A_2 are incompatible (according to optimistic approach). Indeed, in this approach, if there is at least one environment that requests the appropriate input actions in $A_1 \otimes A_2$, and allows the no reachability of illegal states, then A_1 and A_2 can be assembled without producing deadlocks. The composition of A_1 and A_2, denoted by $A_1 || A_2$, is the restriction of their product to the set of states called *compatible*, denoted by $Comp(A_1, A_2)$. They are the states through which the interaction between the two components of A_1 and A_2 passes without having the risk of reaching illegal states by enabling only the locally controllable actions (input and hidden actions). The verification steps in this approach are similar to those described in [1], except that we consider the semantics of actions during the compatibility check by verifying the condition of semantic compatibility between the shared actions.

---

[1] $\oplus$ is XOR.

4 Component Behavioral Contracts and Mismatches

The definitions of component interface mismatches [2,4,5] are essentially due to the reuse of components in a system design which is often harmed by mismatch cases such as: (i) names of exchanged messages between components do not correspond which may lead to deadlock situations, components regularly interact on the same action names; (ii) the orderings of messages or actions in both component protocols do not correspond; (iii) an action in a component that has no counterpart in the other one, or correspond to more than one action.

For component behavioral contracts specified with interface automata, the behavioral mismatch cannot be detected by applying the synchronized product between two composable interface automata as it was defined in Definition 4, because the case where there is no correspondence between the action names leads to them being absent from the set of shared actions. Thus, all of mismatched actions are interleaved asynchronously in the product. To avoid this constraint, our adaptation specification starts by establishing an abstract way to denote the composition requirements. We corroborate the explicit description of interactions between components thanks to *rules*. They relate the mismatched actions used in different components which are supposed to implement some interactions. Rules relate actions even if they do not really label some transitions in the automaton as required by the optimistic approach of interface automata.

The minimal adaptor specification of two interface automata A_1 and A_2 is the set of rules called a *mapping*. The mapping does not represent any behavioural detail about the adaptor.

Definition 6 (Rules and Mappings). *A rule α for two composable interface automata A_1 and A_2, is a pair $\langle L_1, L_2 \rangle \in (2^{\Sigma^O_{A_1}} \times 2^{\Sigma^I_{A_2}}) \cup (2^{\Sigma^I_{A_1}} \times 2^{\Sigma^O_{A_2}})^2$ such that $(L_1 \cup L_2) \cap Shared(A_1, A_2) = \emptyset$ and if $|L_1| > 1$ (or $|L_2| > 1$) then $|L_2| = 1$ (or $|L_1| = 1$);*
A mapping $\Phi(A_1, A_2)$ for two composable interface automata A_1 and A_2 is a set of rules α_i, for $1 \leq i \leq |\Phi(A_1, A_2)|$.

According to the above definition, a rule in our approach deals with one-to-one, many-to-one, and one-to-many correspondences between actions. More clearly, the adaptation may in general relate either an action or a group of actions of one automaton with one action in the other. For instance, a client authenticates itself by sending first its user name and then a password while the server accepts both data in a single login shot. We denote the set of the mismatched actions by $Mismatch_\Phi(A_1, A_2) = \{a \in \Sigma^{ext}_{A_1} \cup \Sigma^{ext}_{A_2} \mid \exists \alpha \in \Phi(A_1, A_2).$ $a \in \Pi_1(\alpha) \vee a \in \Pi_2(\alpha)\}^3$.

---

[2] For some set S, 2^S is its power set.
[3] $\Pi_1(\langle a, b \rangle) = a$ and $\Pi_2(\langle a, b \rangle) = b$ are respectively the projection on the first element and the second element of the couple $\langle a, b \rangle$.

Example 2. To illustrate the mapping relation, we define this latter between the actions of the interface automata Client and server as described in Fig. 1 by: $\Phi(Client,Server) = \{\langle \{login\}, \{usr, pass\}\rangle, \langle\{finish\}, \{close\}\rangle, \langle\{ok\}, \{connected\}\rangle \langle\{req,arg\}, \{open\}\rangle \}$. The set $Shared(A_1, A_2) = \{error,terminate\}$.

Given two composable interface automata A_1 and A_2 and a mapping $\Phi(A_1, A_2)$, if $\Phi(A_1, A_2) = \emptyset$, the adaptation of A_1 and A_2 has no sense and their synchronization is defined by their product $A_1 \otimes A_2$ as it was defined in Sect. 3. Otherwise, we proceed on two steps: (i) we check first the semantic adaptability between the mismatched actions in the mapping $\Phi(A_1, A_2)$. (ii)if the semantic adaptability check was successfully made without giving rise to incompatibilities, we generate the adaptor of A_1 and A_2 according to the mapping $\Phi(A_1, A_2)$. If the generated adaptor is non-empty and it is compatible with both of A_1 and A_2, we say that A_1 and A_2 are *adaptable*.

5   Component Adaptation

In this section we present our approach to adapt components specified with behavioral contracts.

5.1   Semantic Adaptability

The semantic adaptability between the mismatched actions of two composable interface automata has to be made before generating the adaptor. The mismatched actions have to respect some constraints at the level of their semantics. Let us consider two interface automata A_1 and A_2 and a given mapping $\Phi(A_1, A_2)$. To perform the semantic adaptability check between A_1 and A_2 according to $\Phi(A_1, A_2)$, it is required that for each rule $\alpha = \langle L_1, L_2 \rangle \in \Phi(A_1, A_2)$ the following conditions hold:

1. $\sum_{a\in L_1} |P_a^i| = \sum_{b\in L_2} |P_b^i|$;
2. $\sum_{a\in L_1} |P_a^o| = \sum_{b\in L_2} |P_b^o|$;
3. if $|L_1| = 1$ and $|L_2| \geq 1$ where $L_1 = \{a\}$, $L_2 = \{b_1,\ldots,b_{|L_2|}\}$, and $P_a^o = \{o_a\}$ then there exists exactly one action $b_k \in L_2$ $(1\leq k\leq |L_2|)$ such that $P_{b_k}^o = \{o_{b_k}\}$, $P_{b_l}^o = \emptyset$ for $1\leq l\leq |L_2|$ and $l\neq k$, and the two output parameters o_a and o_{b_k} have to satisfy the domain inclusion condition:
   – if $L_1 \subseteq \Sigma_{A_1}^O$, then $D_{o_a} \subseteq D_{o_{b_k}}$;
   – else $D_{o_a} \supseteq D_{o_{b_k}}$;
   θ_α denotes the tuple (a,b_k). If $P_a^o = \{\}$, (a,b_k) is not defined;
4. the condition is analogous to the previous one with $|L_1| \geq 1$ and $|L_2| = 1$ where $L_1 = \{a_1,\ldots,a_{|L_1|}\}$ and $L_2 = \{b\}$;
5. there exists a function $\varphi_\alpha^i \colon \bigcup_{a\in L_1} P_a^i \to \bigcup_{b\in L_2} P_b^i$ that associates each input parameter p of actions in L_1 with an input parameter q of actions in L_2. The function φ_α^i have to satisfy the domain inclusion condition:
   – if $L_1 \subseteq \Sigma_{A_1}^O$, then $D_p \subseteq D_{\varphi_\alpha^i(p)}$ where $p \in \bigcup_{a\in L_1} P_a^i$;
   – else $D_{\varphi_\alpha^i(p)} \subseteq D_p$ where $p \in \bigcup_{a\in L_1} P_a^i$.

The first and the second conditions state that the number of input (respectively output) parameters of actions in L_1 is equal to the number of input (respectively output) parameters of actions in L_2. The third condition states the relations between the output parameter of the action $a \in L_1$ and the one of the action $b_k \in L_2$. We assume that the other actions in $L_2 \setminus \{b_k\}$ have no output parameters. The intuition behind these conditions is to avoid conflicts between the pre and post-conditions during the semantic adaptability check by ensuring the equality between the number of input and output parameters.

The renaming of the input and output parameter in the semantics of actions in $Mismatch_\Phi(A_1, A_2)$ is defined as follows. For all $a \in L_1$ and $b \in L_2$, the parameter renaming is defined by the substitution of each input parameter i of a in $Pre_{\Psi_{A_1}(a)}$ and $Post_{\Psi_{A_1}(a)}$ by $\varphi_\alpha^i(i)$ or the substitution of each input parameter i' of b in $Pre_{\Psi_{A_2}(b)}$ and $Post_{\Psi_{A_2}(b)}$ by $\varphi_\alpha^{i\,-1}(i')^4$. If the couple $\theta_\alpha = (a, b)$ exists, the parameter renaming is defined by the substitution of the output parameter o_a in $Post_{\Psi_{A_1}(a)}$ by o_b or the substitution of the output parameter o_b in $Post_{\Psi_{A_2}(b)}$ by o_a.

We denote by $\Psi_{A_1/\alpha}(a)$ and $\Psi_{A_2/\alpha}(b)$ respectively the semantics of actions in $\Pi_1(\alpha)$ and actions in $\Pi_2(\alpha)$ after the parameter renaming.

Definition 7 (Semantic Adaptability). Given two composable interface automata A_1 and A_2 and an adaptation mapping $\Phi(A_1, A_2)$ such that the conditions 1, 2, 3, 4, and 5 introduced in Sect. 5.1 are satisfied, the *semantic adaptability* $SemAdap_\alpha(A_1, A_2)$ of a rule α in $\Phi(A_1, A_2)$ is satisfied iff the following conditions are fulfilled:

1. If $\Pi_1(\alpha) \subseteq \Sigma_{A_1}^O$, then

$$
\left(
\begin{array}{c}
\bigwedge\limits_{a \in \Pi_1(\alpha)} Pre_{\Psi_{A_1/\alpha}(a)} \Rightarrow \bigwedge\limits_{b \in \Pi_2(\alpha)} Pre_{\Psi_{A_2/\alpha}(b)} \\
\wedge \\
\bigwedge\limits_{a \in \Pi_1(\alpha)} Post_{\Psi_{A_1/\alpha}(a)} \Leftarrow \bigwedge\limits_{b \in \Pi_2(\alpha)} Post_{\Psi_{A_2/\alpha}(b)}
\end{array}
\right)
$$

2. If $\Pi_1(\alpha) \subseteq \Sigma_{A_1}^I$, then the condition is analogous to the previous one by inversing the implications.

We say that A_1 and A_2 are semantically adaptable *according to the mapping* $\Phi(A_1, A_2)$ *if the semantic adaptability of each rule* $\alpha \in \Phi(A_1, A_2)$ *holds.*

The semantic adaptability conditions are stated in a similar way as the semantic compatibility of the shared actions defined in Definition 3 except that for adaptation, we treat sets of mismatched actions associated by the rules of the mapping.

Example 3. To illustrate mismatches between actions belonging to two behavioral contracts, we consider the two composable interface automata *Client* and *Server*, that specify component behavioral contracts, shown in Fig. 1 and a mapping $\Phi(Client, Server)$ as defined in Example 2.

Table 1. The signatures of actions in $Mismatch_\Phi(Client,Server)$

	Client	Server
α_1	login(uname,passwd,lu,lp)→(exist)	usr(username,lengthu)→()
		pass(password,lengthp)→(exist)
α_2	ok(msg)→()	connected(logmsg)→()
α_3	req(read)→()	open(readonly,filename)→(open)
	arg(file)→(status)	
α_4	finish()→(status)	close()→(closed)

Table 2. The semantics of actions in $Mismatch_\Phi(Client,Server)$

Client	Server
$Pre_{\Psi_{Client}(login)} \equiv 1 < lu \le 20 \land 8 \le lp \le 10$	$Pre_{\Psi_{Server}(usr)} \equiv 1 < lengthu \le 30$
$Post_{\Psi_{Client}(login)} \equiv exist = 1 \lor exist = 0$	$Post_{\Psi_{Server}(usr)} \equiv true$
	$Pre_{\Psi_{Server}(pass)} \equiv 6 \le lengthp \le 10$
	$Post_{\Psi_{Server}(pass)} \equiv exist = 1 \lor exist = 0$
$Pre_{\Psi_{Client}(ok)} \equiv true$	$Pre_{\Psi_{Server}(connected)} \equiv true$
$Post_{\Psi_{Client}(ok)} \equiv true$	$Post_{\Psi_{Server}(connected)} \equiv true$
$Pre_{\Psi_{Client}(req)} \equiv read = 0 \lor read = 1$	$Pre_{\Psi_{Server}(open)} \equiv readonly = 0 \lor readonly = 1$
$Post_{\Psi_{Client}(req)} \equiv true$	$Post_{\Psi_{Server}(open)} \equiv open = 0 \lor open = 1$
$Pre_{\Psi_{Client}(arg)} \equiv true$	
$Post_{\Psi_{Client}(arg)} \equiv status = 0 \lor status = 1$	
$Pre_{\Psi_{Client}(finish)} \equiv true$	$Pre_{\Psi_{Server}(close)} \equiv true$
$Post_{\Psi_{Client}(finish)} \equiv status = 0 \lor status = 1$	$Post_{\Psi_{Server}(close)} \equiv closed = 0 \lor closed = 1$

The mismatched actions are described and classified by the rules in Table 1. The function $\varphi^i_{\alpha_2}$ is defined by $\{msg \mapsto logmsg\}$. The function $\varphi^i_{\alpha_4}$ is not defined. The function $\varphi^i_{\alpha_1}$ is defined by and $\{uname \mapsto username,$ $lu \mapsto lengthu,\ passwd \mapsto password,\ lp \mapsto lengthp\}$. The function $\varphi^i_{\alpha_3}$ is defined by $\{read \mapsto readonly,\ file \mapsto filename\}$. The function $\varphi^i_{\alpha_4}$ is empty. $\theta_{\alpha_1} = (login,pass)$, θ_{α_2} is not defined, $\theta_{\alpha_3} = (arg,open)$, and $\theta_{\alpha_4} = (finish,close)$. The parameters $uname$, $passwd$, $username$, $password$, msg, $logmsg$, $file$, and $filename$ are strings. The parameters lu, lp, $lengthu$, $lengthp$, $read$, $readonly$, $status$, $open$, and $closed$ are integers. As the reader can conclude, the conditions to perform the semantic adaptability check hold for all α in $\Phi(A_1, A_2)$:

- for all $\alpha \in \Phi(A_1, A_2)$, $\sum_{a \in \Pi_1(\alpha)} |P^i_a| = \sum_{b \in \Pi_2(\alpha)} |P^i_b|$ and $\sum_{a \in \Pi_1(\alpha)} |P^o_a| = \sum_{b \in \Pi_2(\alpha)} |P^o_b|$;
- the domain inclusion conditions are satisfied for θ_* and φ^i_* where $* \in \Phi(Client, Server)$.

The semantics of the mismatched actions respectively for *Client* and *Server* are listed in Table 2. After unifying the mismatched actions in $Mismatch_\Phi(Client,$

---

[4] f^{-1} is the inverse function of f.

Server), the reader can easily verify the semantic adaptability for all α in $\Phi(\textit{Client}, \textit{Server})$ holds. For example, for the rule α_1,

$Pre_{\Psi_{Client/\alpha_1}}(login) \Rightarrow (Pre_{\Psi_{Server/\alpha_1}}(usr) \wedge Pre_{\Psi_{Server/\alpha_1}}(pass))$ is satisfiable $((1 < \text{lu} \leq 20 \wedge 8 \leq \text{lp} \leq 10) \Rightarrow (1 < \text{lu} \leq 30 \wedge 6 \leq \text{lp} \leq 10))$. Also, $Post_{\Psi_{Client/\alpha_1}}(login) \Leftarrow (Post_{\Psi_{Server/\alpha_1}}(usr) \wedge Post_{\Psi_{Server/\alpha_1}}(pass))$ is satisfiable $((\text{exist} = 1 \vee \text{exist} = 0) \Leftarrow (\text{true} \wedge (\text{exist} = 1 \vee \text{exist} = 0)))$. We can deduce that *Client* and *Server* are semantically adaptable according to $\Phi(\textit{Client}, \textit{Server})$.

5.2   Adaptor Specification and Construction

After verifying the semantic adaptability between two composable interface automata A_1 and A_2 according to a mapping $\Phi(A_1, A_2)$, we treat in this section the interface automaton specification and construction of their adaptor. The adaptor must be composable with A_1 and A_2, and must also satisfy the mapping rules and respect the component protocols specified by A_1 and A_2.

Definition 8 (Adaptor). *Given two composable interface automata A_1, A_2, and a mapping $\Phi(A_1, A_2)$, an adaptor for A_1 and A_2 according to the mapping $\Phi(A_1, A_2)$ is an interface automaton $Ad = \langle\, S_{Ad},\, I_{Ad},\, \Sigma^I_{Ad},\, \Sigma^O_{Ad},\, \Sigma^H_{Ad},\, \delta_{Ad}\,\rangle$ such that*

- $\Sigma^I_{Ad} = \{a \mid a \in Mismatch_\Phi(A_1, A_2) \cap (\Sigma^O_{A_1} \cup \Sigma^O_{A_2})\}$;
  - *For all* $a \in \Sigma^I_{Ad}$, $\Psi_{Ad}(a) = \Psi_{A_1}(a)$ *if* $a \in \Sigma^O_{A_1}$. *Otherwise,* $\Psi_{Ad}(a) = \Psi_{A_2}(a)$;
- $\Sigma^O_{Ad} = \{a \mid a \in Mismatch_\Phi(A_1, A_2) \cap (\Sigma^I_{A_1} \cup \Sigma^I_{A_2})\}$;
  - *For all* $a \in \Sigma^O_{Ad}$, $\Psi_{Ad}(a) = \Psi_{A_1}(a)$ *if* $a \in \Sigma^I_{A_1}$. *Otherwise,* $\Psi_{Ad}(a) = \Psi_{A_2}(a)$;
- $\Sigma^H_{Ad} \subseteq \{\epsilon\}$; *in the adaptor this set represents the internal actions that do nothing, which are associated to input/output actions in mismatched components which are not concerned with the mapping (the adaptation);*
- $\delta_{Ad} \subseteq S_{Ad} \times \Sigma^I_{Ad} \cup \Sigma^O_{Ad} \cup \{\epsilon\} \times S_{Ad}$;
- $Shared(Ad, A_1) = \bigcup_{\alpha \in \Phi(A_1, A_2)} \Pi_1(\alpha)$; $Shared(Ad, A_2) = \bigcup_{\alpha \in \Phi(A_1, A_2)} \Pi_2(\alpha)$;

The adaptor must satisfy the following condition in order to ensure that the mapping rules are respected, therefore the mismatch between components is resolved.

The Condition on the Adaptor Paths: For all execution path $\sigma = s_1 a_1 s_2 a_2 \ldots s_i a_i \ldots s_n$ in the adaptor Ad, such that $s_i \in S_{Ad}$ and $a_i \in \Sigma^O_{Ad} \cup \Sigma^I_{Ad}$, if $\exists \alpha \in \Phi(A_1, A_2)$ such that the output actions (enabled as input in Ad) of α are present in σ then they are succeed, in σ, by there correspondent input actions (enabled as output in Ad).

Property 1. *An adaptor Ad for two interface automata A_1 and A_2 according to a mapping $\Phi(A_1, A_2)$ is composable with A_1 and A_2.*

The property can be easily verified according to Definition 8. Indeed, by considering the set of actions of Ad, Σ^I_{Ad} and Σ^O_{Ad}, the condition of composability, as defined in Sect. 4, can be easily verified with the set of actions of A_1 and A_2.

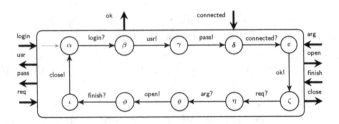

Fig. 2. The adaptor *Adaptor* for *Client* and *Server*

The composition of A_1 and A_2 is performed by synchronizing first Ad with either A_1 or A_2, computing their composition according to our extended approach, and then by composing the resulting composition with the remaining automaton. We suppose that the actions of the adaptor have the same signatures and semantics as actions in $Mismatch_\Phi(A_1, A_2)$. If the composite interface automaton $A_1 \parallel Ad \parallel A_2$ is non empty then A_1 and A_2 are compatible after their adaptation at the protocol and the semantic levels.

To generate the adaptor Ad from A_1, A_2, and the mapping $\Phi(A_1, A_2)$, we have to explore in parallel the states and the transitions of both automata A_1 and A_2. For the lack of space, the details of the algorithm to perform adaptor generation is not described in this paper, however this algorithm is the same as our algorithm in [6] that constructs an adaptor for two composable interface automata A_1, A_2, and a given non empty mapping $\Phi(A_1, A_2)$. In fact the contribution of this paper compared to the approach in [6] is the handling of action semantics in component adaptability thanks to the design of components with behavioral contracts. The step for generating the interface automaton of the adaptor comes after verifying the semantic compatibility between A_1 and A_2. However in [6] we considered only the protocol level in the adaptation. So, the algorithm is basically a loop which reads in parallel A_1 and A_2 and constructs as one goes along the set of states and the set of transitions of the adaptor. The algorithm is executed by respecting the reordering of events of both interfaces A_1 and A_2. The algorithm marks and removes from the generated graph all the fragments of paths that do not respect the condition on the adaptor paths.

The part of the algorithm that constructs the set of states and transitions has the time complexity $\mathbf{O}(|S_{A_1} \times S_{A_2}|.(|\delta_{A_1}| + |\delta_{A_2}|))$. The time complexity of the part that removes the undesired path fragments is linear in the number of the generated states.

Example 4. As the reader can conclude, *Adaptor* is composable with both *Client* and *Server* presented in Example 1 and it satisfies all the items of Definition 8. Our proposed algorithm in [6] generates exactly the same interface automaton shown in Fig. 2. Suppose that the semantic compatibility between the shared actions *error* and *terminate* holds, then *Adaptor* is compatible with both *Client* and *Server*. The composite interface automaton (*Client* $\parallel$ *Adaptor*) $\parallel$ *Server* is non empty which makes *Client* and *Server* compatible after their adaptation.

6   Related Work

Several techniques of adaptation show how to automatically derive adaptors in order to eliminate mismatches between components during their interactions. In [13], the authors propose an interesting approach based on finite state machines to adapt components specified by interfaces describing component protocol and action signatures. This approach deals with one-to-one relations between actions. In [8], the authors propose the Smart Connectors approach which allows the construction of adaptors using the provided and required interfaces of the components in order to resolve partial matching problems in COTS component acquisition. In [2], the authors have proposed a formal approach based on calculus to generate automatically adaptors using the Prolog language. The authors in [3] present an approach based on session types, exploited to specify component behaviors, to adapt heterogeneous components that may present mismatching interaction behaviors. In [7], Hemer has proposed, using template from the CARE language, to define adaptation strategies for modifying and combing components. In [9], the authors have proposed a model of adaptors expressed in the B formal method, allowing to define the interoperability between components. In [11] the authors introduce the concept of parameterized contracts and a model for component interfaces, they also present algorithms and tools for specifying and analyzing component interfaces in order to check interoperability and to generate adapted component interfaces. In [12], the authors propose to generate semi-automatically adaptors, at the protocol level, for concurrent components that are specified with finite state machines. Another approach that deals with the adaptation of component at the protocol level is presented in [10]. The authors proposed an algorithmic approach for checking whether incompatible interaction protocols of component interfaces can be made compatible by inserting a protocol converter between them. The approaches described above propose solutions for the component adaptation based on different specification formalisms of component interfaces. Our approach is different from the others, because we propose a solution to adapt particular components that are specified by interface automata. This formalism allows to exploit optimistic approach [1] to check to component interoperability. This adaptation approach deals with the signature, the semantic, and the protocol levels, and deals also with possibly complex adaptation scenarios: one-to-one and one-to-many correspondences between actions.

7   Conclusion

In this paper, we proposed a formal approach for the automatic development of component adaptors, allowing the elimination of mismatches between interacting components. Our component interfaces are described with behavioral contracts, which allow to handle all component facets for their adaptation, by considering component informations at levels of action signatures, their semantics, and their protocols. So, we proposed a formal framework for component adaptation, based on the following concepts: behavioral contracts, their composability, their synchronization, and their semantic compatibility. Therefore we specified these contracts with interface automata enriched by the action semantics. We exploited the obtained formalism to adapt the interface automata approach to verify compatibility between components specified with behavioral contracts. When components are incompatible due to mismatches, we proposed to specify a correspondence mapping between the mismatched actions of two components as a first abstract specification of the adaptor. This mapping deals with one-to-one and one-to-many correspondences between the actions. Finally, we proposed an approach that generates the adaptor for two composable interface automata according to a fixed mapping. The generated adaptor allows to eliminate mismatches at signature, semantic, and protocol levels.

References

1. Alfaro, L., Henzinger, T.A.: Interface automata. In: 9th Annual Symposium of FSE (Foundations of Software Engineering), pp. 109–120. ACM Press (2001)
2. Bracciali, A., Brogi, A., Canal, C.: A formal approach to component adaptation. J. Syst. Softw. **74**, 45–54 (2005)
3. Brogi, A., Canal, C., Pimentel, E.: Behavioural types and component adaptation. In: Rattray, C., Maharaj, S., Shankland, C. (eds.) AMAST 2004. LNCS, vol. 3116, pp. 42–56. Springer, Heidelberg (2004). https://doi.org/10.1007/978-3-540-27815-3_8
4. Canal, C., Murillo, J., Poizat, P.: Software adaptation. Spec. Issue Softw. Adapt. **12**(1), 9–31 (2006)
5. Canal, C., Poizat, P., Salaün, G.: Synchronizing behavioural mismatch in software composition. In: Gorrieri, R., Wehrheim, H. (eds.) FMOODS 2006. LNCS, vol. 4037, pp. 63–77. Springer, Heidelberg (2006). https://doi.org/10.1007/11768869_7
6. Chouali, S., Mouelhi, S., Mountassir, H.: Adapting component behaviours using interface automata. In: Euromicro SEAA 2010 Conference. IEEE Computer Society Proceedings, September 2010
7. Hemer, D.: A formal approach to component adaptation and composition. In: Proceedings of the Twenty-Eighth Australasian Conference on Computer Science, ACSC 2005, Newcastle, Australia, pp. 259–266 (2005)
8. Min, H.G., Choi, S.W., Kim, S.D.: Using smart connectors to resolve partial matching problems in COTS component acquisition. In: Crnkovic, I., Stafford, J.A., Schmidt, H.W., Wallnau, K. (eds.) CBSE 2004. LNCS, vol. 3054, pp. 40–47. Springer, Heidelberg (2004). https://doi.org/10.1007/978-3-540-24774-6_5
9. Mouakher, I., Lanoix, A., Souquières, J.: Component adaptation: specification and verification. In: 11th International Workshop on Component Oriented Programming (WCOP 2006), ECOOP 2006, Nantes, France, p. 8, July 2006
10. Passerone, R., de Alfaro, L., Henzinger, T.A., Sangiovanni-Vincentelli, A.L.: Convertibility verification and converter synthesis: two faces of the same coin [IP block interfaces]. In: IEEE/ACM ICCAD 2002, pp. 132–139 (2002). https://doi.org/10.1109/ICCAD.2002.1167525
11. Reussner, R.: Automatic component protocol adaptation with the CoConut/J tool suite. Future Gener. Comput. Syst. **19**(5), 627–639 (2003)
12. Schmidt, H.W., Reussner, R.H.: Generating adapters for concurrent component protocol synchronisation. In: Jacobs, B., Rensink, A. (eds.) FMOODS 2002. ITIFIP, vol. 81, pp. 213–229. Springer, Boston, MA (2002). https://doi.org/10.1007/978-0-387-35496-5_15
13. Yellin, D., Strom, R.: Protocol specifications and components adaptors. ACM Trans. Program. Lang. Syst. **19**(2), 292–333 (1997)

Towards Real-Time Semantics for a Distributed Event-Based MOP Language

Mateo Sanabria⬤, Wilmer Garzón Alfonso⬤,
and Luis Daniel Benavides Navarro(✉)⬤

Escuela Colombiana de Ingenierá Julio Garavito, Bogotá, Colombia
mateo.sanabria@mail.escuelaing.edu.co,
{wilmer.garzon,luis.benavides}@escuelaing.edu.co

Abstract. This paper investigates rewriting logic as a suitable means to model the semantics of distributed and concurrent systems implemented using Monitoring Oriented Programming (MOP) frameworks. MOP tools close the gap between specification and implementation, allowing several formal specifications and concrete implementations to be combined into a single executing system. To address real-time monitoring of modern distributed applications, we recently proposed REAL-T, a reactive event-based distributed programming language with explicit support for distributions and time manipulation. REAL-T allows programmers to instrument distributed applications to monitor and enforce specific behavior. It also supports requirements of modern reactive applications (responsiveness, resiliency, elasticity and asynchronous communication). The REAL-T programming model is very flexible, making the semantic specifications very challenging.

Keywords: Rewriting logic · Semantics · Distributed programming
Event oriented programming · Explicit time management

1 Introduction

Designing, implementing, and debugging distributed and concurrent applications is a complex task. Several approaches have been proposed to address such complexity. Objects [16], actors [1], functional programming [23], and other strategies have been investigated as suitable means to model concurrent and distributed systems. However, despite of the programming paradigm, modern reactive applications are full of bugs related to concurrency and distribution. Formal specifications and verification [21,22] have been proposed as techniques to address algorithm accuracy in distributed and concurrent software. Although, correctness may be proved formally, there is no guarantee that the implementation will comply with the specification. Monitoring Oriented Programming (MOP) [9,20] has been proposed to close the gap between formal specifications and implementation, allowing them to create a system together. MOP proposes building a software framework on top of a base application in order to monitor and enforce

© Springer Nature Switzerland AG 2018
E. H. Abdelwahed et al. (Eds.): MEDI 2018 Workshops, CCIS 929, pp. 231–243, 2018.
https://doi.org/10.1007/978-3-030-02852-7_20

desired behavior that has been specified in some formalism, e.g., finite state machines or Linear Temporal Logic.

As mentioned, a MOP framework may enforce specific behavior in the base application, thus altering the original semantics. We argue that such a modification needs to be investigated formally. In this paper, we use rewriting logic to investigate the semantics of systems created by distributed MOP frameworks. Concretely, our investigation examines the semantics of REAL-T [5], a Monitoring Oriented Language designed for distribution and concurrency. REAL-T is a reactive, event-based, distributed programming language with explicit support for distribution and time manipulation. REAL-T allows programmers to instrument distributed applications to monitor and enforce specific behavior.

This paper is organized as follows: Sect. 2 presents the programming model of REAL-T; Sect. 3 presents semantics for a restricted set of the language; Sect. 4 presents related work; and Sect. 5 presents concluding remarks and discusses future work.

2   The Programming Model of REAL-T

REAL-T's programming model has three main components: a distributed base application, a distributed event model, and a time model (a detailed description of the programming model is found in [5]). The distributed base application is where specific behaviors want to be detected or reinforced. The event model describes what events are detected and how messages with event information are exchanged. Time model describes different time management strategies considered in the programming model.

2.1   The Base Application

The base application exchanges messages through the network to achieve its purpose. This application is where specific behaviors want to be detected or reinforced. The base application may possess any or all of the characteristics of modern reactive applications: responsiveness, resiliency, elasticity, and asynchronous communication. REAL-T adapts itself to the topology and architecture of the application, for example, growing and shrinking with it, following its elastic behavior. The programming model does not impose any restrictions on the base application (apart from being a java application). Specific events and patterns of events are detected on the execution trace of the base application at run-time.

2.2   Distributed Event Model

REAL-T detects two types of events: atomic events and complex events. For simplicity, we restrict our study to only one type of atomic event: method calls. Atomic events are defined using a pointcut-like language with explicit support for distribution [4]. Complex events are sequences of atomic events defined using finite deterministic automata (as in [4]), causal predicates [19], or Linear Temporal Logic [14,20].

Atomic events, complex events, and reactions are defined using Event Classes. Instances of those classes are called event monitors, and they are instantiated using a singleton policy, i.e., each event class creates one monitor object on each running node. Monitors consume messages with event information, and they react to those events. The reaction may be a simple notification, e.g., registering the event in a log file, or it may modify the original behavior of the base application.

Atomic event definitions cause the base application to be instrumented by REAL-T's framework. Once instrumented, before executing a method call, a message containing the meta-information of that call is broadcast to the participating nodes in the distributed application. Those messages are consumed by distributed monitors which detect complex patterns of events and react to those patterns. The message containing the meta information does not interfere with the distributed messages of the base application. Furthermore, there is no restriction regarding synchronization among messages with meta information and messages from the base application.

Figure 1 depicts the main concepts explained above. The figure shows five nodes where the distributed application is deployed. In the application, the nodes communicate with each other (solid line). Each node has deployed an event monitor. The monitor detects the events in the application, e.g., sees the instrumented method call represented as a black line in node 3 and broadcasts the event information to other monitors. Those monitors use their constructs to detect complex event patterns. The construct may be a simple predicate, an automaton definition, the automaton augmented with causal guards or a predicate defined using LTL. Note that a node represents a running component of the distributed application; this is a software artifact, not a hardware device. Additionally, the monitor is an instance of an event class definition and there could be more monitors per node, for example, if there are more event-class definitions.

Note that there are two types of messages in the application: regular messages generated by the base distributed application; and messages representing the meta-data of events. Messages containing event meta-data are exchanged over the REAL-T framework, while regular messages are exchanged over the mechanisms defined by the distributed base application.

2.3   Time Model

REAL-T considers three kinds of time models. The first is operational time, where time is modeled defining the order of messages explicitly. The second is logical time [15,19] to address partial orders of events, predicating, for example, over causal relations. Finally, we have declarative time using LTL, where the programmers of event classes define custom models of time and time predicates.

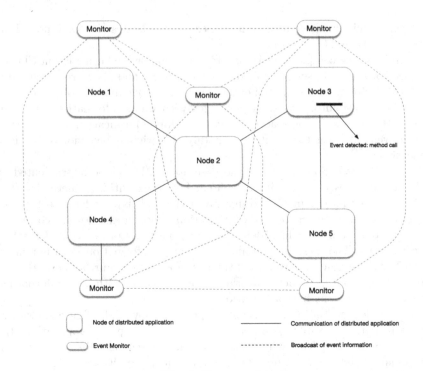

Fig. 1. Event model

Operational Time: Operational time formalisms [13] explicitly describe the evolution of software systems. In our model, we use Deterministic State Automata to describe complex sequences of events. The automaton is concerned only with the next possible transition, thus enforcing specific sequences of events. Each transition on the automaton may be guarded with a boolean guard. Each monitor may have an automaton definition and, depending on the arrival order of messages, each automaton will detect different histories of the distributed computation.

Logical Time: REAL-T allows programmers to write predicates on the causality relationship among events, i.e., when an event has causal influence over another. The causal relation among events is defined (following ideas from [15,19]) considering three concrete cases of distributed events. First, two events a and b are causally related if they are in the same process and a takes place before b. Second, if a represents the event of sending message m while b represents the event of receiving message m, a and b are causally related. Finally, by transitivity, if a is causally related to b and b is causally related to c, hence, a is causally related to c. In any other case, events are considered concurrent [19].

Declarative Time Model (Linear Logical Time): REAL-T incorporates a time model based on Propositional Temporal Logic (PTL) [11]. Using PTL predicates, programmers write temporal predicates asserting temporal relations among events in a sequence of distributed events. Concretely, REAL-T supports the operators described below, where ϕ and ψ are PTL formulas:

- $\bigcirc\phi :=$ "*Next:* In the next moment ϕ is true".
- $\Diamond\phi :=$ "*Eventually:* In some future or present moment ϕ is true".
- $\Box\phi :=$ "*Always:* ϕ is true in all future moments".
- $\phi \cup \psi :=$ "*Until:* ϕ continues being true up until some future moment when ψ is true".
- $\phi \mathrel{W} \psi :=$ "*Unless:* ϕ continues being true unless ψ becomes true (weak until)".

3   Formal Semantics for REAL-T

Figure 2 depicts the main elements of REAL-T's programming model, which is formalized using rewriting logic written in Maude [10]. The first element is the *base application*. In the figure, *node1*, *node2*, and *node3* represent devices executing concurrent components of the base application, and white messages represent regular messages that are exchanged in the base application. The second element is the distributed monitoring framework created with REAL-T. This framework has one monitor attached to each component (e.g., a monitor attached to each Java virtual machine), such monitor may be defined using an LTL formula, a finite state automaton, or a simple boolean predicate. The monitor receives messages containing information of the events occurring in other nodes. Monitors consume messages and react when a specific predicate holds, or when a specific state is reached.

Black messages in the figure are the messages exchanged over REAL-T's framework (not all messages are shown). Note that the network is an unreliable component, messages may be lost, and message order may be altered. Thus, each monitor sees a different history of the computation; at the bottom of the figure, the timeline represents messages as seen by *monitor3*. Finally, at the top of the figure, property P is represented as a meta property, i.e., a property that holds in the entire system. Note that in REAL-T we do not have any guarantee that P holds, programmers may use Deterministic Finite Automata or LTL formulas to define event classes, but as a real-time framework, it does not have access to the full trace of the computation. One of the best features of having the semantics defined in rewriting logic is that we can now analyze what kind of properties may be granted at real-time using REAL-T.

To present the semantics of REAL-T we are going to introduce incrementally some of the features described above. In particular, we are going to specify the base application by means of producers and consumers exchanging messages. First, using a unicast model, then introducing a global clock, and finally creating an asynchronous broadcast model (no global clock). To formalize the event model and the time model we are going to introduce global LTL formulas. Finally, we discuss how to extend the specification to include event classes.

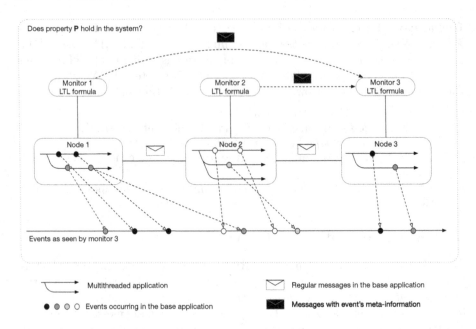

Fig. 2. Main elements of REAL-T's programming model

3.1 The Semantics of the Base Application

Unicast with No Global Time. The state of the computation is modeled with the sort Sys, which is a set of objects in a particular state. This configuration may contain instances of producers and consumers, as well as instances of messages that are in transit between them. The specification of the configuration is shown bellow:

> **sort** Sys .
> **op** {_} : Configuration —> Sys .

Figure 3 shows the specification of the producer. The producer generates messages in the distributed application. A producer has associated five attributes: **frequency** is a natural number representing the speed of message production, the number represents the number of clock ticks before sending a new message. In this example, each object has its own clock. Attribute **count** is used as a clock. The producer can issue a message, the attribute **cnt-prod** will keep track of how many messages the producer has sent. Each producer has a maximum quota of messages, attribute **end**. Attribute **times** stores a list of times, those times are the times associated with message sending.

Likewise, consumers were defined as objects as shown in the Fig. 4. A consumer has five attributes. Like the producers, each consumer has a frequency indicating how fast a consumer can consume messages (**freq-C**). Attribute, **countC** is updated with each clock tick. Attribute **logs** stores the records of messages consumed. Finally, attribute **current-mesg** stores the message being consumed.

```
1  mod PRODUCER is
2    pr NAT . pr STRING . pr LIST{Nat} . inc CONFIGURATION

3    subsort String < Oid .
4    op Unordered–mesg : String Nat Nat –> Msg [ctor].
5    op init–prod : String List{Nat} Nat Nat –> Object .
6    ...
7    var ST : String . var TI : List{Nat} . vars END FR : Nat .
8    eq init–prod(ST,TI,FR,END)
9      = < ST : Producer | cnt–prod: 0 , times: TI , frequency: FR ,
           count: 0 , end: END > .
10 endm
```

Fig. 3. Producer specification no global time

```
1    mod CONSUMER is
2      pr NAT . pr STRING . pr LIST{String} . inc
         CONFIGURATION .
3      subsort String < Oid .
4      ...
5      op init–consumer : String Nat –↠ Object .
6      var ST : String . var FR : Nat .
7      eq init–consumer(ST,FR)
8        = < ST : Consumer | countC: 0 , freq–C: FR , actual–time:
             0 , logs: nil , current–mesg: none > .
9      endm
```

Fig. 4. Consumer specification no global time

Furthermore, system transitions are modeled by seven rewriting rules. During transitions, the producers and consumers update their internal clocks and messages may be consumed by any consumer. We show some of the rules in Fig. 5. Rule [update-frequency-Consumer] updates internal clock of a consumer. While rule [send-msg] makes producer PR to send a message to the system when frequency is matched.

Unicast with Global Time. We now add a global clock to the model, introducing a rule which updates the internal clock of each object in the system at the same time. For this, rule [update-frequency] replaces the aforementioned [update-frequency-Consumer] and [update-frequency-Producer]. Figure 6 shows the definition of the new rule. Rule uses a new operation tick to indicate to the objects of the configuration when to update its internal clock. Figure 7, shows equations and conditional equations defining the behavior of clocks. Contrary to the previous specification this one is not terminating, because the rule [update-frequency] continues to execute indefinitely.

```
1      crl [update–frequency–Consumer] :
2        { < PR : Consumer | ATS , freq–C: FR , countC: CT ,
              current–mesg: none > Con }
3        =>
4        { < PR : Consumer | ATS , freq–C: FR , countC: s(CT) ,
              current–mesg: none > Con }
5        if s(CT) <= FR
6        crl [send–msg]:
7      { < PR : Producer | ATS , cnt–prod: N , times: (L T L') ,
            frequency: FR , count: CT > Con }
8        =>
9        { < PR : Producer | ATS , cnt–prod: s(N) , times: (L T L'),
              frequency: FR , count: 0 > Unordered–mesg(PR,N,T) Con
              }
10     if FR = CT .
```

Fig. 5. Some rules for the system

```
1      crl [update–frequency] :
2      { Con }
3      =>
4      { tick(Con) }
5        .
```

Fig. 6. Rule to update frequency

```
1      ceq tick( < ST : Consumer | Ats, countC: CT , freq–C: FR >
2        Con )
3        =
4        < ST : Consumer | Ats, countC: s(CT) , freq–C: FR > tick(
            Con)
5        if s(CT) <= FR
6        .
7        ...
8      ceq tick( < PR : Producer | Ats , frequency: FR , cnt–frq: CT ,
            end: END , cnt–prod: CT' > Con )
9        =
10       (< PR : Producer | Ats , frequency: FR , cnt–frq: s(CT) , end:
            END , cnt–prod: CT' > tick(Con))
11       if s(CT) <= FR /\ CT' < END
12       .
13     eq tick(Unordered–mesg(ST,N,M) Con ) = ( Unordered–mesg(
            ST,N,M) Con ) .
14     eq tick(none) = none .
```

Fig. 7. Tick operation definition

Broadcast with No Global Time. A more realistic model of the base distributed application will use broadcasting and asynchronous clocks. To model such behavior, messages of the system are defined as shown in Fig. 8. First, line number 1 defines a message sent from a specific producer to one particular consumer. Line number 2 defines a multicast message, sent from a particular producer to a list of consumers. Line number 3 defines broadcast as a message sent from a specific producer, the message is then transformed by a rewriting rule (not shown) into a multicast message to the constant list defined in line 10 (Namesconsumers). The generated multicast message is processed recursively by the equations specified in lines 5 to 8, creating individual messages to each one of the receivers list members. We have shown only a small part of the specification. The interested reader could find the full specification in https://gitlab.com/MaSanaAR/Middleware.

```
1    op msg_from_to_ : Tuple String String -> Msg [ctor] .
2    op multicast_from_to_ : Tuple String Set{String} ->
         Configuration .
3    op broadcast_from_ : Tuple String -> Msg [ctor] .
4    var MC : Tuple . vars SENDER ARECEIVER : String . var
         OTHER–RECEIVERS : Set{String} .
5    eq multicast MC from SENDER to empty = none .
6    eq multicast MC from SENDER to (ARECEIVER , OTHER–
         RECEIVERS) =
7    (msg MC from SENDER to ARECEIVER)
8    (multicast MC from SENDER to OTHER–RECEIVERS) .
9    ...
10   op Names–consumers:_ : Set{String} -> Msg .
```

Fig. 8. Broadcats message definition

3.2   The Event and Message Models

The most simple specification of the event and message models of REAL-T is to represent the framework as a set of properties. Thus, the semantics is the same as that of a verification tool with full access to the global computation trace. We have implemented this specification using the MODEL-CHECKER of Maude and the specification of linear temporal logic. Note that due to the differences in frequencies between producers and consumers it is possible that a message transmitted by a producer is not immediately consumed. As shown in Fig. 10, the property No-msg states that a message has not been consumed. Having this, it is easily verified that the formula $\lozenge No - msg$ (eventually a message will not be consumed) is fulfilled when the system starts with a producer with frequency 4 and two consumers with frequencies 3 and 7 (see Fig. 9).

```
1    reduce in SYSTEM–CHECK : modelCheck({(< "room" :
         Consumer | current–mesg: none,freq–C: 3,actual–time: 0,
         logs: nil,countC:
2    0 > < "room1" : Consumer | current–mesg: none,freq–C: 7,
         actual–time: 0,logs: nil,countC: 0 >) < "lab" : Producer |
3    cnt–prod: 0,times: (5 2 3 5),frequency: 4,cnt–frq: 0,end: 10 >},
         <> No–msg) .
4    rewrites: 6 in 0ms cpu (0ms real) (~ rewrites/second)
5    result Bool: true
```

Fig. 9. Model checker

```
1    op No–msg : –> Prop .
2    ...
3    ceq { MSG < CS : Consumer | Ats , freq–C: FR , countC: CT
         > Con } |= No–msg
4      = true
5      if CT < FR .
6    eq { Con } |= No–msg = false [owise] .
```

Fig. 10. Proposition definition

3.3   Discussion: Implementing the Full Semantics of REAL-T

This research is still a preliminary work, where we have investigated the use of
rewriting logic to specify the semantics of REAL-T. The examples above have
already addressed complex concepts found in distributed applications, namely,
unicasting, multicasting, broadcasting, synchronous and asynchronous clocks,
and LTL formulas. However, we still need to explore the implementation of
event classes, especially allowing them to be defined using one of the formalisms
found in REAL-T (e.g., LT formulas or DFAs). Note that this is very different
to the scenario presented above, what REAL-T does is to have an LTL formula or a DFA instantiated on each monitor, watching a different version of the
computation history. We also need, to implement logical clocks and localization
predicates. Once we have a full representation of the framework, we will explore
the kind of properties that may be granted using REAL-T at runtime.

4   State of the Art

Rewriting logic [21, 22] is proposed as a semantics framework in which many programming languages, models of concurrency, and distributed algorithms can be
represented, executed, and analyzed. Rewriting logic is flexible enough to allow
the specification to be conceptually very close to the application's implementation model. It also has a well-developed foundation with very mature tools. This
makes this formalism ideal to represent real-time features offered by REAL-T.

Even though several researchers have investigated semantics of distributed systems and it has been used to model MOP [9], to the best of our knowledge no MOP framework for real-time distributions exists. The research presented here is a work in progress and we expect to develop more sophisticated contributions in the future. One of the most important points that our approach allows is the investigation of real-time capabilities of distributed MOP frameworks for reactive applications, addressing the needs of modern cloud and mobile applications.

Other formalisms have been investigated as suitable means for modeling concurrent real-time systems [3,7,12,17], including models for distributed and concurrent computations. Those models have been accompanied with verification tools that simulate and verify the behavior of the specified model. For example, In [3], authors used process algebras to define the semantics of an Aspect-Oriented Language for distribution [4] similar to REAL-T. However, as shown in the paper, this approach presents big gap with the implementation. Similarly, Tabareau [24] proposed a calculus based on join calculus as a semantic framework for distributed aspects. This proposal serves as a specification framework to prove properties of the weaved application, however to the best of our knowledge, no verification tool is available.

Note that we have studied a narrow set of semantics for the base application and for the full distributed MOP system, however, the aim of this research is to explore several possible semantics. Once the complete formal model is in place we will be able to explore different semantics for the language. For example, we are interested in studying characteristic properties of synchronous and asynchronous message communications in distributed systems, exploring variants as those proposed in the hierarchy of distributed computations presented by Charron-Bost, Mattern, and Tel in [8]. Such variants may incorporate distinct models for time management (see for example [13,18]), creating several possible complex semantic scenarios. Finally, once the complete toolset is in place we will study methodological approaches using formal models and concrete implementations of REAL-T, to address a full development cycle for distributed systems (similar to those proposed in [2,6]).

5   Conclusions

In this paper, using rewriting logic, we investigate semantics of a real-time, distributed MOP framework. We present the programming model of REAL-T, an event-based programming language with explicit support for distribution, concurrency, and time manipulation. Then we build incrementally, the semantics specification of a reduced set of REAL-T. The specification includes three models for the base application, asynchronous unicast messaging, synchronous (global time) unicast messaging, and asynchronous broadcast messaging. We then present a simplified specification of the event and messaging models introduced in REAL-T. Concretely, we use LTL to represent global properties of the distributed software, and then we discuss the implementation of concrete semantics for the complete model. All the specifications have been implemented in the Maude language.

This work is in its initial steps. We have modeled several of the distributed requirements for a real-time MOP framework. However, we still need to model the full flexibility and non-determinism of the REAL-T language. Particularly, we need to model event classes supporting deterministic finite automata, and LTL formula definitions. We also need to introduce logical clocks allowing the base application to have a different clock from the one used in the base application. We need to support messaging of the base application and messaging of the MOP framework. Once we have modeled all the elements we can analyze to what extent REAL-T can grant a complex distributed and concurrent property in real-time.

References

1. Agha, G.: Concurrent object-oriented programming. Commun. ACM **33**(9), 125–141 (1990)
2. Basu, A., Bensalem, S., Bozga, M., Bourgos, P., Sifakis, J.: Rigorous system design: the BIP approach. In: Kotásek, Z., Bouda, J., Černá, I., Sekanina, L., Vojnar, T., Antoš, D. (eds.) MEMICS 2011. LNCS, vol. 7119, pp. 1–19. Springer, Heidelberg (2012). https://doi.org/10.1007/978-3-642-25929-6_1
3. Benavides Navarro, L.D., Douence, R., Núñez, A., Südholt, M.: LTS-based semantics and property analysis of distributed aspects and invasive patterns. In: Leuven, K.U. (ed.) Workshop on Aspects, Dependencies and Interactions. Technical Report, Belgium, vol. CW 517, pp. 36–45, July 2008. https://doi.org/10.1007/978-3-642-02047-6, https://hal.archives-ouvertes.fr/hal-00469648
4. Benavides Navarro, L.D., Douence, R., Südholt, M.: Debugging and testing middleware with aspect-based control-flow and causal patterns. In: Issarny, V., Schantz, R. (eds.) Middleware 2008. LNCS, vol. 5346, pp. 183–202. Springer, Heidelberg (2008). https://doi.org/10.1007/978-3-540-89856-6_10
5. Benavides Navarro, L.D., et al.: REAL-T: time modularization in reactive distributed applications. In: Serrano, C.J., Martínez-Santos, J. (eds.) CCC 2018. CCIS, vol. 885, pp. 113–127. Springer, Cham (2018). https://doi.org/10.1007/978-3-319-98998-3_9
6. Bensalem, S., Bozga, M., Delahaye, B., Jegourel, C., Legay, A., Nouri, A.: Statistical model checking QoS properties of systems with SBIP. In: Margaria, T., Steffen, B. (eds.) ISoLA 2012. LNCS, vol. 7609, pp. 327–341. Springer, Heidelberg (2012). https://doi.org/10.1007/978-3-642-34026-0_25
7. Bhat, G., Cleaveland, R., Lüttgen, G.: A practical approach to implementing real-time semantics. Ann. Softw. Eng. **7**(1), 127–155 (1999)
8. Charron-Bost, B., Mattern, F., Tel, G.: Synchronous, asynchronous, and causally ordered communication. Distrib. Comput. **9**(4), 173–191 (1996). https://doi.org/10.1007/s004460050018
9. Chen, F., Roşu, G.: MOP: an efficient and generic runtime verification framework. In: ACM SIGPLAN Notices, vol. 42, pp. 569–588. ACM (2007)
10. Clavel, M., et al.: The maude 2.0 system. In: Nieuwenhuis, R. (ed.) RTA 2003. LNCS, vol. 2706, pp. 76–87. Springer, Heidelberg (2003). https://doi.org/10.1007/3-540-44881-0_7
11. Fisher, M.: An Introduction to Practical Formal Methods Using Temporal Logic. Wiley, Hoboken (2011)

12. Fontana, P., Cleaveland, R.: A menagerie of timed automata. ACM Comput. Surv. **46**(3), 40:1–40:56 (2014). https://doi.org/10.1145/2518102
13. Furia, C.A., Mandrioli, D., Morzenti, A., Rossi, M.: Modeling time in computing: a taxonomy and a comparative survey. ACM Comput. Surv. **42**(2), 6:1–6:59 (2010)
14. Haydar, M., Boroday, S., Petrenko, A., Sahraoui, H.: Propositional scopes in linear temporal logic. In: Proceedings of the 5th International Conference on Novelles Technologies de la Repartition (NOTERE 2005) (2005)
15. Lamport, L.: Time, clocks, and the ordering of events in a distributed system. Commun. ACM **21**(7), 558–565 (1978)
16. Le Lann, G.: Distributed systems-towards a formal approach. In: IFIP Congress, Toronto, vol. 7, pp. 155–160 (1977)
17. Magee, J., Kramer, J.: Concurrency: State Models and Java Programs, 2nd edn. Wiley, Hoboken (2006)
18. Mallet, F.: Clock constraint specification language: specifying clock constraints with UML/MARTE. Innov. Syst. Softw. Eng. **4**(3), 309–314 (2008). https://doi.org/10.1007/s11334-008-0055-2
19. Mattern, F., et al.: Virtual time and global states of distributed systems. Parallel Distrib. Algorithms **1**(23), 215–226 (1989)
20. Meredith, P.O., Jin, D., Griffith, D., Chen, F., Roşu, G.: An overview of the mop runtime verification framework. Int. J. Softw. Tools Technol. Transfer **14**(3), 249–289 (2012)
21. Meseguer, J.: Twenty years of rewriting logic. J. Log. Algebr. Program. **81**(7), 721–781 (2012). https://doi.org/10.1016/j.jlap.2012.06.003, http://www.sciencedirect.com/science/article/pii/S1567832612000707, Rewriting Logic and its Applications
22. Roşu, G.: From rewriting logic, to programming language semantics, to program verification. In: Martí-Oliet, N., Ölveczky, P.C., Talcott, C. (eds.) Logic, Rewriting, and Concurrency. LNCS, vol. 9200, pp. 598–616. Springer, Cham (2015). https://doi.org/10.1007/978-3-319-23165-5_28
23. Spiliopoulou, E.: Concurrent and distributed functional systems. Ph.D. thesis, University of Bristol (2000)
24. Tabareau, N.: A theory of distributed aspects. In: Proceedings of the 9th International Conference on Aspect-Oriented Software Development, AOSD 2010, pp. 133–144. ACM, New York (2010). https://doi.org/10.1145/1739230.1739246

Short Paper

Automatic Planning: From Event-B to PDDL

Sabrine Ammar$^{(\boxtimes)}$ and Mohamed Tahar Bhiri

Faculty of Sciences Sfax, Sfax University, Sfax, Tunisia
ammar.sabrine@hotmail.fr, tahar_bhiri@yahoo.fr

Abstract. Automatic planning is a separate discipline of Artificial Intelligence (AI). It aims to formalize the planning problems described by the concept of state space. The Planning Domain Definition Language (PDDL) is a de facto standard language in the field of automatic planning. PDDL-related dynamic analysis tools, namely planners and validators, are insufficient for verifying and validating PDDL descriptions. Such tools make it possible to detect errors a posteriori by means of a test activity. In this article, we recommend a rigorous approach coupling Event-B and PDDL for automatic planning. Event-B is used for formal modeling by stepwise refinement with mathematical proofs of planning problems. A refinement strategy appropriate to planning problems is, then, proposed. The ultimate Event-B model, correct by construction, supposed to be translatable into PDDL, is automatically translated into PDDL using our MDE Event-B2PDDL tool. The obtained PDDL description is submitted to efficient planners for generation of solution plans.

Keywords: Automatic planning · PDDL · Event-B · Correct by construction
Planner · State space · State change operator · MDE

1 Introduction

Automatic planning can describe and solve planning problems. It is applied in various fields such as robotics, management projects, Internet browsing, managing crisis situations, logistics and games. In an informal way, a planning problem can be described by a state space. A state models a stable situation of the processed planning problem. It can be an initial state, final state (also called goal) or intermediate state. Moving from one state to another is governed by transitions. Each transition is labeled by an action. It has a specification showing two parts: its condition of applicability and its effect. A planning problem can accept zero or many solutions. A solution called plan-solution is a sequence of actions that leads from the initial state to the goal state.

The automatic planning community has developed a formal de facto standard Planning Domain Definition Language (PDDL) [1, 2] to formally describe planning problems. In addition, this community has developed solvers (so-called planners) able to calculate solutions to PDDL-formalized planning problems. In addition, it has developed validation tools for verifying whether a given plan-solution can be derived from a PDDL description. In general, PDDL descriptions are difficult to write, read, and evolve. Moreover, the tools associated with the PDDL language, namely the planners and validators, do not allow a rigorous **a priori** analysis of the PDDL

© Springer Nature Switzerland AG 2018
E. H. Abdelwahed et al. (Eds.): MEDI 2018 Workshops, CCIS 929, pp. 247–254, 2018.
https://doi.org/10.1007/978-3-030-02852-7_21

descriptions. Indeed, these tools are used **a posteriori** after establishing PDDL descriptions.

In this work, we advocate the opening of the automatic planning community on the formal methods community through Event-B [3]. To achieve this, we suggest a transformation from Event-B to PDDL. This promotes the development correct by construction [3] of planning problems. The ultimate Event-B model, derived from a chain of refinements with mathematical proofs, is translated into PDDL in order to generate **quality** plans through various planners supporting PDDL.

This article has five sections and one conclusion. The second section presents and evaluates the PDDL language and verification and validation tools associated with this language. The third section proposes an Event-B and PDDL coupling approach. The fourth section provides a refinement strategy for formal modeling of Event-B planning problems. The ultimate Event-B model stemming from this strategy is supposed to be translatable into PDDL. Finally, the fifth section describes our MDE Event-B2PDDL tool. The conclusion draws up the balance sheet of this article and proposes the possible extensions of this work.

2   Planning in Artificial Intelligence

Planning is a separate discipline of AI: planning community with dedicated conferences such as ICAPS (International Conference on Planning and Scheduling). It aims to **formalize** the planning problems described by the concept of state space. Thus, formal languages based on the logic of first-order predicates are proposed and enriched within the framework of the IPC-International Planning Competitions. In the following, we present the fundamental aspects of PDDL considered as de facto standard language in the field of AI planning.

2.1   The PDDL Language

A planning problem formalized using PDDL has two separate parts: domain and problem. The domain construction offered by PDDL makes it possible to describe all the aspects common to a class of problems known as generic domain. The AI planning community, in the IPC framework, has identified more than 50 domains grouped into four broad categories: logistics, robotics, gaming, and business applications. A domain described in PDDL includes types, constants, predicates, numeric functions and actions.

As an example, Listing 1 from [4] describes in PDDL the domain of the sliding puzzle game. The domain of the sliding puzzle game has two types: position and tile. In PDDL, a type does not have a structure and is designated by a name. The predicates at (having two parameters ?tile type tile and ?position type position), neighbor and empty allowing to formalize the concept of state of a sliding puzzle game problem.

Listing 1. State of the application

```
(define (domain n-sliding-puzzle)
 (:types position tile)
 (:predicates (at ?tile -tile ?position -position)
              (neighbor ?p1 -position ?p2 -position)
              (empty ?position -position))
 (:action move
    :parameters (?tile -tile ?from ?to -position)
    :precondition (and (neighbor ?from ?to)
                  (at ?tile ?from) (empty ?to))
    :effect (and (at ?tile ?to) (empty ?from)
                  (not (at ?tile ?from)) (not(empty ?to)))
 )
```

Listing 2. Sliding puzzle game with 8 tiles

```
(define (problem n-sliding-puzzle-bootstrap-33-01)
 (:domain n-sliding-puzzle)
 (:objects p_1_1 p_1_2 p_1_3 p_2_1 p_2_2 p_2_3 p_3_1
           p_3_2 p_3_3 -position t_1 t_2 t_3 t_4 t_5 t_6
           t_7 t_8 -tile)
 (:init
   ;; initial position of the tiles
   (at t_4 p_1_1) (empty p_1_2) (at t_8 p_1_3)
   (at t_6 p_2_1) (at t_3 p_2_2) (at t_2 p_2_3)
   (at t_1 p_3_1) (at t_5 p_3_2) (at t_7 p_3_3)
   ;;framework definition
   (neighbor p_1_1 p_1_2) (neighbor p_1_2 p_1_1)
   (neighbor p_1_2 p_1_3) (neighbor p_1_3 p_1_2)
   (neighbor p_2_1 p_2_2) (neighbor p_2_2 p_2_1)
   (neighbor p_2_2 p_2_3) (neighbor p_2_3 p_2_2)
   (neighbor p_3_1 p_3_2) (neighbor p_3_2 p_3_1)
   (neighbor p_3_2 p_3_3) (neighbor p_3_3 p_3_2)
   (neighbor p_1_1 p_2_1) (neighbor p_2_1 p_1_1)
   (neighbor p_1_2 p_2_2) (neighbor p_2_2 p_1_2)
   (neighbor p_1_3 p_2_3) (neighbor p_2_3 p_1_3)
   (neighbor p_2_1 p_3_1) (neighbor p_3_1 p_2_1)
   (neighbor p_2_2 p_3_2) (neighbor p_3_2 p_2_2)
   (neighbor p_2_3 p_3_3) (neighbor p_3_3 p_2_3))
 (:goal (and
   ;; final position of the tiles
   (at t_1 p_1_1) (at t_2 p_1_2) (at t_3 p_1_3)
   (at t_4 p_2_1) (at t_5 p_2_2) (at t_6 p_2_3)
   (at t_7 p_3_1) (at t_8 p_3_2)))))
```

In PDDL, an action can have parameters typed (**parameters** clause) and defined by a Pre/Post specification: the two **precondition** and **effect** clauses. An operator (action in PDDL) can be applied in a state if and only if all pre-conditions are satisfied in this state. The effect of a PDDL action is defined by the additions and withdrawals of atoms in the current state.

The construction **problem** shown in PDDL makes it possible to formalize a problem belonging to the domain described by the construction **domain**. A problem formalized in PDDL includes the domain of this problem, typed objects (objects), an initial state (init) and a goal state (goal). For example, the Sliding Puzzle game containing 8 tiles from [4] is shown in Listing 2.

A planning problem described using PDDL is solved by a software item called planner. The AI planning community has developed several planners such as FF, LPG [5] and FD. A planner combines exploration and logic. Indeed, it can be seen either as a program that calculates a solution called plan-solution or as a program that **demonstrates** the existence of a solution. For example, the Sliding Puzzle game planning problem described by the two Listings 1 and 2 submitted to the LPG planner provides a plan-solution comprising 52 actions, an extract of which is shown in Listing 3.

Listing 3. Plan-solution extract associated with the 8-tile problem of the Sliding Puzzle game

```
0:        (MOVE T_8 P_1_3 P_1_2)
1:        (MOVE T_2 P_2_3 P_1_3)
2:        (MOVE T_3 P_2_2 P_2_3)
3:        (MOVE T_8 P_1_2 P_2_2)
4:        (MOVE T_2 P_1_3 P_1_2)
5:        (MOVE T_3 P_2_3 P_1_3)
6:        (MOVE T_8 P_2_2 P_2_3)
7:        (MOVE T_6 P_2_1 P_2_2)
8:        (MOVE T_4 P_1_1 P_2_1)
9:        (MOVE T_2 P_1_2 P_1_1)
```

2.2   Evaluation

PDDL offers interesting ways to represent planning problems. Indeed, PDDL supports various representations such as propositional representations, first order logic, both numeric and temporal. This makes it possible to describe the **states** and **actions** of a planning problem. The tools associated with the PDDL language are: planners and validators. Unlike a planner who performs a plan-solutions **production** activity, a validator [6] performs a **verification** activity. From the functional point of view, a validator accepts as input: a PDDL description (**domain** and **problem** file) and one or more plan-solutions files and outputs a verdict. A 'YES' means that plan-solutions can be obtained from the subject PDDL description. A 'NO' means a failure. Validators can be used with profit to appreciate PDDL domains by adopting the functional test. In addition, the validators allow verification by checking the plan-solutions generated by various planners. Finally, a validator can be used as a tool to **objectively** compare the abilities of various planners. The **dynamic** analysis tools associated with PDDL, namely planners and validators, are insufficient for the verification and validation of PDDL descriptions. Indeed, complex PDDL descriptions involving actions with elaborated preconditions and postconditions are prone to errors that are hard to detect **a priori**. In fact, the dynamic analysis tools associated with PDDL makes it possible to detect errors **a posteriori** by means of a test activity.

3 From Event-B to PDDL

The formal Event-B method supports both horizontal and vertical refinement techniques. It allows the modeling of various domains: sequential programs, concurrent programs, distributed programs, reactive systems and recently hybrid systems. It has a platform called Rodin [7] based on Eclipse, including tools for verification (mathematical provers), validation (model-checker, animators and simulators) and code generation. Introduced by Jean-Raymond Abrial, the Event-B method is an evolution of B method [8]. Event-B is used to formally describe systems and reason mathematically about their properties. Event-B supports modeling, correction (or proof) and validation activities. These complementary activities characterize the development of Event-B systems. An Event-B model can only contain contexts (construction CONTEXT), only machines (construction MACHINE) or both. In the first case, the model represents a purely mathematical structure. In the third case, the model is parameterized by the contexts. Finally, the second case represents a model that is not parameterized. Contexts are modeling static properties of the model. Machines (construction MACHINE) are modeling the dynamic behavior of the system. A machine may refine (REFINES relation) and see another one or more contexts (SEES). The state of the machine is defined by variables introduced by the VARIABLES clause. The invariance properties related to these variables are grouped together in the INVARIANT clause. An Event-B machine groups events that affect its state. An event consists of two parts: a "guard" that defines the condition according to it the event may or may not be triggered, and an "action" called body for evolving state variables.

We advocate a rigorous approach combining Event-B and PDDL for automatic planning. Event-B is used for formal modeling by successive refinements with mathematical proofs of planning problems. The refinement of data supported by Event-B can be used profitably to refine the notion of state of a planning problem **step-by-step**. In addition, the one-to-many refinement shown in Event-B is very useful for **determining** the state change operators of a planning problem. Finally, the possibility of reinforcing the guard of an Event supported by Event-B during a refinement step is very useful for incrementally identifying the conditions of applicability of a state change operator of a planning problem.

Proof tools associated with Event-B (generator of proof obligations and provers) guarantee in particular the verification of the consistency of a planning problem described by Event-B. The ProB [9] tool that accepts Event-B offers the possibility of checking the dynamics of a planning problem by using the LTL^e language to specify temporal properties.

The use of Event-B coupled to ProB allows to obtain Event-B model correct by construction (thanks to the Event-B theory: proof obligations) and valid (thanks to ProB) describing a planning problem. Then we have to translate this Event-B model into a PDDL. To achieve this, several refinement steps are required in order to have a model described by **a subset of Event-B**: the data are described by the language of the first-order predicates of Event-B (the theory of sets is discarded because it is not translatable to PDDL) and the processing are described only through deterministic action (:=).

4 Proposed Refinement Strategy

Following numerous Event-B modeling of various planning problems, we have established a refinement strategy that could be reused to model in Event-B various planning problems in several areas [10]. Indeed, all planning problems can be formalized by the concept of **state space**: initial state, goal states, intermediate states and state change operators. Based on all of its common aspects of planning problems, we propose the refinement strategy that includes the steps outlined and justified below.

Step 1: Initial abstract model
The initial abstract model of a planning problem includes elements related to the notion of state, the initial state, and the goal states. These elements are formalized respectively in Event-B by typed variables and having invariant properties, INITIALISATION event and an event called goal having a guard to see if the current state is a goal state. The goal event does nothing (skip action). In addition, the initial abstract model of a planning problem must involve an overly abstract and non-deterministic modeling of the notion of state change operator. This is made possible by the ANTICIPATED status of an Event-B event.

Step 2: Determination of actions by successive refinements
This step includes several successive refinements allowing, ultimately, obtaining an Event-B model with state change operators having deterministic behaviors: The actions (:∈ and :|) are concretised. Each operator contains a guard modeling the condition of applicability of the operator and its action. Refinement techniques supported by Event-B as an event decomposition (one to many) and the strengthening guards are very useful for implementing this step. The state change operators are modeled by events in Event-B whose guards indicate the conditions of application of these operators and the actions that are modeling the changes of state: transition from one state to another in state spaces. To list all of the state change operators related to application, we recommend using parameterized non-deterministic events.

Step 3: Determination of parameters by successive refinements
This step aims to remove the non-determinism related to the parameters introduced in the clause ANY of each operator of states changes. Eventually, we obtain events without parameters. Technically, in this step, the one to many refinement technique and the WITH clause are used with advantage.

Step 4: Reinforcing the conditions of applicability

This step consists in reinforcing the conditions of applicability of the state change operators (WHERE clause) introduced in the previous step. The ultimate model from this step must have state change operators with rigorous semantics. Technically, this step introduces new invariant properties (reinforcement of the invariant) and guards (reinforcement of guards).

Step 5: Realization of data by successive refinements

The purpose of this step is to eventually provide an Event-B model translatable into PDDL. All Event-B set constructions must be realized using the Event-B predicative constructions. To achieve this, data refinement is used via Event-B gluing invariant.

Step 6: Conveying a **reduced** Event-B into PDDL

The reduced Event-B model from Step 5 is translated using our Event-B2PDDL tool introduced in Sect. 5.

This refinement strategy has been successfully applied to the problem of three cannibals and three missionaries.[1]

5   The Event-B2PDDL Tool

Our Event-B2PDDL tool takes as input a reduced Event-B model that is translatable into PDDL and outputs a PDDL description acceptable to planners. Event-B2PDDL is based on simple intuitive rules allowing the systematic translation of Event-B elements to PDDL elements. Event-B2PDDL is made according to MDE technology.

5.1   Event-B to PDDL Transformation Rules

The PDDL description from the Event-B2PDDL tool has two domain and problem constructions (see Sect. 2.1). Thus, in [10], we have respectively established rules allowing the translation of Event-B elements related to the planning domain and the planning problem.

The translation rules for Event-B elements related to the planning domain concern: the translation of abstract sets, constants, Boolean constants or variables, Boolean functions, events and formulas.

The rules for conveying Event-B elements related to the planning problem concern the translation of the constants linked to the sets defined by enumeration and the translation of two INITIALISATION and GOAL events.

5.2   Translation Automation from Event-B to PDDL

Using both MDE Xtext and Xtend tools, we developed the Event-B2PDDL tool based on the transformation rules presented in 5.1. The Xtext tool allowed us to design a DSL for our input language: A reduced Event-B with only those constructions that are taken into account by the transformation. Transformation and generation of PDDL code is programmed in Xtend.

---

[1] https://crocodeal.tn/startbootstrap-resume-gh-pages/.

6 Conclusion

In this work, we proposed an Event-B to PDDL coupling approach. The transition from Event-B to PDDL makes it possible to model correct by construction and efficient planning problems. Event-B ensures the correct by construction of the states change operators. Whereas PDDL ensures the effectiveness of the plan-solutions obtained thanks to the planners associated with PDDL. We proposed, in addition, a refinement strategy which may be appropriate for any planning problem that favors Event-B/PDDL coupling. The transformation of Event-B to PDDL gave rise to an MDE Event-B2PDDL tool. Currently, we are working in two directions: experimentation of the refinement strategy proposed in Sect. 4 on various more or less complex planning problems and development of refinement schemes allowing the realization of Event-B data in PDDL (from set representations to predictive representations). Eventually, such schemes could be automated by adopting the technique of automatic refinement like the BART tool [11] associated with the formal method B.

References

1. McDermott, D., et al.: PDDL-the planning domain definition language. Technical Report CVC TR- 98-003/DCS TR-1165, Yale Center for Computational Vision and Control, New Haven, CI, USA (1998)
2. International Conference on Automated Planning and Scheduling. www.icaps-conference.org
3. Abrial, J.-R.: Modeling in Event-B: Systems and Software Engineering. Cambridge University Press, New York (2010)
4. Bibai, J.: Segmentation et évolution pour la planification: le système Divide-And-Evolve. Université Paris Sud, Paris XI (2010)
5. Gerevini, A., Saetti, A., Serina, I.: User Instructions for LPG-td. http://burglar-game.googlecode.com/svn/branches/burglargameant/planner/lpg/README-LPGTD
6. Howey, R., Long, D., Fox, M.: VAL: automatic plan validation, continuous effects and mixed initiative planning using PDDL. In: Tools with Artificial Intelligence, ICTAI (2004)
7. Voisin, L., Abrial, J.R.: The rodin platform has turned ten. In: Ait Ameur, Y., Schewe, K.D. (eds.) ABZ 2014. LNCS, pp. 1–8. Springer, Heidelberg (2014). https://doi.org/10.1007/978-3-662-43652-3_1
8. Abrial, J.-R.: The B-Book: Assigning Programs to Meanings. Cambridge University Press, New York (1996)
9. Leuschel, M., Butler, M.: ProB: a model checker for B. In: Araki, K., Gnesi, S., Mandrioli, D. (eds.) FME 2003. LNCS, vol. 2805, pp. 855–874. Springer, Heidelberg (2003). https://doi.org/10.1007/978-3-540-45236-2_46
10. Fourati, F.: Contributions à l'analyse statique et dynamique d'architectures logicielles. Faculty of Science of Sfax, Tunisia (2017)
11. Requet, A., BART: a tool for automatic refinement. In: ABZ, p. 345 (2008)

Author Index

Printed in the United States
By Bookmasters